Charles Dicken's

The Bleak House Companion

Includes Study Guide, Historical Context, Biography, and Character Index

BookCaps™ Study Guides

www.bookcaps.com

Table of Contents

Historical Context

Childhood and Youth

Charles Dickens was born in 1812 in Portsmouth, in the southern central coastal area of England, to John and Elizabeth Dickens. By the time he was ten, his family had already moved twice and now resided in Camden, in North London. When Charles was twelve, his father landed in debtors' prison for three months, owing to his inability to support his large family on his small income as a naval clerk. He was followed soon afterwards by his wife and Charles's three youngest siblings. As a result, Charles had to temporarily leave school to work in a boot-blacking factory. Charles's father was released from prison after his mother (Charles's grandmother) died, allowing him to pay off his debts with his inheritance. At that point, Charles returned to school, this time to Wellington House Academy, the model for Salem House and its related characters in *David Copperfield.* In spite of the school's abusive atmosphere and the mediocre education, Dickens's intelligence enabled him to make the most of the experience, winning him the Latin prize by the time he graduated.

Early Career

At fifteen, Dickens worked as an administrative assistant for a lawyer. By 1829, he had learned shorthand and begun working as a reporter, establishing himself in 1831 as a Parliamentary reporter for the *Mirror of Parliament,* a weekly record of Parliamentary debates. In 1834, he began working for the *Morning Chronicle* as a journalist.

Love and Marriage

At seventeen, Dickens fell in love with Maria Beadnell, a banker's daughter. The relationship lasted four years until 1833, in part failing because of her family's objections. Three years later, Dickens married Catherine Hogarth, with whom he fathered ten children and whose father, George Hogarth, edited the *Evening Chronicle,* to which Dickens also contributed. About twenty years later, Dickens fell in love with the young actress Ellen Ternan, causing a final separation between him and his wife a year later. Dickens and Ternan's relationship was not public, and they burned all related letters, but in his will, Dickens left Ternan enough money to support her for the remainder of her life.

Writing career

In 1833, when Dickens was twenty-one, his first story, "A Dinner at Poplar Walk," appeared in the *Monthly Magazine.* From there Dickens went on to publish *Sketches by Boz* (his pen name) and *The Pickwick Papers,* which originally came out in serial form, a technique he used for many of his works. This was the beginning of his prolific output as an author, editor, and sometimes also publisher for various journals, including *Bentley's Miscellany* (1836-1839), *Master Humphrey's Clock* (1840-1841), *Household Words* (1850-1859), and *All the Year Round* (1859-1870). Major works included *Oliver Twist*

(1838), *Nicholas Nickleby* (1839), *The Olde Curiosity Shoppe* (1840), *Barnaby Ridge* (1841), and *A Christmas Carol* (1843). Dickens's so-called dark period, considered his mature period, began in 1848 with the publication of *Donbey and Son,* which was followed by twenty years of extraordinary creative output that would include such masterpieces as *David Copperfield, A Tale of Two Cities,* and *Great Expectations.* Dickens's last work, *The Mystery of Edwin Drood,* was interrupted by his death in 1870.

Conditions of the Times

Most of Dickens's career took place during Queen Victoria's reign, which began in 1837, when he was in his mid-twenties. Contemporary circumstances in England included severe working conditions, child labor, unemployment, and industrialization, which produced significant changes in the economy and labor conditions. Dickens's work as a newspaper, court, and Parliamentary reporter, coupled with his detailed firsthand knowledge of London, thoroughly familiarized him with contemporary events and provided food for his stories.

Political and Charitable Involvement

Dickens himself was passionately opposed to the horrible working conditions of the times, and in 1841, he openly protested the laws that sustained them. In 1847, having returned to London after spending time abroad, he responded to a request for help from Lady Angela Burdett-Coutts, a philanthropist and one of England's wealthiest heiresses. Her idea was to help establish Urania Cottage, a home where former prostitutes could learn a new way of life. Dickens managed the home for a decade. Sometime around 1850, he also became involved in amateur theater, which included many performances for charity.

Miscellaneous and Final Days

In 1842, Dickens and his wife went on their first tour to America, but even though the author was well received, his impressions of the country were negative, which had a negative effect on his popularity. In 1844, the Dickens family spent a year in Genoa, Italy, followed about a year later by six months in Switzerland and Paris, after which they returned to London. In 1858, Dickens began giving public readings, which benefited him economically but wore him down physically, costing him his health. In 1865, on his way back to London from Paris, Dickens, Ternan, and Ternan's mother were involved in the Staplehurst rail accident, a major train disaster that resulted in the derailment of most cars, though it spared their own. The experience had a deep effect on Dickens. In 1867, he embarked on a second hectic tour of the United States, which had to be limited to the East coast because of his failing health. He was again well received in spite of his earlier negative statements on American ways. Back in London in 1868, he went on a final tour of farewell public readings, which also had to be cut short for health reasons. He died of a stroke on June 9, 1870, the same date as the Staplehurst rail disaster five years earlier. He is buried in Westminster Abbey's Poet's Corner.

Background on the Court of Chancery

Function

The Court of Chancery dealt with matters of property, such as wills and estates, as well as issues concerning minors and insane people. There was neither a jury nor witnesses, all matters being handled through various legal representatives who read their written statements in court. Unlike the Court of Law, which dealt with criminal cases and resolved them according to common law, the Court of Chancery presumably relied on its sense of equity, or fairness, in reaching its decisions.

Court Officials

The Court of Chancery (or just "Chancery") was presided over by the Lord Chancellor, whose prestigious position had a triple function that also encompassed cabinet membership and the leadership of the House of Lords. Subordinate to him were the three Vice-Chancellors, the Master of the Rolls, the judges, and the masters. The lawyers presenting the cases were called "barristers," and these were hired by the solicitors, the clients' legal counsel. Barristers and solicitors were just two examples of the many types of legal representatives in the Court of Chancery. In addition, there were clerks, stationers, and copyists, all of whom helped to turn the wheels of the Chancery's often long, drawn-out cases.

Session Terms

The Court of Chancery had four specific session terms, each lasting roughly three weeks. These three-week terms were interspersed irregularly throughout the year and were called Hilary, Easter, Trinity, and Michaelmas Term. Respectively, their starting dates occurred in early January, mid-April, the third week of May, and early November. The four-month period between the last two terms was called "the long vacation."

Locations

During these terms, the Court of Chancery was held in Westminster Hall, with the Lord Chancellor in charge of the proceedings. The year's remaining sessions were held in Lincoln's Inn Hall, one of the Inns of Court. There were four Inns of Court all together, the other three being Gray's Inn, the Inner Temple, and Middle Temple. Together with the Inns of Chancery, which were attached but of a lesser status, the Inns of Court provided a place to live, work, and study for practitioners, students, and apprentices of the law.

Deteriorating Standards

By the time Dickens wrote *Bleak House,* the Court of Chancery had gained a reputation for extreme inefficiency and bureaucracy, not to mention excessive costs. The phrase "in Chancery" had become synonymous with these conditions and with a state of stalemate. The Chancery's original purpose — to provide justice where the law was insufficient to ensure it—had been lost in both its ambition to reap the benefit of its multiplying fees and in its antiquated approach, which resulted in unnecessarily complicated and extended court cases. Some of these cases, like *Bleak House's* Jarndyce and Jarndyce, lasted for decades, during which time the property under dispute was inaccessible.

Plot Summary

Jarndyce and Jarndyce — To say that the story of *Bleak House* revolves around the Jarndyce and Jarndyce suit in the Court of Chancery would be to make an oversimplification. But the suit, which had gone on for decades and in the process become a symbol for the inefficiency and ineptitude of the Chancery Court, provides one of the central threads that weave the novel's many subplots together.

Esther Summerson, one of two narrators — The second connecting thread is the life of Esther Summerson, one of the novel's two main narrators, the other narrator being an anonymous person outside the action.

John Jarndyce — Luckily, Esther's fate is rescued early on by the third major connecting thread, the benevolent John Jarndyce, who becomes Esther's guardian and who brings her and the two other young wards in the Jarndyce case, both cousins of his, to live with him at Bleak House.

Bleak House — In spite of its name, Bleak House is anything but bleak. It got its name from the previous owner, John Jarndyce's uncle, who in trying to unravel the Jarndyce case eventually destroyed himself. In the meantime, his home deteriorated, so he called it "Bleak House." After his uncle's death, John Jarndyce restored the mansion to a warm, welcoming condition, eventually putting Esther in charge of the housekeeping.

A thickening tapestry of stories — The story has many interlacing subplots, all of them somehow connected to one or more of these three main threads. At first, the connections seem tenuous, separated by time and distance, but as the story evolves, the connections become more obvious and the timing faster as the individual lives head toward their inevitable destinies, driven not by "fate" but by the choices people have made and continued to make over the years. The most successful characters always understand that there is an element of choice, and they are able to rise above their past and present circumstances.

Esther's story — Esther's own story unfolds in ever improving ways. She goes from being an orphan girl in a severe household to training as a governess, becoming the housekeeper for Bleak House, being a constant friend to Ada and Richard (Jarndyce's wards), receiving a marriage proposal from John Jarndyce, and finally spending a happy life with those she loves and her husband, the young surgeon, Allan Woodcourt. But though Esther's own life is remarkable, it's the beneficial and inspiring effect she has on others that is her real legacy.

Male counterparts: Jarndyce and Woodcourt — Esther's main male counterpart in wisdom and benevolence is John Jarndyce. His philosophy is that nothing good can come of the Jarndyce and Jarndyce suit — and he's right. Those who expect anything more are eaten up by it. Jarndyce has his own separate source of wealth, which he uses wisely and benevolently, making the most of what he has and helping others whenever he can. In fact, he seems incapable of unkindness. To deal with others' foibles, he instead projects his dismay onto the "east wind" and resolves his issues in the "Growlery," a special room set aside for just that purpose.

Esther's other male counterpart, though less prominent in the story, is the young, dark surgeon, Allan Woodcourt, a strong, steady, benevolent, and deeply committed person, who mostly features at the beginning and end of the novel. Woodcourt and Esther love each other, but they don't admit this until close to the end of the book, when it seems to be too late. Fortunately, John Jarndyce's benevolence comes to the rescue.

Sir Leicester and Lady Dedlock — Other prominent characters include Sir Leicester and Lady Dedlock, the central focus of the fashionably elite aristocracy. But the glitter of wealth and status have their dark side, and aside from the boredom that haunts the lives of many of the aristocracy, the Dedlock mansion, Chesney Wold, is itself haunted by an echoing step on the terrace called the "Ghost's Walk." It is said that the sound of this step signifies family disgrace, and Lady Dedlock does indeed harbor a secret that finally propels her to her tragic ending.

The Rouncewell connection — Chesney Wold's housekeeper, the elderly and dignified Mrs. Rouncewell, has two sons, one of whom became a well-known and prosperous ironmaster while the other — the younger, wilder, but also favorite son — became a soldier and disappeared. This son, George, later reappears in the story and becomes a major suspect in the murder of Mr. Tulkinghorn, Sir Leicester's solicitor. He is later exonerated, but his connection to the case is more intricate: he was once the companion of Captain Hawdon, the former (now dead from opium) and original true love of Lady Dedlock before her marriage to Sir Leicester. It was George's possession of a note by Captain Hawdon, along with the fact that he owed money to greedy Grandfather Smallweed, that got him more closely involved with Tulkinghorn. Immediately before his murder, Tulkinghorn was about to expose Lady Dedlock's prior affair to Sir Leicester, who loved her deeply and forgave her when he did finally find out. But by then, it was too late. Rather than face the situation, Lady Dedlock had already run from it — straight to her death in the wintry cold and wet near Hawdon's grave in a diseased burial ground for the poor. In the meantime, Esther, who had helped in the search for Lady Dedlock, had already known for some time that she was her real mother and Captain Hawdon her father; and Esther and her mother had even connected with each other at one point and had a chance — though brief — to express their love. Sadly, Esther and Inspector Bucket, who led the investigation, arrived too late to save Lady Dedlock.

Multiple subplots — There are more than thirty-five stories that run through the book. There is Jo, the poor boy who shows Lady Dedlock Captain Hawdon's grave. Jo had a special connection with Hawdon, and he, too, dies a sad death after living a sad and difficult life, though he had a good heart. There is Mr. Snagsby, the kind law stationer, who provided Hawdon with work and helped Jo whenever he could. There is Mrs. Snagsby, the ridiculously suspicious wife, and their epileptic servant girl, Guster. There is Mr. Bucket, the police inspector, who finds Lady Dedlock and solves the Tulkinghorn murder case. There is Hortense, Lady Dedlock's former attendant, a Frenchwoman with too much passion and venom for her own good. It is she who murdered Tulkinghorn and then tried to pin the blame on Lady Dedlock. There are the Bagnets, George Rouncewell's wholesome and loyal friends; and it's Mrs. Bagnet — the "old girl" — who finally reconnects George with his aged mother. There is Phil, George's deformed but good-hearted helper, and George's brother the ironmaster, with his prosperous business and happy, prospering family. His son, Watt, will eventually marry Rosa, one of the prettiest girls around and Lady Dedlock's personal maid, who replaced Hortense after the latter was fired. In a full circle, Mr. George returns to Chesney Wold to care for Sir Leicester and be near his own mother in their old age. And there are many more stories, all connected in different ways and weaving a fabric that together reflects the complex society of the times. Some characters, like Mr. Guppy, the inept, pretentious law clerk, provide comic relief; others are inspiring; still others, tragic.

Archetypes—Not all the stories are directly connected to the Jarndyce and Jarndyce suit. Some are symbolic of some aspect of the time or even a larger, more permanent issue. Mrs. Jellyby and others like her show what happens when would-be philanthropists forget what is close by—family and the immediate neighborhood—and think only of long-distance causes or, like Mrs. Pardiggle, force their "philanthropy" on others. Harold Skimpole is the epitome of the careless, self-absorbed artist who considers only his own needs and acts like he's God's gift to creation simply for existing. He gets away with it on charm alone. Mr. Turveydrop is obsessed with his "Deportment" and uses it as an excuse for self-indulgence, though to be fair, he sometimes shows signs of compassion and humanity. The Smallweeds are caricatures of greed, selfishness, and small-mindedness. Mr. Krook is the evil, alcoholic junk shop owner, who dies of spontaneous combustion. And so it goes. Fortunately, these less appealing characters are offset by those with larger, nobler, more compassionate and dedicated natures. Rich and poor, good and bad, sick and healthy, mad and sane—and everything in between— all parade through the pages of *Bleak House,* a timeless, universal human drama as relevant today as it was when Dickens wrote it more than a hundred and fifty years ago.

Conclusions—So what happens in the end? Many of the characters reap what they sow. Some, like the boy Jo, are the victims of circumstances beyond their control, and they lack the means—both inner and outer—to overcome them. The Jarndyce suit, a farce from the beginning, confirms its true nature at the end, when the case is closed because the whole estate has been consumed by legal fees.

And what about the main characters? Richard is exhausted by his obsession with the case and dies without ever seeing his baby. Ada gives birth soon afterwards and is comforted by her child. She and her baby boy spend many of their days with their good friends, Esther, Allan, and John Jarndyce. Mr. George and his mother, Mrs. Rouncewell, take care of Sir Leicester, who regularly visits his late wife's grave. Mr. George brings Phil with him to Chesney Wold, and in the summer, his friends the Bagnets visit him. Charley, Esther's attendant, marries the miller and lives close to Esther. Caddy Jellyby ends up happy and prosperous, and though her family has its problems, she makes the most of things. Esther and Allan live with their two daughters in their own beautiful little Bleak House, a loving gift from Esther's beloved guardian, John Jarndyce, who is always welcome and has his own Growlery there, though he hardly needs it anymore. The moral seems to be that whoever gives love and cares about others receives the same in the end—and much, much more.

Key Themes and Conecpts

The Calm, Efficient Housekeeper

The calm, efficient housekeeper is a theme that comes up repeatedly in Dickens's novels. In this one, it emerges several times, most especially in the form of Esther Summerson, who manages the Bleak House household. But housekeeping is about much more than home economics: the ideal housekeeper, as expressed in the last chapter of Proverbs, is not only a model of efficiency and order but the key to the home's happiness and comfort. When order, freshness, cleanliness, comfort, and beauty are present in the home, the happiness, health, and success of all who live there is assured. The model of such a home presents itself not only in Bleak House itself but in Mrs. Rouncewell's calm touch, Boythorn's welcoming home and garden, Caddy Jellyby's efforts for her family, and in the new "Bleak House," John Jarndyce's gift to Esther and Allan Woodcourt.

Farsighted "Philanthropy"

The opposite of the calm, conscientious housekeeper is symbolized by Mrs. Jellyby, the most prominent of the farsighted "philanthropists." She was so busy with her African project that she couldn't see the suffering caused by her lack of concern for her home and family. Esther's commentary on her was that it seemed wrong to focus on distant concerns when her own home was in disarray. Mrs. Jellyby also seemed oblivious of the real philanthropic opportunities that lay right in front of her on English soil in the form of squalid slums, poverty, poor working conditions, prostitution, and other obvious concerns. She and Mrs. Pardiggle, who shoved her "philanthropic" ideas down others' throats, may have had the right general idea, but they lacked the compassion that is the hallmark of real philanthropy.

The Irresponsible "Artist"

Similar to the farsighted philanthropist, the irresponsible "unworldly" would-be "artist" or person of leisure is likewise lacking in both practical sense and compassion. This archetype is symbolized here by Howard Skimpole, but it arises in other of Dickens's novels as well. Dickens is fully aware of the importance of entertainment and enjoyment as human needs, but the so-called unworldly innocent who focuses only on these things and neglects dealing with basic issues ends up being a hypocrite and a burden on society. Such types often resort to charm to get by, and they profess ignorance and inability to justify their helplessness. Luckily for them, they can often find the support of generous, indulgent friends, but it's not unusual for them to call those same friends "selfish," as Skimpole does later in his memoir.

The Decline of the Aristocracy and the Rise of the Wealthy Industrialist

This trend is most readily symbolized by Sir Leicester and the elder Rouncewell son, respectively. Sir Leicester constantly laments the decline of England, and when Rouncewell's business success earns him an invitation to Parliament (which he declines), to Sir Leicester, it signifies the rapid deterioration of societal and political structures. Sir Leicester's opinion is later confirmed by the difficulties experienced by his side of the political campaign, while Rouncewell's side receives a favorable reception by the public. The same trend is further symbolized by the uselessness of Sir Leicester's cousins' restricted "aristocratic" lifestyle and by the emptiness and silence that ultimately take over Chesney Wold.

The Terror of Shame

The centrality of this theme becomes more obvious as the novel's various subplots start to come together. Its symbol is the echoing step of the Ghost's Walk, which heralds some shameful dark secret in the Dedlock family. That shame, which Lady Dedlock harbors throughout her life and which finally destroys her, is transmitted to her child through Miss Barbary, Lady Dedlock's sister. Mr. George, too, allows shame to prevent him from getting in touch with his family, though in his case, it doesn't stand in the way of a happy ending. The same is true of Esther, who despite a hard beginning and with a lot of outward help and inner resourcefulness, manages to put the past and its scars (mostly) behind her and find happiness. She is able to transmit the same to Caddy Jellyby, who, at first ashamed of her lack of breeding, takes a positive approach and turns what might have been a miserable life into a happy, useful one.

The Power of Love

If shame can convey one useful lesson, it is the power of love to overcome all circumstances. This kind of love is determined and practical. It does not accept the inevitability of a negative outcome but works to change things for the better. Its strength is mercy; its tool, forgiveness. So when Sir Leicester finally discovers Lady Dedlock's painful secret, his reaction is one of compassion and love. Sadly, Lady Dedlock's shame ran so deep that she never discovered the depth of his love and forgiveness. George Rouncewell and Esther Summerson fared better. George's good friend, Mrs. Bagnet, saw to it that his shame would not stand in the way of reuniting with his family, who welcomed him with open arms. Esther caught the eye of the benevolent John Jarndyce early on, and with his generous help and her own determination and many fine qualities, she went on to lead a prosperous, happy, and useful life.

Even when it doesn't fully transform a life, the power of love can begin to lead things in a better direction or provide comfort and moments of happiness to the destitute or suffering. Its effect is always reciprocal, blessing both those who help and those who are helped.

The Chokehold of a Greed-Driven Legal Bureaucracy

The epitome of this idea is, of course, the Jarndyce and Jarndyce case, which in the end is eaten up in legal costs after years of dragging on and on through needless inefficiency and procrastination. The sad irony is that it destroyed a number of lives in the process. By contrast, once it was determined that the case could no longer continue because there was no money to pay the lawyers, the general response in the court was one of laughter. It was true that the case was a farce, but it was also true that the destroyed lives were real. Ironically, some lawyers, like Kenge, saw the process and outcome as a triumph of the English legal system. Others, like Vholes, suddenly lost all interest in "serving" their clients.

Greed As the Root of Many Evils

One of Dickens's most famous tales, *A Christmas Carol*, clearly shows how greed leads to misery and death while generosity leads to happiness and life. One expands; the other contracts. That theme is played out in *Bleak House* through a number of different characters, and those driven by greed are ultimately never successful. Depending on their exact situation, they either grow miserable, go mad, become ill, fail to support themselves, or die—and some even fall prey to all of it. Their lives lack balance and grace, because they forget the things of the heart and soul. Even those who do "succeed" in this regard, like the Chancery Court, create victims all around them and cannot therefore be considered truly wealthy. True success and wealth can only be inclusive, as demonstrated by the generosity of John Jarndyce, who wisely ignores the central symbol of greed—the Jarndyce case—and does his best to make up for the damage it has caused.

Happiness and health as the direct result of unselfishness

A similar theme in reverse is that happiness is the by-product of selflessness and love. It is increased by giving and caring, not by taking and selfishness. Its best examples in the novel are John Jarndyce, who positively beams after doing some kind act; Esther Summerson, who is a source of comfort and kindness to many; Allan Woodcourt, who stays up all night to help the poor, with no thought of return; fresh-faced, honest Mrs. Bagnet, who thinks nothing of traveling miles to help a friend; and the good-hearted trooper, Mr. George, who goes out of his way to make things right. He is warmly received by his equally good-hearted mother and brother. Unlike those driven by greed, the connection between them all has nothing to do with economics and everything to do with love and practical caring.

Darkness and light

Another theme that plays throughout the book is that of darkness and light. Darkness is always equated with foreboding, disease, and death. It haunts the squalid slum, Tom-all-Alone's; hovers over the diseased poor persons' graveyard; takes over Richard and Ada's apartment as Richard succumbs to the Jarndyce case; fills Mr. Tulkinghorn's room following his death; and casts its lengthening shadow over Lady Dedlock's portrait. It seems to follow certain people around — the vampiric Mr. Vholes, who always dresses in black and spends his time in his dark, dingy office; and Mr. Tulkinghorn, who always seems to be lurking in the shadows.

Light, on the other hand, is equated with goodness, life, and true innocence, which can exist even when the first two qualities are overshadowed by outward conditions. This last kind of radiance emanates from Ada's pure love, from the innocence of the brickmaker's dead infant, and from John Jarndyce, who is surrounded by an angelic halo after doing something particularly kind. Goodness, cheer, usefulness, and health are equated with rising early in the morning and, if need be, having the capacity to stay up all night in the service of others. And the welcoming comforts and beauty Bleak House itself, both the old and the new, both home and garden, are clear examples of the effects of freshness and light.

Key People

There are more than thirty-five characters in *Bleak House*, so the following is only a partial listing. Except for the first five (through Sir Leicester), the characters' names are listed in alphabetical order by last name first, if available, and then first name or title.

Esther Summerson

One of two narrators and a central character in the plot, Esther Summerson began life as a lonely orphan who went on to become John Jarndyce's beloved housekeeper and the companion of his two wards. She even nearly becomes his wife until he steps aside to accommodate the mutual love between her and the young doctor, Allan Woodcourt. Esther's selfless and gracious yet practical character earns her the love and respect of virtually all who meet her.

John Jarndyce

Another central connecting thread in the plot, John Jarndyce is the wealthy, generous, compassionate owner of Bleak House who shares his name with the lawsuit that has destroyed so many lives. John Jarndyce transformed Bleak House into a pleasant mansion after his uncle's suicide and took on the care of three young people in an effort to make up for the damage. He is consistently giving and kind, and he has wisely chosen to ignore the Jarndyce suit in the firm belief that nothing good will ever come of it. He is plagued at time by the "east wind," which always appears with any unpleasant occurrence or topic. His resolves these issues by visiting his "Growlery," a special room set aside for airing his concerns. In the end, the east wind disappears forever, and a good west wind blows — the result of a lifetime of kindness and generosity.

Ada Clare, Richard Carstone

Ada Clare and Richard Carstone are the two young wards in the Jarndyce suit. They are also distant cousins, and their fates become inextricably bound by their growing mutual love and, less fortunately, the Jarndyce lawsuit. They meet through John Jarndyce, who adopts them as his wards to make up for the damage caused by the case. They eventually marry in secret, and Ada, who is beautiful, loving, and normally wise, gives her inheritance to help Richard, who has allowed himself to be sucked in by the false hope that the Jarndyce suit will someday make them rich. In the end, he exhausts all his resources and dies before seeing the son Ada is about to bear him. But before he dies, he admits his mistake and reconciles his relationship with John Jarndyce, whom he had falsely accused. Ada then gives birth to their son, who helps her to gradually heal from the tragedy of Richard's life.

Lady Dedlock

The lovely, accomplished wife of Sir Leicester Dedlock, Lady Dedlock is at the center of the fashionable world. But for all the glitter and status, she is thoroughly bored and unhappy. Lady Dedlock also harbors a secret. As a young woman, she was in love with a captain who presumably drowned, and she bore his child — Esther Summerson — out of wedlock. By the time she discovers that the captain did not drown, he is truly dead and buried, having succumbed to an opium habit. Her own life ends in tragedy: unable to deal with the fact that her secret is about to be revealed by the family lawyer, she leaves everything behind and dies in the wintry cold by the gate of the cemetery where her former lover lies buried.

Sir Leicester

Sir Leicester Dedlock, Baronet, was a distinguished member of society and the owner of Chesney Wold, a castle in the Lincolnshire countryside. He married Lady Dedlock out of love, and her beauty, intelligence, and good breeding were the center of his personal life for many years. When she suddenly disappeared, in part out of an unwillingness to shame him, Sir Leicester fell ill and aged tremendously, seemingly overnight. What Lady Dedlock underestimated was the depth of Sir Leicester's love: on learning of her secret, he immediately forgave her, his only desire being to find her and bring her back.

Allan Woodcourt

Allan Woodcourt is the young surgeon who truly cares for people in a consistent, active way, both as a doctor and as a person. For a while, he goes to India but eventually returns, gets a job in Yorkshire, and in the meantime, admits his love for Esther Summerson.

Unlike Richard, who has a tendency to be flighty and unfocused, Woodcourt shows a steadiness, focus, and compassion from the beginning that is ultimately the key to his success and happiness. But Woodcourt does not judge others, and when Esther asks him to befriend Richard for the latter's sake, he does not hesitate to do so. In the end, Esther and Woodcourt marry with John Jarndyce's heartfelt blessing, even though Jarndyce had originally planned to marry Esther himself.

The Bagnets

The Bagnets are Mr. George's close friends. Mr. "Lignum" Bagnet knows George from his soldier days. He married the wholesome, straightforward, down-to-earth, efficient Mrs. Bagnet, who is constantly seen washing greens to feed her family and keep them healthy. The Bagnets have two daughters and a son, whose names — Woolwich, Malta, and Quebec — all reflect Lignum's former military stations. It's

Mrs. Bagnet who finally reunites George with his mother, and the Bagnets and George remain friends for life.

Mr. Bucket

Mr. Bucket is the inspector who shows up on and off throughout the story. He is clearly observant, but the real benevolence of his character doesn't become obvious until the end, when he solves the missing person's case involving Lady Dedlock—though too late—and finds Mr. Tulkinghorn's real killer.

Miss Flite

Miss Flite is the little, old madwoman who is a fixture at the Chancery Court proceedings. Like Ada and Richard, she began many years ago as a ward in Jarndyce. Back then, she was also young, hopeful, and beautiful. But though she maintains her good spirits, the suit takes its toll on all who get involved. In Miss Flite's case, this manifests most clearly through her twenty or so birds, which she keeps caged and literally in the dark. She has given them names like Hope, Beauty, and Youth as well as Dust, Ashes, Death, Sheepskin to reflect the effects of the Jarndyce suit. When the case is finally resolved, she finally sets the birds free.

Mr. Guppy

Mr. Guppy is employed as a law clerk by Kenge and Carboy, John Jarndyce's legal representatives. Though a minor character, he is important in several ways. He falls in love with Esther Summerson and proposes to her more than once. Early on, he notices a striking resemblance between Esther and Lady Dedlock and tries to use the information (unsuccessfully) to gain Esther's favor. He is also friends with both Jobling (aka Weevle) and young Smallweed, which gives him access to certain letters implicating Lady Dedlock. Together with his ridiculous mother, Mr. Guppy's appearances provide a bit of comic relief.

Hortense

Mademoiselle Hortense was Lady Dedlock's first personal attendant, but Lady Dedlock preferred the young, beautiful village girl, Rosa, and ended up firing Hortense. Passionate and rash by nature, Hortense hated Lady Dedlock and hoped to destroy her. After accepting payment from Mr. Tulkinghorn, who was trying to extract information about Lady Dedlock, she felt manipulated by him and ended up murdering him. To help cover her tracks, she got a job with the Buckets, but Mr. and Mrs. Bucket saw through her machinations, and Mr. Bucket finally entrapped and arrested her.

Caddy Jellyby

Caddy Jellyby is the daughter of Mrs. Jellyby, the farsighted "philanthropist." When Caddy first met Esther and Ada, she was unhappy and unhealthy, trapped in a position as her mother's scribe. Determined to escape the woeful lifestyle her mother had imposed on the Jellyby family, Caddy befriends Esther and learns how to be a lady, dance teacher, and good housekeeper. She marries Prince Turveydrop, a dance teacher (to her mother's dismay), and they have a child. The child is sickly, Prince becomes lame, and the elder Mr. Turveydrop is demanding, but Caddy makes the most of it and becomes happy, healthy, and prosperous in spite of her rough beginning and multiple obstacles. Like all of Dickens's best characters, her happiness is not confined to herself but improves the lives of all around her (except her mother, who thinks she's foolish).

Mrs. Jellyby

Mrs. Jellyby is the archetypal long-distance philanthropist, who, no matter how bad things are in her immediate surroundings, can only see what's far away—in her case, her African project. Her husband may be miserable, her children out of control, her servants drunk and quarreling, and her house a mess, but none of that is of any concern to her. Furthermore, there may be pressing issues right at home on English soil—horrible slums, unemployment, pollution, poverty, etc. Mrs. Jellyby does finally take up the women's suffrage issue when her African project goes nowhere. Luckily, her daughter Caddy, whose interests she considers "trivial," manages to improve the lives of her father and little brother, something Mrs. Jellyby never did herself.

Jenny and Liz

Jenny and Liz are the poor brickmakers' wives who represent the opposite end of the societal spectrum in relation to the aristocratic Dedlocks. Their husbands are abusive, and they live in squalid conditions that make survival difficult. Jenny's baby dies early in the story, which prompts Esther to place her handkerchief over its face. Both the handkerchief and Jenny become pivotal when Lady Dedlock, fearing her secret love affair from long ago is about to be disclosed, tries to spare her husband the shame by forsaking all. She retrieves the handkerchief—her only remaining connection to Esther, her beloved child from the affair—and changes clothes with Jenny to avoid detection as she seeks to join her one-time lover in death. Liz is Jenny's compassionate friend.

Jo

Jo is the destitute, illiterate street sweeper boy from London's worst slum. He has a personal connection to the law writer, Nemo (Captain Hawdon), who takes pity on him when he can, as does the kindly Mr.

Snagsby. Later, Lady Dedlock disguises herself and pays Jo to show her Nemo's grave and the other sites related to his last days. Jo ends up getting smallpox, which he transmits to Charley, Esther's maid, who passes it on to Esther after they try to help Jo. He dies a young death after leading a miserable life. But for all the misery of his life, he had a good heart and helped people whenever he could.

Mr. Jobling

Mr. Jobling is Mr. Guppy's friend, who takes over Nemo's job and apartment after the latter's death. He brings his own fashionable flair to Cook's Court, and for a while, the gossip is that he will inherit Krook's supposed fortune. Jobling is mainly important to the story because he is Guppy's main access point to the love letters between Lady Dedlock and Captain Hawdon.

Mr. Krook

Mr. Krook is most interesting because of his strange death by spontaneous combustion, a relatively unknown phenomenon at the time Dickens wrote the novel. Krook is the owner of the rag and bottle shop as well as an evil cat, who is his constant companion. He can neither read nor write yet has taught himself how to copy letters, and he takes a strong interest in the Jarndyce case. It's in Krook's shop that a both a mysterious will and Lady Dedlock's letters are found.

Nemo (Captain Hawdon)

Captain Hawdon was Lady Dedlock's one-time lover many years ago, before she married Sir Leicester. He is also the father of Esther Summerson, but dies before she meets him. This is probably a good thing for her, since he succumbed to an opium addiction, which was the reason for his death. Nemo (which Tulkinghorn pointed out meant "nobody" in Latin), was an excellent copyist and had a soft spot for Jo, who remembers him fondly as being "very good" to him.

Rosa

Rosa is the young, innocent, and beautiful maid-in-training who replaces Hortense as Lady Dedlock's attendant. Lady Dedlock is fond of her but lets her go when she fears her personal secret is about to be disclosed and she feels the need to switch to a cold demeanor. Rosa ends up marrying Watt Rouncewell, the ironmaster's son.

George Rouncewell

George Rouncewell, former trooper and best known as Mr. George, is Mrs. Rouncewell's "vagabond" younger son who became a soldier. For all George's wild ways, he is a strong, compassionate person with a definite sense of right. He owns a shooting gallery, which he maintains with his deformed but good-hearted sidekick, Phil. Later in the story, George is erroneously arrested for the murder of Mr. Tulkinghorn, but he is finally released and ends up closing his shooting gallery and moving to Chesney Wold (where he grew up) to care for Sir Leicester in his old age and to keep his elderly mother company.

Mr. Rouncewell, the ironmaster

Mrs. Rouncewell's older son is the steady, successful ironmaster who settles in northern England and becomes an important figure in business, politics, and the rising non-aristocratic wealthy class. By the time George seeks him out after many years away, the older brother owns his own iron factory, the town bank, and an elegant home. He is happily married, with children whom he insists on educating to their new social level. Yet despite his accomplishments and George's fears of rejection, the elder Rouncewell son welcomes his "vagabond" brother back with heartfelt warmth and generosity.

Mrs. Rouncewell

Mrs. Rouncewell is the dignified elderly widow who manages the housekeeping at Chesney Wold, the Dedlock's Lincolnshire mansion. Mrs. Rouncewell has two sons: George, the younger—her favorite—who ran off to be soldier, was lost, and finally returns; and the elder, who becomes a successful ironmaster. She and her son George support and comfort Sir Leicester in his final years.

Howard Skimpole

Another archetype, Howard Skimpole represents the carefree, "unworldly" artist, who is incapable of any kind of practicality, even though he excels at extracting money for his needs. Rather than attending to practical things, he prefers to play, sing, converse, etc., and he is a master of manipulating to suit his purposes. He gets by on charm for his whole life, but his memoirs reveal another side when he characterizes his kind and generous friend John Jarndyce as selfish.

The Smallweeds

We first meet Bart (young) Smallweed, who, having modeled himself on Mr. Guppy, has managed to escape some of his relatives' nastier characteristics. Unlike the rest of the family, he enjoys life to some extent. He has a twin sister, Judy, whose job is to care for the two grandparents, both parents being dead. The entire family looks old and shriveled, regardless of actual age (Bart and Judy are only in their teens). Grandfather Smallweed is the epitome of greed and selfishness, and Grandmother Smallweed suffers from dementia. Her husband hates her, but she becomes useful to him when, as the sister of Mr. Krook, she inherits Krook's dubious legacy—mostly junk—upon his death. However, among the junk are both Lady Dedlock's letters to her lover and a will that could change the course of the lawsuit, and Grandfather Smallweed sets out to capitalize on these items. His other role is as Mr. George's creditor, and again he tries to extract all he can. Fortunately, those who deal with him are intelligent enough to see their way around his manipulations.

Mr. Snagsby

Mr. Snagsby is the law stationer who lives in Cook's Court and works directly with Mr. Tulkinghorn. He hired Nemo as a copyist and then gave the same position to Jobling after Nemo's death. Mr. Snagsby was a kind, courteous gentleman, who was one of the few to take pity on Jo, periodically providing him with half crowns. He suffered from the suspicions—finally put to rest by Mr. Bucket—of an irrationally jealous wife, and his servant Guster plays an important role because of her interaction with Lady Dedlock shortly before the latter's death.

Mr. Tulkinghorn

Mr. Tulkinghorn is the lawyer for the Dedlock family, among other aristocratic houses, and he is therefore a general repository for aristocratic secrets. He is known for his discretion, but he can also be manipulative and cold, which finally leads to his murder by Hortense, Lady Dedlock's former attendant. Shortly before his death, Mr. Tulkinghorn had infuriated Mr. George with his manipulations and alienated and frightened Lady Dedlock with his threats to disclose her personal secret, all of which complicated the murder investigation.

Mr. Turveydrop

Yet another archetype, Mr. Turveydrop the elder is the owner of the dance school where his son Prince, Caddy's fiancé, now teaches. Turveydrop, however, does not teach dance. That was originally the task of his late wife, who died from exhaustion to support her husband's habit of Deportment. "Deportment" involves playing the role of a gentleman in every imaginable way, which includes posturing, dressing up, dining out, etc. However, the trappings of Deportment conveniently apply only to himself. Esther's initial impression of the elder Turveydrop is that everything about him is false. Yet, though Turveydrop never gives up his concern with Deportment, he does manage to grow past his own self-centeredness enough to embrace his son's marriage and Caddy's family, and in doing so, to bring some small bit of improvement to others' lives, especially those of Caddy's father and her brother Peepy.

Volumnia Dedlock

Volumnia Dedlock is the most developed of Sir Leicester's many aristocratic cousins. She is the symbol, in a comical, tasteless way, of a dying aristocracy. Like the other cousins, she is prevented from earning her living, so she spends her time socializing, attending occasional political events, and otherwise idling her life away. A bit of a caricature, she is represented as clumsy and having a taste for too much rouge and the same worn-out pearl necklace. But she does keep Sir Leicester company in his old age, and for that he is appreciative, even if he sleeps through most of her reading.

Chapter Summaries

Preface

Based in fact — Dickens's main point in the preface to *Bleak House* is that as unbelievable as certain aspects of his story might be, they are based in fact.

Inefficiency of the Court of Chancery — Specifically, he is referring here to the Court of Chancery's reputation for complicating and extending its cases way beyond what is rational or necessary. This milking of the lawsuits under its jurisdiction benefited no one but the multitude of judges, lawyers, and court employees involved, all of whom charged a fee for their services. Dickens's attempt to shame the "parsimonious public," who refused to allow the Court to add more judges to its roster, should therefore be understood as tongue in cheek.

Spontaneous combustion — The second "unbelievable" subject Dickens mentions is spontaneous combustion. In the early 1850s, the general public was still in denial of its existence, which led Dickens to both investigate and defend its actuality by citing various statistics and specific historical cases.

Concluding remarks — Dickens ended the preface with the statement that he deliberately focused on the romantic aspect of "familiar," or ordinary, things, which was also a major aim of his publication *Household Words*. He further rejoiced that his readership numbers were greater than ever. This is especially meaningful since, as mentioned in the introduction to this edition of *Bleak House*,[i] Dickens took a number of literary risks that made the novel critically controversial. He experimented with plot and sentence structure, narrative voice, mystery in storytelling, and the creative, witty use of words and puns. Not least, he dared to say what others were neglecting — to show the darker side of life in Victorian London. But as implied above, while this may have put a dent in his critical acceptance, it had no negative effects on his general popularity.

Chapter 1 — In Chancery

Fog, fog everywhere — In a sense, Chapter 1 is all about fog and mud, starting with Dickens's description of the ubiquitous fog, mud, puddles, and pollution so characteristic of London, at the time the world's largest city. But the fog and mud, and the aggravation they caused, are not just literal in this case. Aside from the external London setting, Dickens's focus here is the Court of Chancery and its grindingly slow, bureaucratic process that killed every case it took on, so that people were actually warned by the lawyers themselves that they would be better off avoiding a lawsuit rather than submitting themselves to the Chancery Court's convoluted ways. Some cases, like the Jarndyce case that is central to *Bleak House,* even dragged on for decades until all resources — financial, emotional, and in some cases, physical — were exhausted, and there was a question as to whether anyone even knew anymore what the case was actually about.

The Chancery's cast of characters — Sitting at the center of all this fog, both literal and figurative, was the Lord High Chancellor, the reigning figure of the Court of Chancery and the holder of one of the highest offices in the land. Around him were the lawyers and judges — the advocates, barristers, solicitors, and masters, each with his own role in the tedious Chancery drama. They were accompanied by the clerks, apprentices, and copyists as well as the newspaper and court reporters, not to mention the odd human fixture such as the elderly madwoman, the jaundiced prisoner, and the man from Shropshire, whose main goal was to corner the Lord Chancellor at the end of the day's proceedings. These last three all frequented the Court in the naïve belief that they eventually stood to gain something from doing so.

The Lord Chancellor sees through the mud to the matter of two young people — Of all those present, Mr. Tangle knew the most about the Jarndyce case. In fact, he had been steeped in it for so long that he seemed to know nothing else. Whether that knowledge was useful was another question, as it seemed to only add to the inefficiency. Somehow, though, the Lord Chancellor managed to make his way through Mr. Tangle's tangled information and useless presentations to deduce that the young boy and girl in his private quarters, both of whom were related to the Jarndyce case, would be living not with their uncle (who was dead) or their grandfather (who suffered from some brain defect) but with a cousin. He even managed to determine that he should broach the matter in court the following morning.

Another day ends in Chancery — And so, after the usual official tasks and the customary, albeit thwarted, attempts by the few sad, stray human fixtures to gain some distant advantage, another day in Chancery came to an end.

Chapter 2 — In Fashion

Sleeping through life — In Dickens's view, the world of fashion, though it had its good points and people, was a sleepy, stagnant world, not so different from the Court of Chancery in the sense that it moved within its own limited rules and sense of things, without much heed for the world around it. While the Chancery Court was bound up in useless precedents, the world of fashion was bound up in fine materials and was incapable of looking outward or forward.

Lady Dedlock — Lady Dedlock is fashion's equivalent of the Lord High Chancellor, and as Chapter 2 opens, she is preparing to leave for Paris, where she plans on staying for an indefinite number of weeks. That, in any case, is the word according to the society columns. She had been staying at her country home, a castle in Lincolnshire, but Lincolnshire is too rainy and dismal to enjoy for the time being.

Sir Leicester Dedlock — Lady Dedlock's husband, Sir Leicester Dedlock, is a member of an ancient and respected family of baronets, a class of commoner higher than an ordinary knight but lower than a baron, the lowest level of the aristocracy. Dickens describes him as "high-spirited" and adamant about matters such as truth and honor, with opinions that emphasize the glory of man above that of nature, which did better when improved upon by mankind. He was in his sixties, at least twenty years older than his wife, whom he still found attractive and to this day treated with great courtesy — his sole romantic quality, according to Dickens, aside from his genuine love for his wife. Lady Dedlock, for her part, began with none of her husband's advantages — possibly even without any family — but she made up for her lack of worldly stature with her beauty, intelligence, and good sense, all of which were enough to capture and keep Sir Leicester's love.

Tired of life — Unfortunately, having achieved the ultimate position in high society, Lady Dedlock appears to have grown tired of it all, and her general demeanor is one of boredom. She wears it well, though, with her classical features and perfect breeding and grooming.

Mr. Tulkinghorn — Sir Leicester and Lady Dedlock are currently staying at their London residence before proceeding to Paris. They are met there by Mr. Tulkinghorn, the family lawyer. Mr. Tulkinghorn is an elderly gentleman of great discretion, and a familiar, though quiet, face among the aristocracy. His silence and discretion are a good thing, too, because he probably harbors more secrets about the aristocracy than anybody else.

Lady Dedlock's illusion — While Mr. Tulkinghorn may have been the main storehouse for the aristocracy's secrets, he was not the only one. Unfortunately, the other storehouses — the servants, tailors, jewelers, booksellers, and other merchants and procurers of the fashionable life — were not as discreet. Lady Dedlock's illusion was that her private thoughts and preferences were known only to her and a handful or two of people who served her needs. It did not occur to her that they passed the information among themselves, with the intention of manipulating her into buying their services. They played into her illusion of being in control, and she never suspected that things might be otherwise.

Lady Dedlock's involvement with Jarndyce and Jarndyce — Lady Dedlock's illusions did not, however, extend to the Court of Chancery, where she was involved in the Jarndyce and Jarndyce case. That, indeed, was the reason for Mr. Tulkinghorn's appearance at the Dedlock's London residence, since he wanted to inform his clients of the latest developments in the case before they left for Paris. He did not pretend, however, on Lady Dedlock's questioning, that anything concrete had transpired, and she knew better than to hope that it had. As for Sir Leicester, he accepted the civilized need for such structures as the Chancery Court, and he took the whole process, inefficiencies and all, in stride—including the fact that marrying Lady Dedlock had given him nothing of a material nature.

Lady Dedlock falls suddenly ill—In any event, Mr. Tulkinghorn proceeded to read the latest legal unfoldments to Lady Dedlock as she sat by the fire. Finding the opening formalities tedious, she moved him along, asking him skip that section. All of a sudden, however, she showed an inexplicable interest in the copyist's script. Meanwhile, Sir Leicester had fallen asleep in his seat by the fire, when he was suddenly awoken by Mr. Tulkinghorn's exclamation that Lady Dedlock had fallen ill. Claiming that she was only faint, she retired to her room, while Mr. Tulkinghorn continued reading the material to Sir Leicester, who mused that his wife's sudden illness must be due to the weather and her recent misery and boredom at their Lincolnshire home.

Chapter 3 — A Progress

Esther Summerson — Chapter 3 introduces Esther Summerson, who now takes over the narrative. Esther's humility — or perhaps, her youthful insecurity — is apparent from the chapter's first sentence, where she informs us of her lack of cleverness and consequent need for the patience of others. In fact, Esther seems unusually shy and a bit lonely, relying on her doll to fill the void. She admits to being observant, but she doubts her ability to interpret her observations and blames herself for the deficiencies she sees in others.

A lonely childhood — Esther was an orphan who was raised by her godmother, described by her as a good, devout woman, though also serious and strict. In fact, her godmother never smiled, which made it hard for Esther to love her and open up to her, so once again, her doll took the place of a human being, and Esther's sense of self suffered.

A stained orphanhood — Esther had no memory or knowledge of her parents, and the servant, Mrs. Rachael, was no help in providing information. Her godmother also refused to reveal anything, which left Esther feeling that she was different and wrong, a feeling that was heightened on her birthday. All the girls at school celebrated their birthdays, but Esther's was ignored, and when she finally pleaded with her godmother to explain, she discovered that she was born in disgrace and therefore never caused anyone any joy, least of all her godmother. She yearned to be loved as she loved her doll, but she found no resonance anywhere. Still, Esther chose to be cheerful and grateful and to do her best to hopefully earn a little love in life by being hardworking, kind, and satisfied with her lot. Her tears therefore didn't last long, but her godmother's coldness on her birthday made the barrier between them seem even thicker.

A mysterious meeting — One day, when Esther was about 12 years old, her godmother called her over instead of ignoring her as usual. She introduced Esther to an unknown gentleman who was obviously well off and who quickly examined Esther and gave her godmother a nod of approval. Esther was then excused and, after a polite curtsy, dutifully went to her room.

Esther's godmother dies suddenly — Esther's next meeting with the gentleman was not until two years later, following her godmother's sudden death. Esther had been reading to her from one of the Gospels one night, when her godmother suddenly stood up and screamed out an entirely different verse — about watching lest the Lord come suddenly. After that, she keeled over and lay in a catatonic state for two weeks until she finally died. During this time, Esther did all she could to watch and pray for some small movement or sign of recognition, but her love and her efforts were futile.

Mr. Conversation Kenge — The unknown gentleman returned the day after the godmother's burial, this time introducing himself as Mr. Conversation Kenge, of Kenge and Carboy, a London law office. He represented Mr. Jarndyce, who, out of his sense of honor and kindness, would provide for Esther's future. She was to be placed in an excellent situation, where she would be cared for and taught how to fulfill the duties of her new station in life. In return, she was simply expected to be loyal, dutiful, and good. Throughout the conversation, Mr. Kenge repeatedly mentioned the Jarndyce suit, and he seemed surprised that Esther had never heard of the historic case. Mrs. Rachael explained that the girl had only been told what was needful and beneficial. Esther herself was so overwhelmed by Mr. Jarndyce's kindness that she couldn't speak.

A new life — Esther was soon on her way to a new life. With her belongings packed and her doll buried in the garden of her former home, she now set out for Reading, leaving Windsor behind forever. The cold farewell from Mrs. Rachael seemed strange to Esther, who was full of warmth and affection. But it matched the cold winter weather, and as Esther's coach drove away into the sunset, it was as though the setting represented a life chapter that had come to a close.

The unknown gentleman — Riding in the coach with Esther was an unknown gentleman who showed an odd mixture of kindness and abruptness. After Esther had cried for a while, he scolded her, telling her to look grateful if she felt it but also gently drying her eyes. He then kindly offered her some cake and pate, only to throw them out the window when she declined them because they were too rich for her. The gentleman exited the coach before Esther and never said who he was.

Greenleaf — At her destination, Esther met Miss Donny, who introduced her to Greenleaf, an exceptionally orderly and well-run boarding school. There, Esther learned to her surprise that Mr. Jarndyce was her guardian and that her new station in life was to be a governess. She soon settled in, making many friends and helping to teach the young girls that went there. Her compassion and gentleness earned everyone's trust, and she was especially sensitive and welcoming to depressed newcomers, though she took no credit for any special qualities and even denied them. But she did notice that her birthdays — in fact, the entire year — were now filled with affection and happiness. This segment of her life lasted six years.

Another transition and a happy farewell — While at Greenleaf, Esther followed Miss Donny's advice, writing twice a year to Mr. Kenge to express her gratitude and happiness. Kenge and Carboy's replies were always curt, informing her that they passed the information on to Mr. Jarndyce. One day, Esther received a letter telling her that she was being transferred to a new position as the companion to Mr. Jarndyce's new ward, per order of the Court of Chancery. She would be picked up the following Monday morning to be driven to the office of Kenge and Carboy. As usual, her reaction was deeply emotional, especially in the wake of all the affection and gifts showered on her by Greenleaf's residents and servants alike. It was clear that her commitment, made six years earlier, to bring some goodness and kindness to the world had earned her ten times the love she ever expected.

Esther leaves Greenleaf — Five days later, Esther was on her way to London. For a while, she sobbed with emotion and gratitude, then finally convinced herself to pull herself together given her new position. Eager to arrive, she wondered when the coach would get to London, but when the streets suddenly became crowded with other coaches and the road turned to stone pavement, she knew they were close.

Esther arrives in London — When the driver finally stopped, Esther was met by a young man, from Kenge and Carboy, who explained that the brown smoke she mistook for the aftereffect of a huge fire was in fact London's famous fog. The dirty streets, crowds, and chaos made no better impression, but things improved as they went through a gate into a peaceful, churchlike setting. Welcoming Esther to the office, the young man offered her a mirror to check her appearance before going before the Lord Chancellor, though she saw no reason to be nervous, and he also pointed out some refreshments left for her by Mr. Kenge. Yet as Esther waited, she noticed that her surroundings seemed strange and unusually dark and dirty. She tried to read, but she was too distracted to concentrate.

Esther meets Mr. Jarndyce's two wards — Finally, Mr. Kenge arrived and was pleased to note how Esther had developed into a fine young woman. He led her to the Lord Chancellor's private quarters, where she met Mr. Jarndyce's wards, the young and lovely Miss Ada Clare and the slightly older Mr. Richard Carstone. They were both standing by a large fire in what was a more comfortable environment than the previous office. Ada extended Esther a warm welcome, and they quickly made friends and sat down together to chat. Esther learned that all three of them were orphans and that although Ada and Richard were distant cousins, they had never met until now. Richard, who was around nineteen, also had a cheerful personality, and all three of them were soon engaged in an enjoyable conversation.

The meeting with the Lord Chancellor — Once the Court had adjourned, the young people were led into the next room, where Mr. Kenge introduced them to the Lord Chancellor, who for all his stature proved to be kind and polite. After a few questions about Mr. Jarndyce and his residence, Bleak House — which according to Mr. Kenge was not bleak — the judge spoke privately with each of the two wards. Having approved of the situation as a whole and of Miss Summerson as a companion for Ada, the Lord Chancellor determined to issue the order.

The little old madwoman — With the meeting now over, the three young people were waiting outside for Mr. Kenge's next instructions, when they were accosted by an elderly lady — one of the fixtures in the Court of Chancery — who was thrilled to meet the young wards in Jarndyce. Richard quickly deduced that she was mad and said so loudly enough for her hear it. She responded that she, too, had once been a ward. Her youth, beauty, and hope did not benefit her, though, but — and here she equated the sixth seal of the Book of Revelation with the Great Seal of Chancery — she still expected a higher judgment to come into effect soon. Luckily for Ada's comfort, the old woman was interrupted by Mr. Kenge, who kindly urged her not to be troublesome. She insisted, though, that her intention was not to trouble but to bless the two young wards. And that was how they left her, smiling, curtsying, and blessing.

Chapter 4 — Telescopic Philanthropy

Mrs. Jellyby — Mr. Kenge thought that Bleak House was too far off to attempt the trip that day, so he arranged for the young people to spend the night at the home of Mrs. Jellyby, a noted philanthropist whose current focus was African coffee cultivation and the English settlement of Borrioboola-Gha in Nigeria. She knew Mr. Jarndyce as a great supporter of philanthropic activity. In fact, Mr. Kenge was surprised that none of them had heard of her. Richard was curious to know more about Mr. Jellyby, but according to Mr. Kenge, Mrs. Jellyby was such an outstanding figure that her husband had simply faded into the woodwork. In fact, her focus on Africa was so intense that she completely neglected the needs of her own home and family, which explained why Dickens labeled her style of philanthropy "telescopic."

Commotion outside the Jellybys' — Having said his goodbyes, Mr. Kenge enlisted the young man, named Mr. Guppy, to accompany the group by coach. On arriving at the Jellybys', they noticed some commotion, and when Esther saw that a little boy had gotten his head stuck in the railing, she immediately asked to be let out so she could help. Two well-meaning townsfolk were already making efforts, but noticing that the boy had a large head, Esther suggested they push his body through instead of pulling it. Her ingenuity helped to extricate the boy, but strangely, once he was free, he started hitting Mr. Guppy for no apparent reason.

No time for the basics — Things were no better inside the house. There were dirty children, one of whom was falling down the stairs as Esther and Ada went up. The whole house and its residents, including Mrs. Jellyby, looked uncared for and in need of patching up. Papers were strewn all about the office, supposedly because Mrs. Jellyby had no time for anything but philanthropy. Richard noticed that her eyes were always focused on some distant object, as though Africa was the closest thing she could see. The fires in the house were untended, leaving it cold; the stairs were dangerous because of a loose carpet; the hot water boiler was broken; and the dinner, which otherwise would have been good, was uncooked. In general, the children were left to fend for themselves, and the two ill-bred and incompetent servants constantly fought. Mrs. Jellyby's oldest daughter, Caddy, who was also her scribe and therefore stuck at her writing post, seemed miserable and unhealthy, while Mr. Jellyby sat in his chair and said nothing. Richard, who sat with him at one point, thought he tried to speak several times, but Mr. Jellyby's sense of self seemed so diminished that he gave up before he began. Matters were not helped by the presence of Mr. Quale, a young self-proclaimed philanthropist who visited in the evenings and kowtowed to Mrs. Jellyby.

The power of caring — In this atmosphere of disarray and neglect, Ada and especially Esther were a welcome sight. Esther could not help taking Peepy — the child who had fallen down the stairs — in her arms as they listened to Mrs. Jellyby dictating her latest philanthropic letter. Mrs. Jellyby even urged Esther to set the child down, calling him "naughty," but this went entirely against Esther's nature. When Peepy fell asleep, Esther eventually took him upstairs and laid him on her bed. Curious, the other children came to see this novel sight and were peeking into the room by the door hinge. Concerned that they might hurt themselves, Esther decided to invite them in and tell them a story on the condition that they were quiet, which they were.

After dinner — That episode took place before dinner, and following dinner, they all gathered in the drawing room, where Mrs. Jellyby once again took center stage with her letter dictation. The children then snuck up to Esther and Ada to ask for more stories, which were delivered in whispers so as not to interrupt the great African enterprise. When it was bedtime, Esther carried Peepy upstairs on his request, and after the children were in bed, Ada and Esther set about making their own room more comfortable. Following that, they returned downstairs, where Esther got the feeling that Mrs. Jellyby didn't think too highly of her concern with comfort and neatness. They finally went back upstairs at around midnight, while Caddy and Mrs. Jellyby, fueled by endless cups of coffee, continued with the African project.

The mystery of Mr. Jarndyce — Once alone, Esther asked Ada for more information about Mr. Jarndyce but discovered that neither Ada nor Richard knew much about him. Ada knew only what her mother had told her, many years earlier before she died, about his goodness and trustworthiness, but she had never seen him. Richard had seen him only once, five years ago. Both had received a letter making the same offer as a way of repairing the damage done by the Jarndyce case, and both had, of course, accepted. But that was all Ada knew.

Caddy's lament — Ada then went to bed, and as Esther sat there musing about Bleak House and her sudden change of fortune, she was interrupted by Caddy, who asked if she could come in. Caddy, it turned out, was so miserable that she made no pretense at happiness or even good manners and instead launched into how much she hated the whole African thing. She admired Esther and Ada and yearned for the same lady's education in etiquette, languages, needlepoint, and so on. But all she could do was write, and she openly wished that Esther could have taught her as she had taught others. She even went so far as to wish she were dead, and when Esther tried to speak, she wouldn't hear of it. In this wretched state, she finally fell asleep, her head buried in Esther's lap. Having covered herself and Caddy with shawls, Esther, too, eventually fell asleep. She awoke early the next morning to see Peepy staring at her, his teeth chattering from the cold.

Chapter 5 — A Morning Adventure

An early morning walk — With Mrs. Jellyby still asleep, Caddy suggested an early morning walk. Breakfast wouldn't be ready till at least an hour after her mother awoke, which would not be soon. Arriving downstairs, they found the house in its usual state, with the tablecloth unchanged and paper, crumbs, and dirt all over. Outside, they ran into Richard, who happily joined them. Following that, they all noticed the Jellybys' cook coming out of the pub, where she had obviously been drinking.

Caddy's anger at her mother and Mr. Quale — By this time, Caddy had reverted to her usual miserable mode, openly complaining about Mr. Quale and her mother's ridiculous focus on Africa. Her mother's complete lack of parental responsibility left Caddy with no sense of filial loyalty. She particularly resented Mr. Quale and wanted nothing to do with him. By this time, Ada and Richard had fallen behind Caddy's fast pace, so only Esther was aware of Caddy's feelings. When they caught up, laughing at the speed of their companions, Caddy shut down again, which finally gave Esther a chance to observe the hustle and bustle of the early London morning.

The little old madwoman reappears — Suddenly they noticed the little old lady from the Chancery Court greeting them again with endless curtsies and smiles. Thrilled to see the young, beautiful, and hopeful Jarndyce wards, she invited them up to her place nearby, convinced their visit would bring her good luck.

Mr. Krook's second-hand shop — The elderly lady lived above a strange, musty second-hand shop that bought — and maybe even occasionally sold — all kinds of things, from waste paper and bones to ink bottles and rusty keys. The owner, Mr. Krook, was the woman's landlord, but to the neighbors he was the "Lord Chancellor," and his shop was known as "the Chancery," evidently because of his unwillingness to part with his strange wares. Mr. Krook himself was a gnarled-looking fellow who was considered eccentric, if not mad, by the little madwoman herself. He had a gray cat named Lady Jane, who would claw and shred rags on cue and was supposedly trained to do the same to anything else Mr. Krook might indicate.

The story of Tom Jarndyce — The elderly lady interrupted Mr. Krook to inform him that both she and her young guests, the Jarndyce wards, were short on time. The information as to who they were made a profound impression on Mr. Krook, who seemed to know a great deal about the case. Learning that Richard's name was Carstone, he ticked off the names Barbary, Clare, and Dedlock as also being involved. From there, his mind turned to Tom Jarndyce, who got so depressed over the interminable proceedings that he shot himself. Yet the Court acted as though nothing had happened, or at least as though they had nothing to do with it.

A sparse apartment — On that cheery note, which understandably left the Jarndyce wards upset, the elderly lady led them upstairs to her apartment, a large, sparse room with a view of Lincoln's Inn Hall. The most prominent items there all had to do with legal proceedings. There wasn't even any food, although Esther noticed a few dishes. Esther felt that the sparseness of the place gave her greater insight into the old woman's state, which she described as "pinched."

The caged birds — The old lady's poverty became more poignant (Richard even quietly left her some money) when she drew aside the curtain to reveal several birdcages containing about twenty birds. Her plan was to set them free once the hoped-for judgment was passed. But she wondered if either she or the birds would make it before the case ended. After all, so many of them had died already. Until the case was over, she would seldom let the birds sing, and she refrained from opening the window for fear that Mr. Krook's malicious cat would devour them.

The old lady hurries to Court — The visit came to an end when, realizing it was already nine-thirty, the old woman hurried her guests out. With such a lucky visit from the wards in Jarndyce, it was especially important to arrive early in Court, before the Lord Chancellor, as he would no doubt address her case first today. On the way down, she tiptoed past the door of the only other tenant, a law writer rumored to have sold his soul to the devil.

Mr. Krook's letters — As they passed through the shop on the way out, Mr. Krook detained Esther, who was following behind the others. He had been drawing some letters on the wall. He wrote only one at a time after erasing the previous one, and he always began at the opposite end from the usual writing method. In this way, he spelled out the words "Jarndyce" and "Bleak House" for Esther. He did all of this from memory, without having learned to read or write. When he was finished, Esther felt that both Mr. Krook and his cat gave her such an evil look that she was glad when Richard came to retrieve her.

Doubts about Chancery — On the way home, Ada and Richard both expressed their misgivings about the Court of Chancery, along with their regret that they might prove a source of pain for other parties involved. At least, the case had brought them together, and they were certainly happy about that.

Back at the Jellybys' — Mrs. Jellyby came down shortly after their return to the house. At breakfast, she was preoccupied with news about her African project, was clearly all that ever concerned her. Even Peepy's disappearance and retrieval by a policeman made no visible dent in her demeanor. Following breakfast, it was back to letter dictation, and at one o'clock, the carriage came to pick up Esther, Ada, and Richard, who were seen off by Caddy's tears, Mrs. Jellyby's regards to Mr. Jarndyce, and a rowdy group of children leaping on and off the coach as it drove away.

Chapter 6 — Quite at Home

On the way to Bleak House — The fog had given way to fresh air by the time they left, and the city appeared more cheerful. Gradually, the excitement of the city turned to suburb, then to country, complete with haystacks, windmills, and rural scenery. Suddenly, a wagon pulled up beside the coach, and the driver delivered three identical notes saying that Mr. Jarndyce looked forward to meeting each of his wards as old friends, on easygoing terms that took "the past for granted." Ada and Richard both had the impression that Mr. Jarndyce had difficulty accepting gratitude and would go out of his way to avoid it. That became the main topic for the rest of the drive, along with questions about their immediate future.

A warm welcome to Bleak House — Eventually, the roads became more difficult, and it was already nighttime as they neared Bleak House. When they finally arrived, Mr. Jarndyce welcomed them at the door with open arms. Jarndyce was a friendly, energetic man of around sixty, and as he asked them about their trip, Esther gradually recognized him as the anonymous man she had met in the coach all those years ago on her way to Greenleaf.

Questions about Mrs. Jellyby — Mr. Jarndyce seemed to read Esther's thoughts, but before she could think much about it, he changed the subject. He wanted to know what they thought of Mrs. Jellyby. Both Ada and Esther answered evasively, but Mr. Jarndyce saw right through their tact. After some encouragement, Esther finally came forward with the group's assessment that Mrs. Jellyby's intense focus on Africa was unjustifiable given the sad state of her home and family.

The east wind — Mr. Jarndyce's own attitude to Mrs. Jellyby's behavior was indulgent and forgiving, though he realized she might not be right in her actions. Then he suddenly started talking about the east wind. Richard mentioned that it was blowing from the north earlier, but Mr. Jarndyce insisted that his "condition" — Richard guessed it was rheumatism — convinced him it came from the east. Something about the Jellyby children reminded him of it, and he wondered if things might be better for them if it "rained" something nice — like sugarplums. Here Ada interrupted, saying that, better than that, it had "rained Esther." To Esther's dismay, Ada proceeded to describe all Esther had done for the Jellyby children, including Caddy. When Ada finished, Mr. Jarndyce noted that the wind was to the north after all.

A tour of the house — But now it was time to see Bleak House. Esther had immediately noticed its old-fashioned character, and its many nooks, crannies, twists, and turns confirmed that. Each of their rooms had its own special sense of comfort and interest. Esther's room had many little corners and a tiled hearth with a roaring fire; Ada's had a spacious view; and Richard's was an interesting, comfortable mix of bedroom, library, and sitting room. Ada and Esther also had their own little sitting room with a flower-garden view. The least comfortable was Jarndyce's own bedroom, with the bed in the center, a perpetually open window, and a cold bath in an adjoining room. The rooms were all linked by a maze of confusing passageways.

The furnishings — The furniture was as charming as the house — old-fashioned, though not old. Each room had a different theme, and there was an eclectic mix of decorations, paintings, mirrors, linens, lavender and rose petals, and whatever else added to the home's comfort, brightness, and orderliness.

Describing Mr. Skimpole — John Jarndyce was happy that his young companions enjoyed their new home, and he was convinced that their own brightness and youth would add to its charm. On that note, he informed them that dinner would be served in half an hour, when they would meet another guest, a man his own age but with the innocence of a child. He was a talented man who could have been a professional musician or artist, except that things had not turned out well for him. In response to Richard's question about whether Skimpole had any children, Mr. Jarndyce informed them that he had about six that he had never taken care of, the excuse being that he was too much of a child himself. Mr. Skimpole also knew Mrs. Jellyby.

Esther is given charge of the household keys — The whole subject must have made Mr. Jarndyce uncomfortable, because his thoughts suddenly turned to the east wind again. By then, though, the luggage had arrived, so Esther went up to change. While she was unpacking, a maid came in with a basket containing the housekeeping keys, which would now be Esther's responsibility. That surprised her, though she was grateful for the trust.

Mr. Skimpole — Richard was already chatting with Mr. Skimpole when Esther and Ada came down to dinner. To Esther, Skimpole looked and acted more like a young man ravaged by life than a well-preserved older man. That impression matched his attitudes and experience. Trained as a physician, Mr. Skimpole had once been employed by a German prince but had proved so negligent and inept that he was eventually fired. It didn't surprise him, since he admitted to having no practical sense for things like money and time. He did manage to fall in love and marry, and various friends, including Mr. Jarndyce, had tried to get him a job.

A dedicated artist and romantic — Mr. Skimpole knew his strong points, and they had nothing to do with business. Among other things, he enjoyed conversing, drawing, reading the paper, drinking coffee and wine, and walking in nature. He was not like Mrs. Jellyby, who was passionate about business details, and he didn't know whether drawing, his primary talent, was useful to anyone. But it was what he did best and most readily, and he believed the world should just accept and support him. Fortunately, Mr. Jarndyce did. This all seemed odd to Esther, who had always assumed that obligations were a part of life.

Mr. Skimpole's winning manner — But Mr. Skimpole's charming, carefree ways were convincing, even though Esther had difficulty reconciling his viewpoint to her own. The only feelings of envy Mr. Skimpole admitted to were toward the young wards, but he even turned that situation around, claiming they should feel grateful to him, that he had been placed on the earth to bless them. His manner was so winning and lighthearted that they all felt charmed, and he ultimately won Esther over when he spoke of Ada in glowing terms, comparing her to the morning and proclaiming her a blessed child of the universe. Mr. Jarndyce doubted that the universe made the most caring parent, but Mr. Skimpole insisted on taking a poetic rather than a worldly view of life.

A glimpse into the future — Mr. Jarndyce treated this comment with indulgence, patting Mr. Skimpole on the head. He then looked thoughtfully at Ada and Richard, who were over by the piano. Afterwards, he quickly glanced at Esther, as though wanting to communicate his desire to eventually see his two young wards in a more intimate relationship. In the dim room, by the flickering firelight,

Esther could hear the moaning of the wind accompanying Ada's soft singing and playing, and in that scene, she read some omen of the future.

A surprise arrest—Following tea, the group enjoyed Ada's singing and Mr. Skimpole's cello and piano playing. But at one point, Esther noticed that both Skimpole and Richard had left, and then the maid appeared, discreetly informing her that Mr. Skimpole was "took" and asking her to please come upstairs. It turned out that Mr. Skimpole had been arrested for a debt of about £24 and that if he didn't pay, he would end up either in jail or in "Coavinses," the detainment house that gave debtors time to repay their debts. From then on, "Coavinses" became the arresting officer's nickname.

Esther and Richard come to the rescue—Esther found it strange that Mr. Skimpole seemed to suffer no unease in relation to this situation. His idea was to have the young Jarndyce wards pledge part of their inheritance, since he didn't feel comfortable asking Mr. Jarndyce for any more help. But according to the officer, there was no provision for such a pledge. Mr. Skimpole therefore appealed to Richard and Esther as his only hope, since the world owed him the right to live free as a butterfly. In response, Richard gave him his only £10, and Esther gave her life savings of £15, originally set aside for a rainy day.

Transferring the guilt—Once the matter was settled, Mr. Skimpole wanted to know whether "Coavinses," the arresting officer, had even an inkling of regret or a sense of romance about his mission. But the officer, being a working man and not a romantic, had no interest in Skimpole's view and considered thinking about his work a waste of time—he was busy enough.

Back downstairs again, the group resumed the evening's entertainments, such as learning backgammon and playing music. But Esther couldn't help thinking how strange it was that Skimpole seemed completely carefree, while she and Richard felt like they were the guilty parties who had just been arrested.

Mr. Jarndyce's dismay—It was past midnight when Mr. Skimpole finally went to bed. Shortly afterwards, Mr. Jarndyce entered all perturbed, complaining about the east wind and rubbing himself to allay the pain. He had heard about what had happened with Skimpole and wanted to make immediate amends to Richard and Esther. He could not think of going to bed until then. He wanted to know how much he owed them, but Richard felt uncomfortable breaking Mr. Skimpole's trust. Mr. Jarndyce explained that Mr. Skimpole was always in financial trouble—he was born that way, he would be that way again next week, and he entrusted his debts to anyone and everyone.

A gentle reminder brings relief—Esther gently reminded Mr. Jarndyce that Mr. Skimpole was a child and could not be held responsible. The thought seemed to bring Mr. Jarndyce great relief, as though he could now forgive Skimpole and rest easy. He did, however, make Esther, Richard, and Ada promise that they would never again indulge Mr. Skimpole by giving him money. **Symbolism of the wind; a growing affection—**With the matter resolved, Mr. Jarndyce announced that the wind was actually from the south and that the east wind had been a false alarm. It was obvious to Esther and Ada that Mr. Jarndyce's preoccupation with the east wind was just his way of dealing with difficult situations, since he was uneasy blaming anyone, even for real faults. Later, when she was alone, Esther recognized her growing affection for this man, whom she had wondered about for so long, and sometimes she even secretly thought he might be her father. But in the end, she brushed those thoughts aside and reminded herself of her motto to be grateful, cheerful, and to attend to her duties.

Chapter 7 — The Ghost's Walk

Back in Lincolnshire — Meanwhile, back at Chesney Wold, the Dedlock's Lincolnshire estate, the dreary, rainy weather continued. Fortunately, for their sakes, the Dedlocks were still in Paris.

Animal dreams — Dickens takes a moment here to imagine what the Dedlocks' animals were thinking. He speculates that the horses, dogs, and other animals dreamt of brighter, livelier times, when the weather was fair and the house full of people, when the hunt was on and the plants fresh — and all this despite their own dull, mournful exteriors. Whether this was true or not, their human counterparts, the servants, lacked any imagination except for an occasional reference to ghosts.

Mrs. Rouncewell — The Dedlocks' housekeeper was Mrs. Rouncewell, who had been with the family fifty years. She was a straight-backed, orderly widow from the market town, whose sole concern was the management of the house, which was closed down in the winter season. During that time, she spent her days in her room, adjacent to the courtyard.

Mrs. Rouncewell's sons — Mrs. Rouncewell had two sons. The younger one became a soldier, considered shameful back then, and never returned home. In spite of this, his mother spoke highly of him, but the whole episode troubled her. Her other son always liked creating engineering projects, which worried his mother because it seemed rebellious, so she took the matter up with Sir Leicester. Sir Leicester had no tolerance for such things and suggested sending him to the ironworks in northern England, away from Chesney Wold. Her older son survived, however, eventually marrying and having his own son, who, having completed his ironworking apprenticeship abroad, was now visiting his grandmother at the estate. His name was Watt, and his grandmother remarked how much he was like George, her younger son, though Watt protested that others said he was more like his own father, now a thriving ironworker.

Rosa — Watt, however, was more interested the pretty, dark-haired girl he saw earlier with his grandmother. Her name was Rosa, and she was a widow's daughter from the town. Mrs. Rouncewell had decided to ensure her proper training as a maid by starting early, which explained why the girl was so young. Rosa was beautiful as well as was shy and modest, increasingly unusual qualities, according to Mrs. Rouncewell. She was also learning well, and Mrs. Rouncewell was pleased with her.

Two gentleman visitors — As they were speaking, Rosa herself knocked on the door to inform Mrs. Rouncewell that two gentlemen claiming to be lawyers were requesting permission to see the house. One of them had sent his card, which Mrs. Rouncewell instructed Rosa to hand to Watt. Coming in from the rain, Rosa looked particularly fresh and beautiful, and there was an awkward moment when, after shyly extending the card, she dropped it, and she and Watt almost hit each other retrieving it. The card simply read "Mr. Guppy." Since Mrs. Rouncewell had never heard of him, Rosa explained that the two men were on business in the area and had some extra time. Hearing of Chesney Wold, they decided to see if they could visit it. Mr. Guppy had also taken the liberty of mentioning Mr. Tulkinghorn's name, in case that helped.

Tour of the Dedlock home — Mr. Tulkinghorn's name proved to be the magic access key for Mr.

Guppy and his associate. With Mrs. Rouncewell's permission, Rosa led them on a tour of the house as the gardener accompanied them, opening the shutters to shed more light on the rooms. Mrs. Rouncewell also went along, as did Watt, who was curious to see the house. Dickens describes the young lawyers' reactions as typical of those who do estate tours: they take an interest in all the wrong things, ignore whatever is of real interest, and generally behave depressed and "knocked up," meaning exhausted.

Lady Dedlock's portrait — Mr. Guppy's mood, however, suddenly changed when he saw Lady Dedlock's portrait. He immediately asked who it was, convinced he had seen it before. Yet when he asked whether it had been reproduced for popular use, the answer was a firm no — Sir Leicester would not allow that. Throughout the remainder of the tour, Mr. Guppy could not get Lady Dedlock's portrait out of his mind, and he wondered whether he had seen it in a dream.

The Ghost's Walk — On completing the tour, Rosa informed the guests that the terrace in the courtyard was called "the Ghost's Walk." Intrigued, Mr. Guppy was curious to hear the story behind it, but Mrs. Rouncewell, the only one who knew it, declined to give details, saying it was a private family story.

The story behind the name — Once the guests had left, Mrs. Rouncewell explained the history of the name "Ghost's Walk" to Rosa and Watt. Back in the 1600s, during the reign of Charles I, Sir Morbury Dedlock was married to a lady who had relatives among the King's dissenters. According to the story, she was their informant, so when the loyalists met at Chesney Wold, she was always close by, listening in.

A strange sound on the pavement; the story continues — Mrs. Rouncewell paused to direct Watt's attention to a sound on the terrace, and he admitted to hearing an echo-like sound, like a faltering footstep, through the noise of the rain. Mrs. Rouncewell continued. Sir Morbury's relationship with his wife, which was already difficult, got worse when a near relation of her husband killed her brother during England's civil wars. After that, she took to crippling the horses to prevent the loyalists from riding out. One night, her husband caught her and grabbed her wrist, and though no one knows how, she too became crippled from a fall.

Following that, her health deteriorated, yet she insisted on taking daily walks on the terrace despite the pain, which she bore in silence. One day, she fell down, and when her husband tried to help her up, she insisted on dying there and swore to keep walking the terrace forever after, with the warning that the sound of her footstep would be an omen of impending misfortune. Mrs. Rouncewell quoted the Lady's dying curse as including the word "disgrace," yet Mrs. Rouncewell denied that Chesney Wold ever experienced disgrace, and Watt felt compelled to agree.

A definite sound heard only occasionally — One curious aspect of the sound, noticed also by the current Lady Dedlock, was that it was impossible to ignore. It was also heard only in the dark and then only occasionally. Though it wasn't quite dark yet, as a test, Mrs. Rouncewell asked her grandson to activate the French clock. She then told him to listen through the clock's loud ticking and music. Could he hear the strange, disturbing echo? He was sure he could. And so, his grandmother assured him, could Lady Dedlock.

Chapter 8 — Covering a Multitude of Sins

Esther learns about her new housekeeping manager position — The next morning, Esther's first task was to learn the details of her new housekeeping role, so she took notes about where the dishes, foods, and other things were stored. It also was her job to prepare the tea for breakfast, but since the others hadn't come down yet, she went outside to inspect the driveway and gardens, where she discovered the flower garden, kitchen garden, farmyard, haystack area, and horse paddock. The house itself had a quaint look, with its three-peaked roof, windows of many shapes and sizes, and flowering trellises.

The Growlery — After breakfast, Esther's housekeeping duties were interrupted by Mr. Jarndyce, who wanted to show her the "Growlery," a small room adjacent to his bedroom where he went to vent his frustrations. To Esther's surprise, Mr. Jarndyce claimed it was the most used room in the house and an escape from the dreaded east wind. He then noticed that Esther was shaking as she kissed his hand in gratitude and affection. But Jarndyce assured her it was natural to adopt an orphan out of compassion and that her development and trust were more than enough reward.

Mr. Jarndyce explains the history of the Jarndyce case — Mr. Jarndyce next asked Esther what she understood about the Jarndyce case, explaining that it all began when a Jarndyce ancestor willed a large amount of money to his heirs. However, the case became so convoluted that its only remaining purpose over the years seemed to be to create lawyers' fees, and the man made responsible for sorting it out knew nothing about what everyone else already understood. The resulting accumulation of paper, legal proceedings, and costs created nothing but misery for the heirs, so that all who became involved had no way out other than that taken by Tom Jarndyce, who shot himself in the head after years of trying to fix the mess.

How Bleak House got its name — Before that, Bleak House had been called "the Peaks," but Tom Jarndyce, John Jarndyce's uncle, was too engrossed in trying to resolve the case to take care of the house he dubbed "Bleak House." Consequently, both the house and garden fell into disrepair. After his uncle's death, John Jarndyce inherited Bleak House and set about restoring it to its current pleasant condition. But he was dismayed that the Jarndyce will included several London properties in sad condition. Nor did there seem to be any hope for them, now that the Chancery Court had gotten its clutches on them.

Jarndyce's faith in Esther — Esther remarked several times how Bleak House had changed since her guardian's arrival, a comment that made him grateful for her positive focus, which he saw as wisdom. Esther herself was not as convinced of her own wisdom, but Jarndyce believed her effect on the house might someday even make the Growlery obsolete. He also left it up to her whether to tell Ada and Richard about their conversation, since outside the Growlery, John himself never even contemplated the things discussed there.

Another job for Esther — The subject next changed to Richard's future, and once again Esther found herself unexpectedly entrusted with an important job, this time of helping Richard make a career choice, though Jarndyce was sure that the Chancery would have its say in exchange for worthless ceremony, hefty fees, and general uselessness — a process he called "Wiglomeration." This was evidently not a happy subject, as it brought on the east wind.

A growing mutual trust — With their Growlery time nearly over for the day, Jarndyce asked Esther if she had any questions. To this she gave a confident "no." She was sure he would communicate whatever was important without her prompting, and from then on, she felt comfortable in his presence.

An introduction to "philanthropy" — Life at Bleak House was busy, owing to the many people who knew Mr. Jarndyce and usually wanted some of his money. Esther and Ada, who helped sort and respond to his mail, found that many of these petitioners were women who were passionately involved in some charitable cause. Some even came from as far away as America. Mr. Jarndyce classified these charitable petitioners into two groups: those who made a lot of noise and accomplished little and those who made no noise and accomplished a lot.

Mrs. Pardiggle and her miserable family — Esther guessed that Mrs. Pardiggle, one of the most prodigious letter writers, was in the first group, as her name always brought on the east wind. This suspicion was born out one day when Mrs. Pardiggle arrived at Bleak House in person with her five young sons. Esther and Ada, who were alone at the time, observed that she was loud and needed a lot of space, since she tended to knock things over. Unlike Mrs. Jellyby, Mrs. Pardiggle insisted on bringing her boys everywhere. In addition, she was training them to be young philanthropists and give away what little allowance money they had. Understandably, her boys were all miserable, though this escaped their mother's notice. Mrs. Pardiggle had also convinced Mr. Pardiggle to add his contribution of £1. In fact, everything seemed to be "under her direction," although she acted as if her boys and husband were pleased to volunteer their resources.

Mrs. Pardiggle's love of staying busy — Mrs. Pardiggle's main concern in life was "business," meaning whatever work she was engaged in. Even Bleak House became in her mind a potential venue for a public speech. And unlike her husband and children, who were tired after a long day, Mrs. Pardiggle had an endless capacity for work, another fact that did little for her children's happiness.

Mrs. Pardiggle ropes in Esther and Ada — Mrs. Pardiggle also prided herself on her frank speech, and she now informed Esther and Ada that she expected them to help her with her visiting rounds. Esther was the more immediate target, and though she made a number of excuses about why she couldn't do it, none of them made an impact on Mrs. Pardiggle, who finally cornered the two young women into accompanying her then and there to a brickmaker's home.

Esther's horrible experience with the Pardiggle children — Since Mrs. Pardiggle had grabbed Ada to walk beside her, Esther was left to walk with the children, normally a good experience for her. In this case, however, the boys were so disgruntled that Esther found their company more like a nightmare. The oldest one immediately demanded a shilling from her and spoke disrespectfully of his mother. When Esther pointed that out, three of the boys pinched her arms, another stepped on her toes, and the youngest, who had "voluntarily" sworn to refrain for life from cakes and cookies as well as tobacco, turned purple as they passed a bakery. Esther was relieved to reach the brickmaker's house in spite of its squalid surroundings, complete with pigsties, mud, and broken windows.

The brickmaker's home — When they arrived, the brickmaker was lying on the floor smoking a pipe, having spent the last few days drinking. His wife was nursing the baby, his daughter was doing laundry, and his son was putting a collar on the dog. The brickmaker himself was hardly pleased to see Mrs. Pardiggle, but his attitude didn't appear to ruffle her. She took it more as a challenge to work harder—her favorite thing. But the brickmaker preferred to see her leave as soon as possible, so he rattled off the answers to her questions before she even had a chance to ask them. Yes, he had been drinking alcohol, which was after all better than the brown, filthy laundry water his daughter was using to wash their clothes. Yes, his wife got her black eye from him, even if she said otherwise. Yes, the house was dirty—that was how they lived, and if their children died (as five already had in their infancy), so much the better. No, he hadn't read the book she left—none of them could read, anyway … and so on. Mrs. Pardiggle had gotten a word in earlier, but Esther and Ada both thought her approach was too businesslike and overbearing, and they felt uncomfortable being there.

The baby dies in its mother's arms—Once done with her visit, Mrs. Pardiggle and her boys headed to their next stop. Instead of following, as Mrs. Pardiggle expected, Esther and Ada stayed behind out of concern for the baby's health. But as Ada went to touch the infant, both she and Esther saw it die. A neighbor came by to console the heartbroken mother, whose name was Jenny, and as Esther watched how the friend embraced the mourning mother, repeating "Jenny" over and over again, she noticed how the woman's ugly and abused features became more beautiful because of her compassion.

Esther and Ada return to the mourning mother—Once back home, Esther and Ada decided they would return that evening with some small gifts. Richard accompanied them most of the way, and they were all struck by how the rest of the family seemed unaffected by the sad event. The mother, however, lay on her bed with her dead baby on her breast, and her compassionate friend stood watch by the door, though she risked displeasing her own husband by doing so. Earlier, Esther had covered the baby with her own handkerchief, and now the mother's friend laid their gifts near the bed as Esther and Ada paid their respects. They could see that the baby, in contrast to the filthy surroundings, had been washed and clothed in clean linen—they guessed by Jenny's caring friend. As Ada and Esther lifted the handkerchief to look at the infant, Esther imagined she saw a halo around the baby. That handkerchief would eventually make its way to another troubled figure, but at the time, Esther had no inkling of this. After that, the two young women left, and on their way out, they gratefully blessed the mourning mother's caring friend—much to her surprise.

Chapter 9 — Signs and Tokens

Richard and Ada fall in love — Esther and Ada had been spending busy days at Bleak House, and later in the day, they were usually joined by Richard, who was fast falling in love with Ada and vice versa, while Esther tried hard to be discreet about it.

Esther's special effect — Esther had all sorts of nicknames — "Dame Durden," "Mother Hubbard," "Little Cobweb, "little old woman," among others — all references to her housekeeper status. These were used freely by Richard and Ada, who found her a comforting regular presence in their lives. Richard would visit her as she worked outside in the morning, and Ada would confide in her at night.

Richard's career prospects — As far as Richard's career was concerned, there was talk of his becoming a seaman, something he had always dreamed of. To help him in his career, Mr. Jarndyce wrote to Sir Leicester, but neither Sir Leicester nor Lady Dedlock, both Richard's distant relations, felt they could do much for him. Richard therefore concluded he would have to make his way on his own.

Richard's carefree approach to money — Richard's character was lighthearted and energetic, which also amounted to a certain recklessness with money, though he didn't see it that way. If he gave money away and then got it back — as with Harold Skimpole's debt, which Mr. Jarndyce repaid — he saw it as a gain, even though the actual gain was zero. And because Richard had gained it easily, he would donate or spend it easily. In fact, he gave half the regained money to the brickmaker and spent most of the other half on a roundtrip to London. But in his mind, with £1 left over, he had come out ahead. In spite of that flaw, his courage, passion, and gentleness made him good company.

A letter to Jarndyce from an old friend — One morning, Mr. Jarndyce received a letter from an old friend, Mr. Lawrence Boythorn, who was on his way to visit them. Jarndyce described Boythorn as a large, loud, hardy man with a warm, passionate personality that some people found abrasive because of his tendency to express himself in extremes. He and Mr. Jarndyce went back forty-five years to their schooldays, when Boythorn knocked the teeth out of a bully who was bothering Jarndyce. That protective streak was still there — but Mr. Jarndyce didn't want to reveal too much for fear of spoiling the fun of meeting him.

Mr. Lawrence Boythorn — Boythorn arrived much later than expected, bursting in and loudly declaring how his coach had been deliberately misled. He added that if Jarndyce had been married, he never would have bothered him so late, preferring instead to head for the distant Himalayas. Mr. Jarndyce's answers were modest, rational one-liners, especially compared with Boythorn's exaggerated proclamations and loud laughter, which could be heard throughout the house. But Esther, Ada, and Richard were even more impressed by Boythorn's appearance. About ten years older than Mr. Jarndyce, Boythorn was handsome, tall, upright, and large as well as gentlemanly, kind, and frank.

Boythorn's canary — Mr. Boythorn had a canary, in his opinion the most extraordinary bird in Europe. He had even made provision for it in his will. The bird was well domesticated, and after flying around the room once, it landed on its master's head, where it sat eating out of his hand. Later, Boythorn let it hop about on the table, and for all the difference in their sizes, the bird seemed perfectly comfortable with his master.

An offer to shake up the Chancery — The subject next turned to the Chancery, which infuriated Mr. Boythorn. In his opinion, the Chancery masters should all have their money shaken out of their pockets, and he even offered to do it for Mr. Jarndyce, though Jarndyce himself didn't think it would do any good at this point. The other solution, in Boythorn's mind, was to blow up the Chancery, together with every record and every person who belonged to it — not to mention its originator, the Devil himself. This image made everyone laugh, including Boythorn himself, whose bellowing roar seemed to reverberate throughout England.

A right-of-way dispute with his neighbors, the Dedlocks — Mr. Jarndyce inquired about Boythorn's ongoing argument with his neighbors about a right-of-way issue. It turned out Boythorn's neighbors were Sir Leicester ("Sir Lucifer" to Boythorn) and Lady Dedlock. The dispute revolved around a piece of property supposedly belonging to Chesney Wold's parks, but since Boythorn owned it, he beat off anyone else who tried to use it. Moreover, he considered the Dedlock family line the worst bunch of arrogant "blockheads," though he acknowledged Lady Dedlock as being the most impressive woman alive. He realized that Richard and Ada were distantly related to the Dedlocks, and he was relieved that they were amused, adding that he would have apologized if they had felt differently. But, he stressed, with his own background of bold action, he was not about to be run over by any "Sir Lucifers."

A question about Boythorn's past — That night, while Mr. Boythorn sat listening to the piano, Esther noticed a gentleness in him as he contemplated Ada and Richard. That prompted her to quietly ask Mr. Jarndyce whether Boythorn had ever been married. Mr. Jarndyce answered that he had once come close, an incident that changed his life forever, for never again did he venture in that direction. Noticing that the subject made her guardian uncomfortable, Esther dropped it.

Mr. Boythorn gets a letter from Kenge and Carboy — The next morning, Boythorn received a letter from Kenge and Carboy. He had business to attend to and would meet with the lawyers that day after being escorted there by their clerk, Mr. Guppy. Richard, Ada, and Mr. Jarndyce also decided to go out because of the excellent weather. Esther, however, had to stay home to pay bills and run the household.

Mr. Guppy's changed appearance — When Mr. Guppy arrived for Mr. Boythorn, Esther barely recognized him. She noticed that he was much better dressed and that he took special care with his grooming. She was also struck by the way he kept scrutinizing her, which she could feel even though she avoided looking at him.

Mr. Guppy meets with Mr. Boythorn upstairs — Instead of going out, Mr. Boythorn had Mr. Guppy go upstairs to see him. It took a while before he returned, and from a distance, Esther could occasionally hear Mr. Boythorn yelling at Mr. Guppy. When Guppy finally did return, he looked a little worn and even commented on Mr. Boythorn's warlike nature.

A nervous lunch — In the meantime, Esther had ordered lunch to be brought for Mr. Guppy, per Mr. Jarndyce's request. She had told this to Mr. Guppy before he went up, and he had bowed awkwardly and asked if she would still be there, to which she replied yes. Throughout their interaction, she noticed a lot of nervous movements on his part, along with the fact that he kept looking at her intensely. Now, at the lunch table, he kept asking her if she would join him, but she declined. Finally, he got up the nerve to mention that he had something to tell her in confidence, and he wanted to verify that she would keep it to herself. Esther agreed, even though she was unsure what to make of his statement. But before Mr. Guppy could bring himself to reveal his secret, he had to take several more glasses of wine.

Mr. Guppy's proposal — Mr. Guppy started by telling Esther how he had gotten several raises since they had first met, and he went on to describe his prospects in the next year. Then he described his mother's prospects and qualities, saying that she was perfectly suited to being a mother-in-law. Finally, he burst out saying that he adored Esther and, going down on his knees, asked her to marry him.

Esther's rejection — Esther, however, was offended by this display, which she thought was ridiculous, and she ordered him to get up before she rang the bell for the servants. But Mr. Guppy was not so easily put off. He kept pleading with her to hear him out as he kept trying to convince her. He even admitted that the interview with Boythorn had been nothing more than an excuse to see her. But Esther was adamant, and Guppy's efforts were pointless. Finally, she rang the servants' bell to have him seen out. In a last-ditch effort, Guppy left her his card and mentioned both his own and his mother's address.

Old feelings reawaken in Esther — After Mr. Guppy left, Esther finished her day's business. Her focus was total, and she accomplished a lot. Later, though, when she was done with the day's work and alone in her room, she found herself first laughing and then crying. Something long dormant in her — since her childhood days with her doll — had been uncomfortably triggered.

Chapter 10 — The Law Writer

Mr. Snagsby's office — Mr. Snagsby was a law stationer who lived off Chancery Lane in Cook's Court. Dickens gives a long and detailed description of the bureaucratic paraphernalia found in Mr. Snagsby's office, from different types of paper to inkwells, notebooks, and the red tape used for binding documents — the origin of the current phrase for excessive bureaucracy.

Mr. Peffer's legacy — The sign on Mr. Snagsby's door read "Peffer and Snagsby." It changed from just "Peffer" when Mr. Snagsby joined him upon completing his apprenticeship, but in fact Mr. Peffer died twenty-five years ago, leaving Mr. Snagsby with both the business and Peffer's niece, whom Snagsby married.

Mr. and Mrs. Snagsby — Dickens describes Mr. Peffer's niece as a small, savvy woman with a sharp nose. Her tiny figure was supposedly partly due to her mother's determination to tie her daughter's corset too tight for "perfection's" sake. But she caught Snagsby's eye in any case, and they married at the same time that he became her uncle's partner. She was also far more vocal than her husband, a shy, quiet, balding, overweight man who seldom spoke. Much of the time, he could be found in the shop with his two apprentices, while his wife could be heard below, yelling at the servant girl.

Guster — The servant girl's name was Guster, possibly short for Augusta. She had come to the Snagsbys from a workhouse, known in those days for their horrible conditions. After being hired her out to the Snagsbys, Guster's fear of being sent back drove her to work continuously. Other than looking old for her age, which was about twenty-three, her main problem was that she was prone to seizures. On the whole, though, Guster was exceptionally pleased with her current environment, and the Snagsbys and their associates were content with her.

More on the Snagsbys — In describing the Snagsbys, Dickens constantly refers to the gossip that regularly flies about Cook's Court and colors people's opinions. Mrs. Snagsby was considered the most privileged housewife in the area, since her duties included whatever Mr. Snagsby didn't deal with in his business. That meant handling the money, the taxes, the religious outings, and whatever else fell under the heading of domestic and personal issues. But the gossip mills also said she was meddlesome and possessive, and though this troubled Mr. Snagsby, he was too weak-willed to object to her behavior. But that was probably a negative view. Mr. Snagsby was in fact a reflective sort who loved to walk in the nearby gardens and think about the olden days, when the area was still pure countryside. So it was no surprise when one evening at dusk as he stood in the doorway of his shop and looked at the sky, he noticed a crow flying westward. The narrator continues that the crow flew over Chancery Lane, all the way to Lincoln's Inn Fields, the residence and workplace of Mr. Tulkinghorn.

Mr. Tulkinghorn — Mr. Tulkinghorn, as mentioned earlier, was a highly regarded lawyer among the wealthy and aristocratic members of society. He was also inscrutable. Dickens describes him as being an "Oyster," an impenetrable old-school lawyer. His rooms, too, were old school, with their allegorical ceiling paintings, heavy furniture, and worn carpet. There, amidst his manuscripts, with only one clerk (which was all he wanted), he would ponder what Dickens calls "the train of indecision" that was his habitual state of mind. On this day, after several rounds of this, he suddenly decided to pick up his manuscript and pay a visit to Mr. Snagsby.

Nemo — Mr. Tulkinghorn's main interest in visiting Mr. Snagsby was to discover who had copied the particular manuscript he brought with him. He liked the work, and though he didn't say this outright to Mr. Snagsby, he wanted to hire the person for additional work. Mr. Snagsby, who was always happy to see Mr. Tulkinghorn because he stood for wealth and influence, obligingly interrupted his tea hour to help solve the question. They found from the roster that the copyist went by the name of "Nemo," which Mr. Tulkinghorn noticed meant "nobody" in Latin. Nemo was the mysterious tenant who lived above Mr. Krook's junk shop. He was a remarkably fast and reliable copyist, and though he was known to have posted for-hire notices, no one ever saw him.

Mr. Tulkinghorn visits the law writer's place — After Mr. Snagsby showed Mr. Tulkinghorn the way to Mr. Krook's shop, the two men left the place and went their separate ways. But Mr. Tulkinghorn suddenly turned back, and after finding Mr. Krook and his cat in the back of the shop, he asked to see the mysterious male tenant. Mr. Krook informed him that it was unlikely that he would come down, so Mr. Tulkinghorn, armed with a candle, made his way up to the law writer's apartment. Mr. Krook also mentioned that the man was rumored to have sold himself to the devil, but this didn't seem to faze Mr. Tulkinghorn.

A dark, strange sight — By himself again, Mr. Tulkinghorn now opened the door of the room after getting no response to his knocking. At that moment, his candle went out, and he found himself peering into a dark, soot-covered room with a low fire in the hearth. Everything in it showed signs of neglect, including the man Mr. Tulkinghorn now noticed lying on the bed. His hair and beard were scraggly, his feet were bare, and his overall look appeared yellow in the candlelight. Mr. Tulkinghorn believed the man's eyes were open, even though his own banging on the door with the candlestick had gotten no response. Throughout the chapter, there are allusions to death, even if only in phrases like "bored to death." Dickens now describes the candle as having melted into the shape of a shroud, and it occurred to Mr. Tulkinghorn that the strange, bitter smell permeating the room was opium.

Chapter 11 — Our Dear Brother

Mr. Snagsby's office — By candlelight, both men could see that the person on the bed, whose eyes were still open, was dead. In a state of panic, Mr. Krook yelled at Mr. Tulkinghorn to call for Miss Flite, the upstairs tenant, to fetch the doctor as fast possible. While Mr. Tulkinghorn was calling her, Mr. Krook secretly snuck over to the dead man's suitcase (which doubled as his dresser) before anyone else noticed.

Dead from an opium overdose — When the doctor arrived, he estimated that the man on the bed had died three hours earlier. This was corroborated by the young surgeon who had also arrived on the scene. Realizing that another medical person was present, the physician, who had interrupted his dinner, excused himself and left. The surgeon, who recognized Nemo as having bought opium from him for the last year and a half, determined that he had died from an overdose. He did not think it was deliberate but added that there was enough in the room to kill twelve people.

A word about Victorian surgeons — At that time, surgeons were considered lower-ranking than physicians, in part because they lacked the physicians' medical knowledge and therefore their ability to prescribe medication. They mainly did amputations without anesthesia, which hadn't been invented yet. That put them in the category of manual laborer and associated them with images of patients howling in pain. The common substitutes for anesthesia were opium and alcohol, which explains why Nemo could purchase opium from the surgeon.

The surgeon's compassion and the other's reactions — Apart from his examination of the corpse, the surgeon clearly had compassion for Nemo, commenting that he must have once been handsome and better positioned in life. Mr. Krook could not verify this, as he claimed to know nothing except that Nemo owed him six weeks' rent and kept to himself. Mr. Tulkinghorn was his usual expressionless self, and Miss Flite was too dumbstruck to say anything — not that she knew much.

Snagsby's account of Nemo — Now, however, Mr. Tulkinghorn volunteered that he had come that day intending to offer Nemo work. He had never met him before but knew his work through Mr. Snagsby. Maybe Snagsby could tell them something. Hearing that, Miss Flite went to fetch the stationer. However, Snagsby could only tell them that Nemo had first appeared in his shop about a year and half before, when he started renting from Mr. Krook. Nemo had first met Mrs. Snagsby, who was alone in the shop that day, and he had told her that he was in dire need and looking for copying work. Snagsby added that though his wife usually disliked strangers and avoided needy people, something about Nemo had struck her, and after that she constantly reminded her husband about him until Nemo got regular work. Snagsby also mentioned the speed with which Nemo worked, delivering thirty-five pages of copying work overnight, which meant that he had been working all night.

Checking the room for papers — Mr. Tulkinghorn next suggested that Snagsby check the apartment for relevant papers, since Mr. Krook couldn't read and there would certainly be an investigation. This would ensure that everything was legally above board and also prevent trouble for Mr. Krook, whom Tulkinghorn offered to represent, if necessary. Agreeing, Snagsby first pointed out the suitcase, which Tulkinghorn seemed not to have noticed till then. But the suitcase contained little of interest — just clothes, receipts, tickets, old notes about Nemo's opium intake, and some news articles about coroners' inquests. Beyond that, there was nothing much either in the room or on Nemo's person.

Flying gossip and the inept beadle — With nothing more to be done, Miss Flite took Snagsby's suggestion and ran off to fetch the beadle, while the rest of them went their separate ways. Meanwhile, the Cook's Court residents emerged to gossip about the incident. A policeman arrived on the scene and checked out the room, and a group of boys pressed their noses against Krook's shop window while they all waited for the beadle. By that time, beadles were more or less outdated and therefore looked down on by policemen, who merely tolerated them. Once the beadle did arrive, the townsfolk weren't too helpful, and his investigation turned up nothing. It didn't help that he was inept and inefficient, which brought on harassment from the townspeople, especially the boys. Eventually, the policeman did his job, got rid of the boys, and restored some degree of order and quiet to the area. By nightfall, the beadle had finally managed to notify the witnesses, serve his mostly misspelled summons to the jurors, and organize some paupers to help with the burial. Still, little to nothing was known about the dead man, who now lay all alone, as he had spent his life.

General excitement equals big business — Big news was also big business as people made the most of the excitement the event created. That was helped by the fact that the coroner held the inquest at Sol's Arms, the local pub, a common practice in those days. In fact, Dickens figured the coroner was the reigning expert on pubs. Using it as a meeting place meant the pub was busier than usual. The local (bad) comic singer took advantage of the performance opportunity, and the pieman, who catered to the children in the area, set up his stand outside and sold out of brandy balls.

The inquest — The coroner, the jurors, the witnesses, and the stenographers now having settled into this venerable environment, the inquest began. First, the coroner accompanied the jury to Mr. Krook's to view the dead man's body. By the time they returned, Mr. Tulkinghorn had also arrived at the pub. However, the jurors were instructed to not bother "the distinguished gentleman," since he had no new information to add to what they had already heard from the other witnesses — the surgeon, Mr. Krook, Miss Flite, and Mr. Snagsby.

The jury rules accidental death; a homeless orphan gives additional information — Upon listening to a few more useless jurors, the coroner presented the evidence before the jury, who ruled accidental death. One juror, however, seemed more significant: Jo, the little sweeper boy who had had some sort of relationship with the dead man. He was an illiterate, homeless orphan, whose lack of general knowledge made his account seem useless at first, but after the jury and witnesses had been dismissed, Mr. Tulkinghorn and the coroner decided to ask Jo a few more questions. By now, Jo had recognized the dead man by his black hair and yellow features. He recalled how when Nemo was broke, he would commiserate with Jo, and when he had a little money, he would share it with the boy. Once he even gave him enough for a meal and a room for the night, and Jo kept repeating how good Nemo had been to him. As Jo was leaving after the interview, Mr. Snagsby, who had been waiting for him, quietly snuck him a half crown, with the request that Jo should never mention it in the presence of Mrs. Snagsby.

The party after the inquest — In keeping with the festive atmosphere of the event, the inquest was followed by socializing and entertainment by Little Swills, the chubby red-faced singer who entertained the coroner and the other gentlemen in the same room where the inquest had taken place. The room was called the "Harmonic Meeting Room," complete with piano, and the evening's so-called "first-rate" musical entertainment was a bad imitation of the day's proceedings.

After the party — Here the scene shifts to Nemo's room, where everything was quiet again after a day of activity. There he lay in his dark little room, alone, forsaken, and forgotten by all, except for one little boy who shared his misery and humanity for a moment. There had even been a woman who once loved him and whom he loved, but she was nowhere in sight.

Good night, dear Nemo — The arrival of the new day brought with it Nemo's burial, conducted by the beadle and the band of paupers he had gathered to help him. Nemo's corpse was laid directly upon another recently buried corpse, a part of the overcrowding that made the graveyard a source of stench, rot, and disease — so disgusting even the most savage brute would reject it. Nemo's death was, in short, as tragic as his life. But through the murk and mire, one tiny figure cared enough to peer through the cemetery gate and sweep the entrance clean in remembrance of his only friend.

Chapter 12 — On the Watch

Mrs. Rouncewell prepares for the Dedlock's return — Mrs. Rouncewell had learned that the Dedlocks were returning to England from Paris and that they planned to host an exclusive party at their home in Lincolnshire. She was therefore busy preparing for their arrival.

Lady Dedlock's reaction to the mention of the copyist — Meanwhile, Sir Leicester and Lady Dedlock's carriage was pulling away from Paris, which, despite its glitter and ceaseless entertainments, had been unable to relieve Lady Dedlock's boredom. One thing did get her attention, though. Sir Leicester was going through his mail, and Lady Dedlock idly mentioned that she had noticed a communication from Mr. Tulkinghorn. She learned from Sir Leicester that Mr. Tulkinghorn wanted to speak with her when they returned, and when she found out that it had to do with the copyist of the Chancery document that had captured her attention several months earlier in Lincolnshire, she expressed a sudden urge to take a walk. The walk was brief, but Lady Dedlock leapt out of the carriage and walked away so quickly that it took Sir Leicester a few minutes to catch up, at which point she graciously received him, and they walked back to the carriage arm in arm. In fact, their interaction was generally so gracious that wherever they went, their admirers couldn't help remarking how much they loved each other despite their obvious age difference.

The return to Chesney Wold; Lady Dedlock notices Rosa — The Dedlocks spent only one night in London and then drove on to Lincolnshire through Chesney Wold's woods and park until they reached the castle, where they were welcomed by Mrs. Rouncewell. Rosa also happened to be standing behind Mrs. Rouncewell, and when Lady Dedlock spotted her, she took an obvious interest in the girl. Lady Dedlock was especially struck by Rosa's beauty, which Rosa herself seemed unaware of. When Lady Dedlock discovered Rosa was only nineteen, she gently touched her cheek and admonished her to not let herself be spoiled by flattery. After Lady Dedlock retired upstairs, Rosa went on and on about her many fine qualities. Mrs. Rouncewell, who was careful never to sound negative about any Dedlock, agreed with most of it but believed Lady Dedlock might profit from being a little warmer and friendlier.

Mrs. Rouncewell's speculation; Watt's interest in Rosa — Mrs. Rouncewell commented that the only thing that might improve the Lady's otherwise remarkable life would be the presence of a grown daughter. The topic then switched to Watt's request to stay an extra few days. He claimed he was interested in learning more about the beautiful neighborhood, but it was obvious that Rosa's beauty was a major draw. Rosa herself was too shy to acknowledge this, but Lady Dedlock's maid Hortense, who had arrived in the meantime, was acutely aware of it and wasted no time tearing Rosa down because of it.

Mademoiselle Hortense — Hortense was a dark, black-haired woman from the South of France, with a tight jaw and an acute sense of observation that she did not necessarily put to good use. She had been serving Lady Dedlock for five years and had never had the type of attention Rosa received on barely arriving at Chesney Wold — and that in spite of Hortense's good taste, excellent command of English, and outstanding knowledge of her job. Unfortunately, Hortense's manners and consideration did not match her training, and she relentlessly ridiculed Rosa for attracting Lady Dedlock's attention.

The grand party — Chesney Wold quickly transformed into a hub of activity as the distinguished guests arrived in their carriages for the grand occasion. Individuals of every age, elite description, and talent filled the lit, mirrored hall at night, guns went off during the day, and on Sundays, the church was packed.

Dandyist tendencies in the guise of religion — But for all the talent and excellence that filled the halls of Chesney Wold for those weeks, something seemed not quite right. The narrator wonders whether it was the influence of Dandyism, though there were no overt signs of it. Dickens states, however, that there was a subtle version of it, expressed in one group of guests' approach to religion. The movement he is alluding to here is the nineteenth-century movement within the Anglican Church called the Oxford movement, which saw Anglicanism as a branch of Catholicism and was seeking to reinstate Catholic elements. For various reasons, including mysticism, ritualism, and allegations of homosexuality, the Oxford movement became equated with Dandyism, even though its own members did not see it that way.

More Dandyism in the form of elegance and political talk — The second group that was "not quite right" cultivated a lackadaisical elegance and lightness that they applied to everything, from the arts to their appearance and conversation. Finally, there was the third group, the earnest gentlemen who discussed government and politics around the table. The leaders of these conversations were Lord Boodle and the Right Honourable William Buffy, M.P., and they and their train of followers were the only ones allowed to take the stage. These qualities, too, Dickens equates with the unhealthy behavior patterns of Dandyism.

Lady Dedlock awaits Mr. Tulkinghorn — Amid all the bustle at Chesney Wold, one person was still missing. It was Mr. Tulkinghorn, whose small, spare room remained empty, being reserved for him at all times. Lady Dedlock had been watching for him throughout the day and night at different times, but so far, he hadn't come.

Mr. Tulkinghorn arrives and discusses the Boythorn business with Sir Leicester — Mr. Tulkinghorn finally arrived at dusk one day when Sir Leicester and Lady Dedlock were walking by themselves on the Ghost's Walk, everyone else having already left the terrace. He had his usual unruffled, unhurried demeanor, and he and Sir Leicester discussed the case involving Boythorn, whom Sir Leicester considered a savage and to whom he was determined to yield nothing, no matter how much trouble Boythorn caused.

Lady Dedlock asks about the unknown copyist — Since night was falling and the air was getting cooler, Sir Leicester advised that they go inside. It was now Lady Dedlock's turn to talk to Tulkinghorn, and she brought up the subject of the copyist's script. She figured she must have had some connection with it, but she couldn't imagine what. She was also impressed that Mr. Tulkinghorn had actually taken the trouble to find the copyist. Mr. Tulkinghorn then revealed the strange fact that he had found the copyist dead. Sir Leicester broke in here and tried to discourage any further discussion, but Lady Dedlock would not allow any interruption. She wanted to know the rest. Mr. Tulkinghorn continued, saying that they did not know for sure whether the man had committed suicide but that his death was ruled an accidental self-poisoning. His body was in a miserable state, though the surgeon thought he had seen better days. Also, the copyist's real name was unknown. Only the name he went by was known to anyone, though Mr. Tulkinghorn never said what it was. Nor did he specifically mention the opium, though he did tell them about the relatively empty suitcase. That was all he claimed to know.

Lady Dedlock and Mr. Tulkinghorn keep their secrets to themselves — Neither Lady Dedlock nor Mr. Tulkinghorn had veered from their usual demeanors during this conversation, though they were focused on each other. The subject being finished, Sir Leicester once again insisted on its inappropriateness, especially in relation to Lady Dedlock, whose exalted station in life couldn't possibly be related to anything so distasteful. In the coming days, both Lady Dedlock and Mr. Tulkinghorn took their regular places among the rest of the company — Lady Dedlock as her graceful but bored self and Mr. Tulkinghorn with his usual air of confidential reserve. They seemed to ignore each other, but that was just a veneer, for each secretly harbored the wish to know what the other held inside.

Chapter 13 — Esther's Narrative

Richard finally decides to become a surgeon — Mr. Jarndyce was convinced that Richard's association since birth with the Jarndyce case had influenced his perception of reality so that he saw indecision and procrastination as normal. Even his excellent education hadn't been able to change this. Consequently, he and those helping him choose a career could easily pinpoint his interests and skills, but linking them to a suitable profession was more problematic.

Another issue was Richard's lighthearted approach to everything. Any career suggestion made by Mr. Jarndyce was received by Richard with immediate enthusiasm, though Esther had the impression that he didn't always give the ideas much thought. But the notion of being a surgeon resonated with him more than the other suggestions, and his enthusiasm quickly turned to determination. Mr. Jarndyce wisely recommended that Richard take his time making such a serious decision, but Richard seemed intent on sticking with it.

Boythorn's opinion and Kenge's help — Mr. Boythorn also considered it a fine career choice, though he was angry at the disrespectful treatment of naval surgeons in particular as well as at the low pay that surgeons received in general. But Richard was determined, so with the help of Mr. Kenge, the lawyer, they found a suitable apprenticeship situation with Kenge's cousin, a London medical practitioner. Jarndyce and his wards therefore decided to pay Kenge's cousin a visit and see London at the same time.

The visit to London; Esther is stalked by Mr. Guppy — Once in London, the group enjoyed visiting the city's sights, including its many worthwhile theaters. It was at the theater that Esther became aware that she was being stared at from the pit by Mr. Guppy, who had a despondent look on his face. This made Esther uncomfortable and self-conscious, which ruined the play for her. Even worse, Mr. Guppy appeared at every play they attended, followed them outside afterwards, and even pursued them to their temporary residence on Oxford Street, where he would watch for Esther from down below. Esther was relieved that Mr. Guppy had to work during the day, because otherwise she would never have had any relief from his stalking. None of her ideas for dissuading him seemed ideal, so she decided to do nothing about it.

Mr. Badger receives Richard as his apprentice — Mr. Kenge's surgeon cousin, Mr. Bayham Badger, was happy to take Richard as an apprentice, and since they liked each other, Richard would be living with him in Chelsea, a residential area for intellectuals and professionals. To celebrate the new relationship, Mr. Badger and his wife invited Mr. Jarndyce and his charges for dinner.

Dinner at the Badgers' — Mrs. Badger was a talented woman who dabbled in various things, including singing, painting, playing the piano, harp, and guitar, reading, writing poetry, and growing plants as well as "working" (which presumably meant managing the household). On top of that, she had the distinction of being previously married to two fine gentleman, a naval captain and a European professor. Fortunately, her current husband, who was quite a bit younger than his wife — estimated to be a youthful fifty — was also proud of this. In fact, Captain Swosser, Mrs. Badger's first husband, and Professor Dingo, her second husband, seemed to accompany the guests throughout the evening. They were the subject of Mr. Badger's dinner conversation with Ada and Esther, and afterwards, when the ladies moved to the drawing room, Mrs. Badger told the girls stories from her younger years.

Ada admits she and Richard are in love — Esther had recently noticed that Ada and Richard were sticking close to each other, which made sense, given their affectionate relationship and the fact that Richard was leaving soon. Later that night, back at Oxford Street, Ada confided to Esther that Richard had proclaimed his love for her. Ada seemed to think this was a huge secret and was astonished that Esther had picked up on it months ago. But there was more: they were thinking about getting married.

Richard and Ada confide in Esther — Richard had been waiting at the door during Ada's revelation, and now both sought her advice, talking far into the night about what this meant for their lives. Both Richard and Ada promised to work hard for each other, and both understood the importance of faithfulness.

Advice from Cousin John — Ada and Richard had also entrusted Esther with telling Mr. Jarndyce the next morning. Jarndyce had anticipated this months ago, though not so soon, so they all gathered together as he dispensed his fatherly advice. They were young now, but if their love should ever wane, they should not feel bad, and they could always confide in him. Richard should also never forget the importance of steadfast effort. Life did not yield its results without it, and love, too, would fall by the wayside if he did not take care of other things. Richard should therefore work hard to earn Ada's love, and except for occasional visits, they could love each other from a distance while Richard worked at his apprenticeship. But now it would be best if Richard and Ada took a walk together by themselves.

Mr. Jarndyce thinks of Esther's happiness — As Mr. Jarndyce and Esther watched the two cousins walk out together, Jarndyce mentioned that Esther's happiness should not go forgotten in the meantime. Esther replied that she was happy — that caring for others gave her great joy, to which Jarndyce replied that she would be the most remembered of all in the end.

The other dinner guest — As Esther ends the chapter, her thoughts drift back to the previous night's dinner at the Badgers'. There had been another guest as well, whom Esther hadn't mentioned. He was a dark, young, reserved surgeon, whom both Esther and Ada found pleasant and rational.

Chapter 14 — Deportment

Richard leaves for his apprenticeship — With Richard leaving so soon, Ada and Esther would both miss him, so the three of them made arrangements for keeping in touch, with plans by Ada and Richard to always keep Esther in their lives — as a guardian, guide, bridesmaid, housekeeper, and beloved friend.

Ada has misgivings about the Jarndyce settlement — Richard suggested that if the Jarndyce case ever made them rich … Here Ada's face darkened — she didn't think they should count on it. Doing so would only make them miserable. Richard ultimately agreed, but that didn't change his usual glib outlook, and he left for his new life as cheerful as ever.

Caddy Jellyby visits Esther and Ada — Since coming to London, Mr. Jarndyce and his wards had tried calling on Mrs. Jellyby, but she was always out on some African business. However, the day after Richard's departure, Caddy appeared at the Oxford Street residence with Peepy. In spite of Caddy's efforts, Peepy's appearance spoke of his mother's neglect, although Caddy's own appearance was much improved and even pretty. Mr. Jarndyce's immediate reaction to their arrival was to note the presence of a strong east wind. Still, Esther and Ada graciously welcomed Caddy, who politely relayed her mother's business to Mr. Jarndyce. Eventually, Mr. Jarndyce escaped to the Oxford Street version of the Growlery, leaving Ada and Esther alone with their guests.

Caddy's misery — Having sent Peepy to the other side of the room to play, Caddy confided to Ada and Esther that her father would soon be bankrupt. It was all her mother's fault that things were in such disarray — but her mother obviously didn't care, so the disastrous effects of her neglect would serve her right. Esther tried to soothe her and reason with her, but Caddy refused to hear it. It was futile, and her father was clearly miserable, too.

Caddy is secretly engaged — But there was more. Caddy, who trusted Esther, now informed them that she was engaged. Her family didn't know, and Caddy felt justified in this. She needed to escape from the awful situation created by her mother, and her intention was to benefit her family when they came to see her after her marriage.

The story behind the engagement — The change in Caddy started when Esther and Ada first visited the Jellybys', which left Caddy feeling ashamed and resolved to improve herself. Her mother was unsupportive, but Caddy still decided to learn how to dance, which was how she met Mr. Prince Turveydrop of Turveydrop's Dance Academy. The engagement was a secret — even her fiancé's widower father didn't know about it. The only one who did know anything was Miss Flite, who had provided her apartment as a place for Caddy and her fiancé to meet briefly.

Caddy asks Esther to come to her dance lesson — Caddy also hoped that Esther would accompany her to her lesson, which was her next stop. Feeling responsible for Caddy and hoping to influence her in a good direction, Esther agreed and then arranged for them all to meet at Miss Flite's afterwards. She also stipulated that Peepy and Caddy should come for dinner — a suggestion that was readily accepted.

The dance academy and Mr. Prince Turveydrop — The Academy on Newman street was in a run-down house that also had a drawing studio, a lithography studio, and a coal merchant. The most prominent sign was Mr. Turveydrop's, and the dance studio was full of young ladies ranging in age from their early teens to their early twenties. Amid the bustle, Esther met Mr. Prince Turveydrop, a young, slight man, whose delicate manner made Esther think that he probably resembled his late mother and that neither had been treated too kindly.

The older Mr. Turveydrop — The older Mr. Turveydrop did not teach, but he was known for his excellent deportment. Esther noticed that everything about him seemed false or forced — his skin, teeth, hair, and whiskers all appeared fake, and his corpulent, middle-aged body seemed shoved into his tight, though elegant, clothes. Seeing his father, the son introduced him to Esther, who was graciously acknowledged by the older Mr. Turveydrop, after which he commanded his son to begin the lesson. The father himself did nothing but stand by the fire, practicing his deportment, while his son ran the whole lesson.

An elderly lady rants about the older Mr. Turveydrop — Esther was observing all this from her seat on the bench, when the elderly lady sitting next to her interrupted her thoughts. According to her, the older Mr. Turveydrop was a vain, selfish fool who had taken advantage of his wife's love and admiration, just as he was now taking advantage of his son. Mr. Turveydrop's wife had been the previous dance teacher and had literally worked herself to death for him, while he spent the money she earned on elegant clothing and fashionable entertainments. As far as the elderly lady knew, he had no skills other than his capacity for elegant deportment. In her view, he deserved to be transported to a penal colony.

Mr. Turveydrop approaches Esther — As Esther sat there half-amused, listening to elderly lady's ranting yet having to admit to herself that her observations seemed true, the master of deportment himself sat down next to her. After flattering her, which she ignored, he informed her that the dance school was devoted to the constant polishing of the young ladies' skills. He added that age had not been kind to him and that his own deportment had gone downhill. In fact, deportment in general was fading fast from the English landscape, and true gentlemen were increasingly hard to find. Even his own son, who had mastered so much, lacked that indefinable quality that could not be taught.

Unequal mutual treatment between father and son — Esther then noticed that the lesson had come to an end. It was now two o'clock (as the father determined from his gold watch, the son, meanwhile, having no timepiece), and the father reminded the son that he needed to be at his school in Kensington at three. He should eat some dinner first and then rush out, and there was a cold mutton chop for him on the table. The father, of course, would do his fashionable rounds and then dine out. Unlike the elderly lady and Esther herself, neither the father nor the son seemed to see anything strange in their unequal treatment of each other — the son showing only admiration and devotion, while the father exhibited a self-satisfied condescension.

Caddy and Esther leave, escorted by the older Mr. Turveydrop — The young Mr. Turveydrop having said his goodbyes, the older one now gallantly escorted Esther and Caddy outside, where he parted from them to go on his aristocratic way. Esther was so distracted by the whole scene that she found it hard to concentrate, though she finally got a handle on herself.

Caddy confides in Esther about Prince's lack of education — Caddy lamented that Prince had spent so much time teaching dance that his education had lagged, though she could make up for both of them when it came to writing. And who was she to criticize him, being herself so deficient in so many things, thanks to her mother's negligence? Besides, the most important thing was that Prince was pleasant, even if his education was lacking.

Caddy tells Esther how Miss Flite is teaching her housekeeping skills — Caddy added that she had been frustrated trying to learn housekeeping skills in her own family home, but she was lucky to have found a teacher in Miss Flite. In the interest of being a good wife to Prince, she had been practicing her new skills by helping Miss Flite. She admitted that her sewing still need help, but in addition to all the practical housekeeping skills she had learned, she was happy that her overall temperament had improved and that she found it easier to forgive her mother. Esther found herself feeling more and more affection for Caddy, and she suggested they be friends. They could talk about these things more often and together find the best solutions to Caddy's issues.

Caddy and Esther look inside the room where Nemo died — By this point, Caddy and Esther had arrived at Miss Flite's building, and as they passed the second-floor apartment where Nemo died, they looked in. Caddy remarked that Esther looked pale and cold, and Esther admitted — to herself, at least — that the dark, desolate atmosphere of the room had given her chills.

Miss Flite is recovering from a nervous reaction to the presence of death — Miss Flite, too, had suffered from the presence of death in the building. A doctor was in attendance, the same young, dark doctor who witnessed at Nemo's inquest. Mr. Jarndyce and Ada were also there, and Miss Flite was pleased to once again be honored by the company of the wards in Jarndyce, not to mention Mr. Jarndyce himself.

Miss Flite's windfall — Miss Flite was delighted to add that a sudden, unexpected windfall had come her way. She thought it had something to do with the Jarndyce case but couldn't point to the exact source, though she had her theories. In any case, either Mr. Kenge or Mr. Guppy had been coming on a weekly basis and delivering a paper to her containing seven shillings, which Caddy, whom she had dubbed "Fitz-Jarndyce," would then put to good use for her. Hearing this, Esther looked over at Mr. Jarndyce, who was nonchalantly studying the birds.

Mr. Krook edges his way into the conversation — Suddenly, Miss Flite turned her attention to the door. Mr. Krook had been standing behind it, listening, and she demanded to know why. Of course, he denied it, claiming he had just arrived. Miss Flite also wanted to know why he had come while she had company. Mr. Krook's strange response was that he equated himself with the Lord Chancellor and claimed to know a great deal about the Jarndyce case. It was therefore of great interest to him to meet Mr. Jarndyce, who made it a point to never attend the Court of Chancery. He continued moving into the room until he was right next to Mr. Jarndyce, who still stood by the birdcages. With Miss Flite's permission, Krook then revealed the names of all the birds to the guests. There were about twenty all together, and their names represented all the qualities that marched through the Court of Chancery at one time or another — from Youth and Hope to Death, Despair, Sheepskin, and Plunder. If there ever were a judgment, all the birds would be released, only to be killed — in his opinion — by the wild birds.

Mr. Krook eyes Mr. Jarndyce as he shows the guests his strange activities — Ever since Mr. Krook's arrival, the east wind had been making its presence felt, and it was a particularly bad one today. Mr. Krook had also latched onto the guests, especially Mr. Jarndyce, from whom he rarely removed his eyes. He insisted on showing them his own strange version of the Chancery Court and the room where he was teaching himself to read and write, something he entrusted only to himself.

Dr. Woodcourt discounts Mr. Krook's madness — Once the group had finally managed to escape the house, Mr. Jarndyce asked Dr. Woodcourt, the young, dark surgeon, whether Mr. Krook was insane. Dr. Woodcourt didn't think so, though it was clear from the smell in the back of his shop that he drank plenty of gin. That and his suspiciousness, which the doctor equated with ignorance, might combine to make him look crazy, but he didn't think that was actually the case.

Dinner at Oxford Street; Esther notices the young surgeon again — Following the visit, they all went back to dinner at Oxford Street. That included the young surgeon, whom Esther coyly refers to in her final paragraphs — but she never finishes her full statement, leaving the reader with the definite impression that she's holding something back.

Chapter 15 — Bell Yard

The philanthropists — The excitable people Esther mentions at the beginning of the chapter are the philanthropists discussed earlier in the story, whose self-aggrandizing charitable efforts only brought forth the east wind whenever Mr. Jarndyce came in contact with them. He preferred the company of Mr. Skimpole, who was at least straightforward about who he was.

Skimpole visits Jarndyce's London residence — Mr. Skimpole lived in London but had been sick with liver complaint from too much alcohol, so Mr. Jarndyce and his wards hadn't seen him. Now, however, he appeared on their doorstep with his usual notions about money. It was all right for him to not pay the doctor, the butcher, or whomever. His intention to pay was good enough, since he didn't have the money, anyway. The doctor and the butcher already had whatever they were providing, so it wasn't the same situation.

The impending visit to Boythorn's — Mr. Jarndyce was amused but unconvinced by Mr. Skimpole's convenient double standard, and Skimpole soon switched to the subject to Mr. Boythorn. Skimpole had heard that the Jarndyce party would be visiting Boythorn in Lincolnshire, and Boythorn had invited Mr. Skimpole to his place as well and even offered to pay his roundtrip fare. But he and Mr. Boythorn were so different that there was a question in Skimpole's mind as to whether they could get along. However, he reassured himself that two angels, Ada and Esther, would act as a buffer.

Coavinses dies and leaves three orphans — Mr. Skimpole then informed them that Coavinses had died (been "arrested by the great Bailiff"), which shocked Esther and stirred up the east wind for Mr. Jarndyce. Mr. Skimpole had learned the news from Coavinses's replacement, who had come to take possession of Skimpole's house. Jarndyce became increasingly perturbed as he learned that Coavinses had left behind three children and no wife. Furthermore, his children's future was compromised by their father's former profession, which got him a lot of enemies.

Jarndyce's compassion — Mr. Skimpole seemed curiously unaffected by the suffering caused by the situation, as he interjected a piano chord between each phrase and then finished with a song. Mr. Jarndyce interrupted him. This wasn't right. Mr. Coavinses was only doing a job made necessary by the foibles of others. Mr. Jarndyce wanted to know more, so Skimpole suggested that they visit the station headquarters, and off they all went.

The Jarndyce party is confronted by Gridley — At the station, Mr. Jarndyce discovered that Coavinses's real name had been Neckett and that he had lived above the chandler's shop in Bell Yard. On entering the chandler's shop, the group was directed upstairs by the landlady, who gave Esther a key. Halfway up, they were confronted by an angry-looking man named Gridley, who had heard the noise on the stairs and asked what they wanted. Gridley was tall and strong-looking, though obviously aging, and Esther noticed a mess of papers in his room as they passed.

Coavinses's struggling children — Once at the top floor, they found that the children were locked in. After unlocking the door, Esther opened it to a little boy holding a toddler. The boy explained that there were three of them, but the third, his sister Charley, was out working as a washerwoman. For safety, she locked them in when she left, and they didn't mind. Esther noticed that the apartment was cold, with no fire to warm it, and the children's clothing wasn't enough to ward off the rawness.

Charley Neckett — Just then, Charley herself appeared. Charley was at least thirteen years old, though small for her age, but her clothing and her responsible manner were suited to her role as the caretaker of her family. It was obvious from the soap suds on her arms that she had just come from her washing job. As she entered, the baby, Emma, reached out to her, and Charley took the baby in her arms, just like a mature woman.

Mr. Jarndyce interviews Charley — Moved with compassion, Mr. Jarndyce wondered how such a small child could take responsibility for a family. Questioning Charley, he learned various details of the children's lives, including that Charley, on her father's advice, had taken over the household responsibilities after her mother died following Emma's birth. She was proud that she was able to support them with the money she earned. Tom, the little boy, was also happy to cooperate and take care of Emma while Charley was away. They made do with what they had and were happy to share, though it was clear their life was hard.

Mrs. Blinder's report — Meanwhile, the landlady, Mrs. Blinder, had come upstairs. She was sympathetic to the children's situation and didn't mind waiving the rent for them. She also confirmed Charley's remarkable strength and industry, but things were harder for the children because of their late father's profession. Even Mrs. Blinder had nearly evicted him when she discovered he was one of the sheriff's "followers." But seeing Mr. Neckett's steady and upright character, she relented and convinced the reluctant Gridley to approve of his presence. She then dealt with the rest of the Bell Yard residents, who generally disliked having an arresting officer in their midst, but she didn't much care at that point, having made up her mind to be fair.

When asked how the children had generally been treated, Mrs. Blinder added that their father and others had provided for them. The neighbors' reaction was mixed, including towards Charley. But Charley was smart, patient, and resourceful, and in general, things could have been worse.

Mr. Gridley reveals his involvement with the Chancery Court — Mrs. Blinder's account was followed , the arrival of Mr. Gridley, who had always shown compassion toward the children.. His love for the children was obvious, but he made no attempt at first to ingratiate himself to the adult guests. It soon came out that the source of his anger was a long Chancery suit that was still unresolved and that was a joke in the court. When he learned that Mr. Jarndyce also had firsthand experience with the Chancery Court, he admitted that Jarndyce dealt with the matter more gracefully but added that if he didn't express his own anger, the whole thing would drive him mad.

Mr. Gridley's rage at "the system" — Anger was a weak word to describe Mr. Gridley's rage. Unlike Jarndyce and Jarndyce, which involved thousands of people, his suit had been a simple affair between himself and his brother, a matter of less than £300 having to do with his father's will. The Chancery Court had dragged it out for so long that not only the £300 but the entire estate had been eaten up by legal costs, and what had begun as a simple suit ended up involving hundreds of people. Furthermore, no one would take responsibility: only "the system" was at fault, and all the legal types had to serve the system, which of course rewarded them plentifully while it sucked everyone else dry. Even Gridley's brother, who had instigated the lawsuit, would have loved to be released. But now they were both stuck, neither would see a penny, and both had already lost everything to the Court's insatiable appetite for fees.

Mr. Gridley's inability to temper his rage — Mr. Jarndyce was sympathetic, but nothing he said seemed to soothe Mr. Gridley and only stirred up his rage. Gridley admitted it was a problem. He had landed in jail many times because of it, and he would no doubt create trouble again. He had been told by the Lord Chancellor and others that he would be better off returning to Shropshire and focusing on earning his living. But even though he had once been an even-tempered man, he could no longer bring himself to do that — his rage would certainly drive him mad. But he hadn't come there to talk about this. He had come to bring the two youngest children down to his room to play and maybe even find a gingerbread soldier. With that, he excused himself and took them downstairs.

Mr. Skimpole's distorted views — Mr. Gridley's vehement but honest account of his own struggles had provided Mr. Skimpole with plenty of food for his theories on Gridley's life. Mr. Skimpole's opinion that the Chancery Court filled a need in Mr. Gridley exhibited a lack of normal human compassion and a flighty, romanticized view of life. His view of Coavinses was equally skewed. But whereas Skimpole once would have preferred to see Coavinses done away with, now that he had met his lovely children, he elevated himself to the level of benevolent patron of Coavinses's family.

The party leaves and Charley returns to work — Luckily for Skimpole, his charm overrode whatever came out of his mouth, and he made Mr. Jarndyce smile. Mr. Jarndyce had been quietly speaking with Mrs. Blinder, but now the group was preparing to leave, so they all kissed Charley goodbye and watched her disappear down the walkway.

Chapter 16 — Tom-all-Alone's

Lady Dedlock's restlessness — Lady Dedlock was unusually restless these days, to the point that the informants for elite society had trouble keeping tabs on her movements. She seemed to be all over — Lincolnshire, London, out of the country. Even Sir Leicester had trouble keeping up, though to be fair, he was hampered by a bout of arthritic pain, an exclusive ailment inherited from his exclusive ancestors. And with Lady Dedlock in London again, Sir Leicester was by himself, looking out on his estate, with only his Lady's and his ancestors' portraits to keep him company.

The home of Jo the sweeper boy — Here the scene shifts to Jo, the sweeper boy, who knows nothing about anything except how to sweep his own crossing, and even that can be difficult in muddy weather. Jo's home is the opposite of the Chesney Wold estate. He lives in one of the most squalid areas of London, a place infested with vermin and disease, run down to the point of ruin, full of darkness and decay. "Run down" here doesn't mean broken in places: it means that the houses are on the verge of crumbling, as they sometimes do, leaving human casualties in their wake. The name of this dismal place is Tom-all-Alone's, and like so many other things, it is stuck in the clutches of the Chancery Court — though why, in this case, nobody knows.

The world according to Jo — The world from Jo's point of view is a completely different experience from that of most people. First, he's illiterate, which means that most of what is common knowledge to others is to him a great mystery. Second, he has been cast aside and treated as less than human, a condition he's used to but that makes him feel like an outcast.

A day in Jo's life — This particular day is market day, so after Jo trundles out from his dank, dark habitation, munching on a soiled piece of bread, he watches the area around his corner slowly come to life. Overworked oxen bump into things and get into trouble. A herd dog takes a break from the sheep he normally guards. His master has gone into the butcher's shop, which might explain why some of the sheep are missing. Amidst the bustle of the market — the music, the noise, the movement — Jo feels more like the animals than like the human beings who resemble him only in the general form of their appearance. Not knowing how to read or write, and not having the buffer of a civilized life, Jo's reactions to his surroundings are more basic and direct than those of his fellow humans.

The view from Mr. Tulkinghorn's — Mr. Tulkinghorn has a completely different experience. He sits in his room, remote from the sights, sounds, and smells. Today he had to deal with that nuisance, Gridley, and he is determined to keep him at bay however he can. From his ivory tower, Mr. Tulkinghorn can easily dismiss whatever doesn't require his immediate attention. He therefore has no reason to look out the window at the woman now walking by. Women, after all, are of little use, being mostly trouble — though at least, being trouble, they bring in more income for lawyers.

The mysterious woman — This woman, however, is different. She has already turned several heads because of the incongruousness of her appearance. Her dress is like that of an upper-class servant, but her demeanor, though veiled, is unmistakably that of a lady. Yet she herself is not concerned with the people who stare at her, being solely focused on her goal — to approach the little sweeper boy.

The mysterious lady's mission — Why would a lady of such refined demeanor want to approach an illiterate creature more on a par with the animals than with his fellow human beings? The mysterious lady has a secret mission — to discover the last places in the life of a wretched, nearly forgotten copyist, who now lies buried beneath the ground in a dark, diseased graveyard. For that she is willing to pay good money and make her delicate way through some of the worst parts of London. But she has to do it in disguise under cover of night, and so, she waits till evening to approach Jo.

Retracing Nemo's last days — From the moment the lady neared Jo, it was clear that she would be control of their interaction. He was not to come too close (she found him too wretched and disgusting). He was simply to answer her questions and show her where the copyist had spent the last days of his existence. So Jo took her first to Cook's Court to show her who had employed him. From the outside, he then pointed out the copyist's apartment in Krook's building. He showed the lady the pub where the inquest had taken place. And finally, he took her to the graveyard and explained how they had buried Nemo on top of other bodies and had to stomp on the ground to make sure he fit.

Conclusion of the visit — Going to the graveyard meant going to another squalid area of London, complete with vermin and filth — not what the lady was used to. In the meantime, Jo had figured out that she was a lady, despite her denials, and their interaction confirmed his hunch. Seeing the horrible condition of the graveyard, the lady asked whether it had been blessed, but Jo couldn't imagine that it had. It seemed more likely to have been cursed. The lady having completed her business, she gave Jo a gold crown (to his surprise) and disappeared.

Conclusion to the day — That night, Lady Dedlock attended a dinner and several balls in London. Jo kept reexamining his gold coin to make sure it was real. Sir Leicester, meanwhile, was still in Lincolnshire, alone in his room, trying to read and ignore the pain of his arthritis. And Mrs. Rouncewell informed Rosa that the haunting footsteps on the Ghost's Walk had never been so distinct, even through the rain.

Chapter 17 — Esther's Narrative

Richard's lack of seriousness — Esther had grown fond of Richard's charming, lighthearted ways, but she wondered whether he had the seriousness to succeed in a career, while her guardian still maintained that Richard's long-time association with the Chancery Court had influenced his character too much.

Mrs. Badger's opinion — They were not the only ones to observe these things. Mrs. Badger's association with her first two husbands had given her many opportunities to observe young men. Richard, in her opinion, seemed deficient in the passion and commitment needed to succeed as a surgeon, and she wondered how seriously he had considered his career path. By contrast, Mr. Woodcourt, the young, dark surgeon, possessed the determination, earnestness, and focus to withstand the difficulties of the career — the low pay, the heavy workload, the thanklessness. Mr. Badger, who hadn't thought about the situation till then, felt compelled to agree.

Esther and Ada resolve to talk to Richard — Hearing this, Ada and Esther resolved to talk to Richard when he arrived the next morning. But the next morning, by the time Richard and Ada had had their private time, Esther noticed — as anticipated — that Ada had adjusted her opinion and was ready to support Richard in anything. It therefore fell to Esther to play the role of wise advisor.

Richard decides to try law instead — Richard readily admitted that he didn't care for the profession of surgeon, but in addition to his lack of seriousness and focus, he was unconvinced as to the worthwhileness of it all. All careers seemed the same to him, though he had fortunately thought about an alternate — the law. Unfortunately, that choice betrayed his irrational fixation on winning the Jarndyce suit in spite of everyone's warnings.

Mr. Jarndyce advises a trial run — Mr. Jarndyce was receptive to this new development, but he counseled Richard to take things slowly. They should give the new venture a trial run before making a final decision. Richard needed to remember, after all, that his decisions impacted not only himself but Ada, too.

Mr. Jarndyce assures Ada that he thinks no less of Richard — Ada needed assurance that Mr. Jarndyce did not think less of Richard because of his instability, but Jarndyce assured her that that would only happen if Richard's actions had a negative effect on her. Even then, he would be more likely to blame himself — after all, he introduced them. As Ada went off to bed, Esther noticed a troubled look on her guardian's face as he looked Ada and then at her.

Unable to sleep, Esther finds Mr. Jarndyce is also up — Ada slept peacefully and happily that night, evidently dreaming of Richard, about whom she had only good things to say. Esther, on the other hand, had difficulty sleeping. Something was disturbing her, and though she had some idea of what it was, she wouldn't admit it to herself. She was also depressed, but after giving herself a pep talk, she resolved to work on some decorative sewing until she could no longer keep her eyes open. To complete the project, she needed to retrieve some silk from the temporary Growlery, where she found Mr. Jarndyce also still awake, his hair all tousled from rubbing his head, as he did whenever he was troubled. Surprised to see him, Esther asked what was bothering him, but he said it wasn't anything she would understand. Yet the way he said it seemed different to her, and it made her think. Seeing his surprise that she was still awake, too, Esther explained that she couldn't sleep and had decided to work instead.

Mr. Jarndyce tells Esther about her past — By now, Jarndyce had waved the troubled look off his face as he told Esther it was time she learned about her background. That way, at least she could have some perspective in case anyone tried to attach anything negative to her. As Esther sat down, she tried to remain calm while audibly recalling how Miss Barbary had called her a disgrace to her mother, and vice versa. Her guardian had saved her from the sadness and loneliness of her childhood, and she was forever grateful for that. But Mr. Jarndyce motioned to her to stop — he didn't want to be thanked.

Mr. Jarndyce then told Esther about the letter he had received nine years earlier, when Esther was twelve. Miss Barbary, which was not her real name, had written him with the intention of providing for Esther in the event that she (Miss Barbary) died before the girl became an adult. She was actually Esther's aunt and had raised her since the time she was born. But she would disclose no further details about the child's birth, refused to see Mr. Jarndyce in person, and had cut herself off from the rest of the world to raise the girl in secret. It seemed to Mr. Jarndyce that her view was unnecessarily dark and that the little girl was being punished for something she had no control over, so he sent Mr. Kenge to meet with the woman and assure the child of a decent future. That was all he knew.

A tender goodnight — Mr. Jarndyce cheerfully added that he had regularly checked up on Esther and that his efforts had been repaid many times over. Esther had been holding is hand, which she kissed in gratitude, and now she thanked him for his fatherly care. When she mentioned the word "father," his face suddenly looked troubled again. But it was only for a moment, though it made her wonder. He then gave her a fatherly goodnight kiss, and Esther went to her room and slept well, thanking heaven for all the good she had received.

The young, dark surgeon leaves for India — The following day, Mr. Allan Woodcourt, the young, dark surgeon, visited the Jarndyce London residence to inform them that he would be leaving on a long journey for India. He had few prospects here, not being wealthy, and this was his best option. He had enjoyed his visits with them, and this time he also brought his mother, a black-eyed Welsh woman who told stories about their famous ancestor, a renowned Welsh hero, and admonished her son to not marry beneath his pedigree. Esther found herself wondering for a moment whether her background would pass muster but then quickly dismissed the thought as irrelevant. Allan himself was uncomfortable with his mother's speeches, but he was too kind to say anything. He was known for his gentleness, skill, and compassion for the poor, and his personality shone through in this instance, too. His main goal in coming that day, other than to say goodbye, was to thank Mr. Jarndyce for his hospitality.

Caddy brings a mysterious bouquet — Later that day, Caddy showed up with a surprise — a small bouquet of flowers left by Mr. Woodcourt at Miss Flite's. They were for Esther, and Caddy never said who left them, only that "somebody" who had been kind to Miss Flite and was leaving to board a ship had left them for Esther. How she knew they were for Esther was unclear, but she seemed convinced. The scene ends as Ada teases Esther about the romantic implications.

Chapter 18 — Lady Dedlock

Richard's continued indecision delays his apprenticeship — For all his enthusiasm and determination, Richard had not yet chosen between law and medicine. Surgery didn't seem so bad after all, and for a month, he threw himself into his books and learned a lot, but then his passion waned, and he was back to his usual indifference and indecision. By the time he started his apprenticeship with Mr. Kenge, it was already the start of summer.

A place in town and irrational spending habits — Apprenticing with Kenge meant finding Richard an apartment in town, since by now the Jarndyce group had returned to Bleak House. Eventually, they found Richard a small furnished place in a quiet, decent neighborhood, but the move unfortunately brought out Richard's irrational attitudes about money, as he promptly spent too much on unnecessary trinkets. His reasoning was that he might have spent the money on something more expensive and that he therefore gained in the process. As a result, he was soon broke.

Mr. Skimpole's convenient ways — Richard stayed behind when the others went to visit Mr. Boythorn in Lincolnshire, having now set himself the task of unraveling the Jarndyce case. But whatever entertainment was missing because of Richard's absence was made up for by Mr. Skimpole. Skimpole explained that his furniture had all been possessed since the officer came to his home. He liked the freedom of no furniture, but he simply couldn't understand why his landlord would want to possess something that hadn't been paid for. To Skimpole, the thought that he should pay his own way for anything — whether furniture, food, or travel expenses — never occurred to him, and he was always ready to shunt the cost over to Mr. Jarndyce, who took it all with good grace.

Meeting Mr. Boythorn — It was a beautiful summer's day as the coach traveled past wheat fields and wildflowers till finally arriving in a sleepy little market town. Mr. Boythorn met his guests at the town inn, and since the coach was twenty-five minutes late, he ranted and raved about how the driver deserved to die for delaying them. That being said, he suddenly changed his demeanor and became a complete gentleman as he helped the ladies transfer to his open-air carriage, which was to take them the rest of the way.

Boythorn's refusal to set foot in Chesney Wold — The trip home, however, did not include going through Chesney Wold, which would have been the direct route. That was something Boythorn had sworn never to do for as long as he lived, given his negative relationship with Sir Leicester. He could not understand why Lady Dedlock ever married that numbskull, Sir Leicester, whose stiff, self-satisfied ways irritated him to no end.

Jarndyce's desire to visit the estate — Mr. Jarndyce asked whether the Dedlocks were there at the moment. According to Boythorn, Sir Leicester was there, and Lady Dedlock was expected but had not yet shown. Jarndyce then wanted to know whether the group might visit Chesney Wold's park. From the hill, they could see how beautiful and peaceful it looked, and their interests lay solely in sightseeing. Mr. Jarndyce, anyway, had no expectation of meeting Sir Leicester. Mr. Boythorn did not feel it was his place to prevent them from doing so, as long as he wasn't accompanying them.

Mr. Boythorn points out Watt — As they entered the small village near the estate, Mr. Boythorn pointed out Watt Rouncewell sitting next to some fishing tackle. He came there several times a week to fish — a statement that brought on loud laughter from Boythorn. He added that the young man was in love with a girl who worked for Mrs. Rouncewell and that Lady Dedlock herself had taken a great interest in this lovely young girl and planned to engage her more closely.

Mr. Boythorn's house and garden — Mr. Boythorn lived in a beautiful old home with an abundant and well-maintained walled garden, full of fruit trees and bushes of all kinds, in addition to a kitchen garden, flower garden, and lawn. There was even an herb garden, and the fresh scents from there and the nearby meadows added to the impression of abundance and well-being. The house itself was not as orderly as the garden, yet it had all the charm of an old house, with its brick floors and ceiling beams.

Boythorn's attempts to fend off trespassers — Adjacent to it was the land that was the ostensible cause of Mr. Boythorn's argument with Sir Leicester, and Boythorn had taken various measures to guard it, including the placement of a sentry, a bulldog, and threatening signs referring to either the bulldog, a loaded gun, lurking traps, personal punishment measures, or legal prosecution. Mr. Skimpole could not believe that Boythorn was serious about any of this, but Mr. Boythorn protested that he could not be more serious. He would have trained a lion if he thought he could have done so successfully, and he was ready to meet Sir Leicester in single combat.

The congregation — The next day was Sunday, and since the church was within the estate, the group had to walk through Chesney Wold's park to arrive there. The small congregation was mostly made up of country folk, many of them servants from the estate. Mrs. Rouncewell was there, as were Watt, Rosa, and Hortense.

Esther's eyes meet Lady Dedlock's — Esther was observing that it was a dark little church with an earthy smell, when her thoughts were interrupted by the arrival of the Dedlocks. A stir went through the congregation, and an even greater stir passed through Esther as her eyes met Lady Dedlock's. The sight of Esther pulled Lady Dedlock out of her indifference and moved Esther in a way she could not explain, if only for a moment. Thoughts of her childhood with Miss Barbary flashed through her mind — yet she was sure she had never seen Lady Dedlock before. She tried to concentrate on the reader's words but still found images from her childhood mingling with the present, and her own and her godmother's face seemed intertwined with the face of this beautiful, proud lady.

More convenient views from Mr. Skimpole — Following the service, Mr. Skimpole remarked that Sir Leicester had surveyed the congregation as someone surveying his domain, and Skimpole theorized about how he could take advantage of such a person by agreeing to agree with him and hoping the great man would throw something his way. On Boythorn's questioning, Skimpole added that he had no qualms about taking the same approach with the man's enemy. His own role in life was to be in harmony with everyone, and if he got something out of it, so much the better.

Boythorn's hospitality and Jarndyce's graceful humor avert potential disaster — Boythorn's reaction to this was to turn red, strike the ground with his stick, and insist that there must be some principle to things. But Boythorn's vehemence did not perturb Skimpole in the least. He had no clue about principles, nor was he interested, his childlike nature once again being his excuse.

Throughout this conversation — and there were many like it — Skimpole acted pleasant, cheerful, and oblivious of such things as conscience or responsibility. In fact, Esther couldn't help noticing how his wife and children never factored into his considerations. Fortunately, between Mr. Jarndyce's enjoyment of Skimpole's company and Boythorn's insistence on being a good host, whatever might have erupted between Boythorn and Skimpole did not.

Ada, Esther, and Mr. Jarndyce take cover in Chesney Wold's woods — The next week was hot, so Ada, Esther, and Mr. Jarndyce spent much of their time in Chesney Wold's woods. The following Saturday, they were again in their favorite moss-covered spot, when a sudden storm broke out, forcing them to run for cover. Fortunately, the groundskeeper's lodge was nearby. They had noticed its dark, ivy-covered walls before, and now they took shelter near the door. A man appeared from inside the lodge and brought two chairs for Esther and Ada.

Lady Dedlock emerges from within — As they sat there watching the drama of the thunderstorm, a voice inquired whether it wasn't dangerous to sit in such an exposed area. Thinking it was Esther, Ada answered no. Meanwhile, Esther's heart started pounding, and once again, childhood images arose in her mind. Lady Dedlock had come up behind Esther and put her hand on her chair. She asked whether she had frightened them, but they denied it. She then turned to Mr. Jarndyce, whom she recognized, and apologized that the land dispute (which she did not attribute to her husband) had interfered with a proper reception. She seemed respectful and well-disposed toward Mr. Jarndyce, and their conversation was amiable, though Lady Dedlock rarely veered from her usual state of indifferent grace and nobility. Without ever mentioning names, she asked whether Richard's issues had been resolved, regretting that Sir Leicester had been unable to help. Perceiving that Ada was the other Jarndyce ward, she asked to be introduced and then turned toward Esther with the same intention.

Lady Dedlock continues her conversation with Mr. Jarndyce — Mr. Jarndyce explained that Esther was his true ward, having nothing to do with the Jarndyce case. Perceiving that Esther was an orphan, Lady Dedlock commented on her good fortune at having Mr. Jarndyce as her guardian. After looking at each other full on, Lady Dedlock suddenly turned from Esther, as though something was wrong. She then mentioned to Mr. Jarndyce how long it had been since they had last seen each other, and Mr. Jarndyce observed that her appearance had hardly changed. She laughed when she heard this, attributing it to flattery and wondering that he, too, should feel compelled to adulate her. There was a moment of silence, in which Esther noticed how composed Lady Dedlock was and how little the presence of others seemed to affect her. Lady Dedlock then resumed her conversation with Mr. Jarndyce. She knew he had been more in touch with her sister over the years than with her. She and her sister were quite different, and she regretted that they had to part but added that they had had no choice.

Lady Dedlock bids them goodbye and rides off with Rosa, leaving Hortense behind — By now, the storm had cleared, and soon a little carriage appeared with Rosa and Hortense inside. Hortense emerged first, proud and confident. The messenger had called for Lady Dedlock's attendant, and as far as she was concerned, that was her role. Rosa was more timid but expressed her belief that Lady Dedlock had meant for her to come, so she did. Lady Dedlock confirmed her statement, ignoring Hortense. She then bid farewell to Ada and Mr. Jarndyce, without even looking at Esther. She offered to send a carriage, but Mr. Jarndyce declined. She also regretted that they would no longer be meeting.

She and Rosa then got into the carriage, leaving Hortense behind. Hortense's reaction was to remove her shoes and walk barefoot through the wet grass, which made Mr. Jarndyce wonder whether she had lost her mind. But the keeper and his wife said she wasn't the type. They assumed it was her reaction to receiving her notice while Rosa was promoted. It was probably her way of cooling down. The keeper's wife added that Hortense, with her temperament, would probably just as soon walk through blood.

A peaceful sight — After that, the Jarndyce group left and was soon passing the estate house, which looked bright and even more peaceful than before, now that it had been washed by the rain. And there, off in the distance, was Hortense, crossing the wet grass with her bare feet.

Chapter 19—Moving On

The long vacation—Summertime meant the onset of the long vacation, when the courts closed and the clerks and ticket porters had nothing to do. Only one judge came in to work a couple of times a week, and even he didn't bother with the usual wigs, robes, and attendants. Instead, he was dressed in a white leisure suit, looking tanned and relaxed. The rest of his peers were either off somewhere else in the world or simply enjoying the English seaside.

The Snagsbys entertain the Chadbands—Mr. Snagsby also had less to do now, which meant that he and his wife had time to entertain. Guster had therefore been cleaning and was now setting the tea table with plenty of food for Mr. Chadband, who liked to eat. He and his wife were expected at six that evening.

The Chadbands—Reverend Chadband was portly, awkward, and yellow, as though he drank too much lamplighting fluid. He often wiped his sweaty head, and instead of speaking normally, he preferred making sanctimonious speeches. Even a simple greeting or description of the tea table transformed into a speech about high principles.

The constable asks Mr. Snagsby to confirm Jo's story—Meanwhile, the constable had arrived at the shop with Jo the sweeper boy. He had been referred there by a young man who vouched for Mr. Snagsby's respectability. The constable was complaining that Jo refused to move on, no matter how many times he was told. Jo tried explaining his side of the story, but the constable didn't believe him, so here he was at the stationer's to hopefully resolve the issue. By now, the whole party had gathered on the stairs to listen, and they were soon joined by the young man mentioned above, who turned out to be Mr. Guppy.

Jo tells about the mysterious lady—Mr. Snagsby confirmed that he did, in fact, know Jo and considered him harmless, but to avoid trouble with his wife, he was careful to avoid mentioning the half crowns he had given him. The constable, however, believed Jo had stolen the half crowns. In his mind, their presence did not match the boy's poverty-stricken condition. In his own defense, Jo told them about the mysterious lady who had asked to see where the deceased law writer had spent his final days. His story left the constable unconvinced, but it captured the others' interest, particularly that of Mr. Guppy.

Mr. Guppy cross-examines Jo—The constable having stated his case and enlisted Mr. Snagsby's help to get Jo to move on, he left. At that point, Mr. Guppy decided to question Jo further. This was so interesting to the assembled ladies and gentlemen that Mrs. Snagsby invited Mr. Guppy upstairs for tea, and Jo, being the interviewee, also came along. After a lengthy examination, Mr. Guppy determined that either Jo simply wasn't budging from his story or that something extremely unusual had taken place. Kenge and Carboy had certainly never seen anything like it—at least, not in Mr. Guppy's time.

The Kenge and Carboy connection—Hearing the name Kenge and Carboy, Mrs. Chadband whispered something to Mrs. Snagsby. As it happened, she had been associated with that office many years ago, when she was put in charge of a child called Esther Summerson. This caught Mr. Guppy's attention, but before he could do anything, Mr. Chadband rose to speak. Mrs. Snagsby, who was always ready to hear his preaching, therefore hushed everyone up.

Reverend Chadband's speech to Jo—Jo had been standing in the doorway the whole time Mr. Guppy was interviewing him, but now he came forward on Mr. Chadband's request. Mr. Chadband then proceeded to announce that Jo, to them, was a diamond by virtue of his being human. He went on and on like this, sermonizing on the subject with great eloquence. At one point, Jo, who was uncomfortable and unsure of the whole scene, wiped his face with his arm and yawned, which prompted Mrs. Snagsby to equate him with demon spawn. Mr. Chadband, however, had a more elevated point of view. This was another opportunity for the reverend to redeem himself from some minor ill—even if only in thought—and for that, he was immensely grateful.

Mr. Chadband invites Jo to hear more speeches—Mr. Chadband, who loved to hear himself talk, invited Jo to see him again, preferably in a receptive state. Jo agreed to this, though he seemed more intent on leaving, and Guster finally escorted him out with plenty of meat scraps that Mr. Snagsby had collected from the tea table.

Jo moves on—Jo's next stop was Blackfriars Bridge. From his nook, where he settled down to eat his meal of leftovers, he could watch the river and the crowds going by. But such meager comforts never lasted long, and Jo was soon prodded to move on again.

Chapter 20 — A New Lodger

Idle days at Kenge and Carboy — The idleness of the long vacation gave Mr. Guppy plenty of time to stab his desk with his penknife and plot unnecessary defenses against unsuspecting apprentices, especially young gentleman like Richard. But Richard himself was too embroiled in the Jarndyce case to notice.

Young Smallweed — Young Smallweed was the articled clerk at Kenge and Carboy. Even though he was under fifteen, Smallweed had a shriveled appearance. His main goal in life was to imitate Mr. Guppy, and otherwise he spent his time giving Guppy occasional personal advice or running errands for the office, which included important tasks like fixing fizzy drinks.

Mr. Jobling — One of Mr. Guppy's entertainments during this languid time was to look out the upper-story window, and on this particular day, he found his friend Mr. Jobling looking back. Jobling was in need of money for a meal, so he called up to Guppy to throw him down a half crown. Guppy obliged and invited him to dinner as well.

Mr. Smallweed takes them to his favorite restaurant — Once downstairs, Mr. Guppy quickly fended off his friend's questions about how "she" was doing. That subject was off limits, since its effect on certain "chords" of the mind was too painful to bear. In the meantime, Smallweed had joined them downstairs and now led the others to his favorite cheap restaurant. He was obviously a regular there: he had his choice of booths, demanded the best food, and expected all the newspapers to be reserved for him. He also smoked and drank and seemed unusually worldly for his age.

Jobling devours several meals and dessert — Jobling, who had the faded appearance of a gentleman fallen on hard times, ate his meal twice as fast as the others and needed no additional prompting when asked by Guppy if he wanted another. As Jobling — also called Tony — began to relax, Guppy commented that he had regained his manhood, to which Jobling replied that he'd only just begun. But by the time he'd had another vegetable, pudding, and rum, he announced that he finally felt like a fully grown man again.

Jobling still sees enlisting as his best option — Now that Jobling had fully satisfied himself, Guppy wanted to know whether he still thought enlisting was a good career move. Jobling replied that he needed to eat, and enlisting seemed like the best solution for now, admitting that he had been betting on the wrong horse.

Mr. Guppy suggests Jobling take over where Nemo left off — In the meantime, Mr. Guppy had the idea that Jobling could take on copying work to support himself. It was not the best living, but it was better than nothing, and Guppy's acquaintance with the Snagsbys would make things easier, even if Jobling had been fired from Lincoln's Inn. Neither Guppy nor Smallwood had mentioned this — it was Jobling himself who brought it up. And both Guppy and Smallweed refused to put it in those terms, saying instead that he had left.

Guppy informs Jobling of the vacant room at Krook's — There was also the possibility of renting the vacant room at Mr. Krook's. Guppy also told Jobling that he would be greatly interested in finding out more about Mr. Krook, should Jobling end up living there. There were rumors that Krook was extremely rich, and Guppy was interested to know what shady businesses he was involved in. Finally, he mentioned that the room's previous tenant had died there, though it was ruled an accidental death.

Guppy and Jobling wake up Mr. Krook — With Jobling agreeing to the situation in spite of all this, he and Guppy proceeded to Krook's, leaving Smallweed behind to admire the waitress and read the newspaper. They found Mr. Krook sleeping soundly on a chair in the back of his shop, with an empty bottle of gin in front of him and the whole back area smelling of alcohol. Waking Krook was next to impossible, and even when he did get up, it took him a while to figure out what was going on.

Guppy fills Krook's empty bottle with high-quality gin — Krook's first suspicion was that they had been nipping his gin, when he saw that the bottle was empty. But this impression was soon fixed by Mr. Guppy, who ran over to the pub to get more. Not only that — he got Mr. Krook the high-quality gin rather than his usual kind, which instantly won Krook over.

A new room and a new employer — With Mr. Krook on his good side, Guppy now felt ready to broach the matter of renting the empty second-floor room. Krook was immediately amenable and took them upstairs. The room had since been washed and freshly furnished with added pieces, and they agreed that Mr. Weevle (Jobling's new assumed name) should move in the next day. Following the visit, Guppy and Jobling's next stop was the stationer's place, where both Mr. and Mrs. Snagsby approved of him.

Jobling moves in — Jobling moved into his new room over the next few days, bringing what little he had with him. Unlike his predecessor, he took care of himself, cooking, cleaning, and reinventing his space. With his basic skills, he created curtains, constructed shelves, and finally hung up his most prized possessions, his portraits of fashionable women. In fact, fashion was his great interest in life. Aside from sporting fashionable whiskers, Jobling loved to read about the activities of the fashionable elite. In the evenings, when he wasn't socializing with either Guppy, Smallweed, or Mr. Krook, he would freely converse with others in the court. He soon developed a favorable reputation, and the gossip among the Cook's Court ladies centered around Jobling's fashionable whiskers and the thought that Krook's rumored fortune might end up going to him.

Chapter 21 — The Smallweed Family

The Smallweeds — Smallweed, whose first name was Bart, lived with his remaining family in an area that for centuries had been a dumping ground for garbage and human waste. By the 1800s, the Mount Pleasant dumping ground had been converted to a prison, though the smell of sewage still prevailed. Unlike its name, the area was not pleasant, and like the Smallweeds themselves, there was nothing fresh about it. The only childlike trait in that family was the mental and physical helplessness of Bart's grandmother. His grandfather, on the other hand, though he had more or less lost the use of his limbs, still had his mind intact — at least, to the extent that he had developed it, which was only in one direction: money.

Family trends — Bart's great-grandfather's life had revolved around maximizing his money through "compound interest," probably a euphemism for usury, judging from his habit of using entrapment to get his clients. His money fixation ultimately led to no good and cost him his career. Moreover, he had no concern for matters of the heart or character, and the family's trend of working young and marrying late started with him. Bart's grandfather followed in his father's footsteps, starting work young, first as an office clerk and later a money lender. He, too, married late and produced a son with the same mindset.

A dull lifestyle — This "lean and anxious" mentality meant that enjoyment and fantasy had no place amid practical issues. It also meant that the family grew slowly, and to Dickens, it explained why the children all looked old and the family had monkeylike features.

Bart's twin sister, Judy — Bart also had a twin sister, Judy, with the same old, shriveled, monkeylike features. Dickens explains Judy's old looks by the fact that she had no childhood to speak of — no dolls, no fairy tales, no laughter. Even as a child, she herself had had no great love of other children, and they didn't much like her. Her brother had the same sort of upbringing, but his association with Mr. Guppy, his model in life, had opened up other horizons.

A no-frills home — The lean, no-frills approach carried over to the Smallweeds' home. The basement-level parlor was dark, and whatever décor it had was cheap, basic, and minimal. Grandfather and Grandmother Smallweed sat facing each other, propped in their chairs, which also protected them from drafts. Grandfather Smallweed had a drawer full of "property" beneath his chair, and if Grandmother Smallweed mentioned anything about money, he would throw his pillow at her. It was Judy's job to look after the two elderly Smallweeds, and part of that was to prop them both up again after Grandfather Smallweed had thrown a pillow at this wife.

A stingy mentality — Being teatime, Grandfather Smallweed asked about Bart's whereabouts, since he was late, and now he also inquired where "the girl" was. "The girl" turned out to be Charley, who was busy cleaning house until Judy called her to check on her progress. Before and after Charley's arrival in the parlor, the conversation had largely revolved around maximizing every penny, without consideration for anything else. The result of this mentality was that none of the Smallweeds now present were ever too generous with either their money or their opinions of others, especially if those others were not careful with their own money.

Bart joins his family for tea; the grandfather babbles about family history—While they were talking, Bart arrived and joined them for tea. It came out that Bart and Judy's father, who had finally laid the foundation of a long-awaited house, died of a fever fifteen years ago. He had certainly learned to stretch every penny, and the grandfather was obviously proud of his son. Their mother had also gradually faded and died after giving birth to the twins. Judy and Bart therefore stood to inherit all their grandfather had, which was rumored to be a lot of money. But he was glad they had both learned a trade early on—Bart, the law, and Judy, the art of making artificial flowers—since that meant they could build on their inheritance rather than spending it.

Judy's poor treatment of Charley—Judy had heard all this before, so she busied herself with consolidating the leftover tea and scraps of old bread for Charley's teatime. Charley was to eat in the parlor, since Judy didn't trust that she wouldn't take too long a break. Her whole attitude toward Charley was negative, and she thought nothing of maligning her for the slightest thing, even when Charley was completely innocent.

Mr. George—While Charley was eating, the doorbell rang, so she got up to answer it. It was Mr. George, a strong, handsome, dark man of about fifty, who looked like he might have once had a moustache and been a trooper. In every way, he was the opposite of the Smallweeds. He was also compassionate, unlike most of them. When the grandfather cursed the grandmother, Mr. George took pity on her, propped her up, and counseled her husband to imagine his own mother if he couldn't sympathize with his wife. That prompted Grandfather Smallweed to comment that Mr. George must have been an outstanding son, but Mr. George denied it. He saw himself as a terrible son, though he didn't mean to be and wasn't proud of it.

Mutual business—But Mr. George hadn't come to socialize. He had two months' interest to pay to Grandfather Smallweed, who on taking the money, studied every inch of the accompanying legal document and then locked it in a leather case inside a bureau. In return for the payment, Grandfather Smallweed treated Mr. Smallweed to a pipe and some brandy.

Strange bedfellows—The business being concluded and the pipe on the way, Mr. George and Grandfather Smallweed socialized with each other amid veiled threats and denials that the old man's friend, a money lender from London's financial district, would sell out Mr. George if he was ever late with his payment. At one point, the grandmother woke up from her nap and started screeching about huge sums of money and interest, causing the old man to let fly with his pillow and a string of curses. The whole show left Mr. George flabbergasted, so when the grandfather asked him to prop him up, he roughed him up a bit in the process, leaving the old man winded and skeptical of Mr. George's goodwill.

Old man Smallweed questions Mr. George—Following this drama, the conversation continued while Mr. George enjoyed his pipe and brandy. Their talk was in fact mostly about general business, though with personal touches here and there, and it was clear from their muttered interjections that their relationship was not built on trust, despite the veneer of friendly exchanges. So far, though, Mr. George was the only person to have ever extracted any perks, such as a pipe and brandy, from Grandfather Smallweed. Even the old man was impressed. That sort of practicality, he said, might yet lead to better fortune. Grandpa Smallweed wondered whether Mr. George had any well-off relatives who could vouch for him. Just two names might get him a larger loan from his friend in the financial district. Mr. George explained that it wasn't his style to seek out his relatives after being gone so long — better to stay away. Besides, he'd already caused them enough problems.

Mutual memories of Captain Hawdon — The conversation turned to the subject of Captain Hawdon, who had owed old man Smallweed and his London associate huge amounts of money. Grandfather Smallweed indicated that some wealthy relations might have bailed him out, but his animosity toward Hawdon's memory was still obvious. Mr. George had also known Captain Hawdon, in both good times and bad — when he was still strong and active, and later, when he was so down he was about to shoot himself in the head. But he never saw him at his worst, when he no longer resembled the man he had once been. In fact, Mr. George believed Captain Hawdon had drowned at sea a long time ago.

Getting ready to leave — By this time, Judy had come into the room and stayed at her grandfather's side at his request (he didn't want to be shaken up again if he needed propping), so Mr. George handed her his pipe and prepared to leave. Mr. George, who had examined her a fair amount, was not impressed with her looks, but the one time Charley appeared in the room, he commended her for bringing some youth and freshness to the place.

The old man's true colors — Once Mr. George had left, old man Smallweed quickly dropped his veneer of friendliness and snarled at the door after it shut. Having promised to entrap Mr. George sooner or later, the old man and his lunatic wife reverted to their dull routine of sitting in their chairs facing each other.

Mr. George's evening — By this time, it was evening, and Mr. George decided to go to the theater, which back then was more like the circus, with its horses, acrobats, and clowns. Following that, he went to his own place, George's Shooting Gallery by Leicester Square and Haymarket, an area known for its foreign influences, sports or game venues, and odd exhibitions.

Mr. George returns home — Entering the shop, Mr. George found Phil, the deformed little shop attendant and one-time vagabond, sleeping on the floor. Mr. George woke him up, asked about the evening's events, and then ordered him to close up shop. Despite his many deformities and lameness, Phil was strong and moved quickly. Once the shop was closed, he brought out two mattresses with bedclothes, and having made their own beds and gone through their individual routines, the two men went to sleep.

Chapter 22 — Mr. Bucket

Mr. Tulkinghorn's evening — Mr. Tulkinghorn's solution to the hot summer evenings was to fling open his two windows to let in the cooling breezes. Doing so also let in the dust, but that was nothing new to Mr. Tulkinghorn's already dust-covered apartment. Sitting there by the window in the benign, cool darkness, Mr. Tulkinghorn enjoyed his glass of aged port, which he kept stashed in the cellar — one of the many secrets, both personal and professional, he kept safely tucked away from the world.

Mr. Snagsby tells Mr. Tulkinghorn Jo's story — This evening, however, Mr. Tulkinghorn had a visitor. It was Mr. Snagsby. On this and the previous evening, Snagsby's wife had gone to hear Mr. Chadband, so Mr. Snagsby had taken advantage of her absence and gone to tell Mr. Tulkinghorn about Jo's recent meeting with the mysterious lady. He was just finishing when he suddenly noticed another man standing in the room.

Mr. Bucket — Like Mr. Tulkinghorn, Mr. Bucket was calm and self-possessed. He was portly and middle-aged, and his attentive look indicated an acute interest and intelligence in matters like the one just relayed by Mr. Snagsby. Mr. Tulkinghorn explained that Mr. Bucket was a detective and that Mr. Snagsby was to accompany him to Tom-all-Alone's to show the Bucket where Jo lived. They could then bring Jo himself to Mr. Tulkinghorn's. Seeing Mr. Snagsby's hesitation, Mr. Bucket assured him that Jo would not be hurt and that he would be paid for his efforts. Taking Mr. Snagsby aside, Mr. Bucket then added that the matter should be kept strictly confidential. He suspected that Jo's mysterious woman might have had designs on some property willed to the dead man. That statement, however, confused Mr. Snagsby.

On the way to Tom-all-Alone's — Having agreed on most everything, Mr. Bucket and Mr. Snagsby set out for Tom-all-Alone's. Once outside, Mr. Bucket asked Snagsby if he knew Mr. Gridley, but Snagsby didn't. Gridley had gotten out of hand again with his threats toward certain "respectable" persons (evidently Mr. Tulkinghorn), and Mr. Bucket had a warrant for his arrest. As they walked together, Mr. Snagsby noticed that Mr. Bucket had a lot of strange mannerisms. He had a tendency to lurk, to change direction suddenly, and to pretend to not see other policemen. And through all this his expression never changed.

Tom-all-Alone's — Tom-all-Alone's was dark, so on arriving there, Mr. Bucket and the policeman on duty by the slum got out their lanterns and escorted Mr. Snagsby through the filth, stench, and mud of the streets. Seeing a raucous crowd approaching, they moved to the side on Mr. Bucket's caution. The crowd was carrying a palanquin, but there were too many people to see who was on it. As the crowd dispersed, the slum's residents surrounded the three men but then gradually evaporated, only to reappear again whenever the men would stop for a moment. Between the slum residents' faces, the horrible filth and stench, and the warning whistles and screeches, the whole experience was like a nightmare, and Snagsby, being unused to such places, was having trouble breathing.

The search for Jo — Mr. Bucket asked the policeman whether the ruins they were looking at were the "fever-houses." The policeman answered that they were and that the people staying there were dying by the dozen. The group then asked around for Jo at different houses, but the search became a guessing game because the people there didn't go by their real names. Finally, they concluded that "Toughy," also known as "Tough Subject," might be Jo. He was running an errand for a sick resident but would be back shortly.

Liz , Jenny, and the baby — The sick woman, Liz, was one of two women just arrived the day before looking for work. She and her friend, Jenny, were there with their husbands, both brickmakers (see Chapter 8), who lay sleeping on the floor in the same room. In her arms, Liz held a baby, barely three weeks old. Jenny, too, had had a baby, but it died, and though Jenny had grieved much, Liz wondered whether her own child might not also be better off dying. She would do her best for the child, but she worried that that might not be enough — that her difficult life and her husband's abusiveness, evident from the bruises on her chest, might change both her and her child for the worse. There, in the darkness and the squalor, as Mr. Bucket shone his light on the woman with her child, Mr. Snagsby recalled images he had seen of the Christ Child — though Dickens never says this directly, only mentioning them as pictures of "another infant, surrounded by light."

Jo accompanies the men — As though to complete the scene's message of goodness amidst darkness and hopelessness, Jo, aka "Toughy," returned from his errand of mercy. Afraid at first that he was in trouble, he agreed to go with the policemen after first learning why they had come and giving the woman her medicine. Jo and the three men emerged from the slum as though emerging from hell into quieter, lighter, safer, cleaner streets, leaving the horrid squalor and crowd behind them. The policeman on duty took back his lanterns and resumed his post, and the two other men and the boy continued to Mr. Tulkinghorn's.

A confusion of ladies — As they entered the apartment, Jo suddenly stopped. Mr. Tulkinghorn was not there, but standing in the middle of the room was the woman Jo had seen — or so he thought. At least, she was dressed the same way, and her height was the same. But on further investigation, when she took off her glove and spoke to him, Jo realized that something was amiss. The hand he remembered was whiter, smaller, and more delicate, and the voice was different, too. The previous woman had also worn some obviously expensive rings on her fingers, and this woman did not.

Mr. Bucket's conclusion — Hearing that, Mr. Bucket drew his conclusions, paid Jo five shillings, and brought him outside. Mr. Tulkinghorn then entered the room, and the veiled woman revealed herself to be Hortense, Lady Dedlock's former maid. She had agreed to cooperate in exchange for a recommendation from Mr. Tulkinghorn, and now she excused herself, having no more to do. Mr. Bucket had come back in the meantime, and having escorted Hortense downstairs and returned again, he explained that Jo's statement convinced him that the mysterious woman was not Hortense but the other woman in disguise.

Mr. Snagsby returns home — Meanwhile, Mr. Snagsby, concerned that his wife might be worried, now also excused himself. Mr. Bucket escorted him downstairs as well and thanked him profusely for his discretion. Mr. Snagsby then walked home in a state of utter confusion. On arriving there, he found that his wife had sent Guster to notify the police that he was missing and that, between all her trouble and her fainting, she felt unappreciated.

Chapter 23 — Esther's Narrative

A pleasant stay at Boythorn's — The Jarndyce party stayed for six pleasant weeks at Mr. Boythorn's before returning home to Bleak House. Much of their time was spent roaming the woods or park at Chesney Wold, though from then on they only saw Lady Dedlock in church. She still exerted a strange fascination over Esther, who always found herself thinking about her childhood whenever she saw Lady Dedlock, and Esther imagined at times that the feeling was mutual, though there was never any outward evidence of that.

Hortense's offer — One odd event was Hortense's offer to work for Esther. Hortense had requested a meeting with Esther and braved Chesney Wold's breakfast room, even though she was no longer employed there. She had determined that Esther was good, beautiful, skilled, and well-bred, and she wanted to work for such a person, even if it meant both lower status and pay. But there was something strange in the intensity of Hortense's approach, and Esther was in no position to hire her, nor did she want to. Hortense even offered her services for free after Esther rejected her the first time, but she finally backed off. On parting, she mentioned an oath she had made, which she meant to keep, though she never said what it was.

Richard's flightiness — With the Jarndyce group back at Bleak House, Ada and Esther saw Richard regularly. His great focus in life was still the Jarndyce suit, having convinced himself that it would someday be settled in his and Ada's favor. To this, neither Ada nor Mr. Jarndyce said anything. Ada was too in love, and Mr. Jarndyce just kept his thoughts to himself, though Esther noticed an increase both in the presence of the east wind and in time spent in the Growlery. But Esther was concerned about Richard, so she determined to speak to him herself.

Esther speaks to Richard — Esther's chance to see Richard arrived when Caddy invited her to London, so on the day of their appointment, Esther arranged to meet Richard at the station. Her main question was whether he had "settled" in his career. Initially, he answered with his usual cheery, evasive flightiness, but he finally admitted that he was not settled. That mindset did not come naturally to him. By now, he had also grown tired of the law, his only interest being the settlement of the lawsuit. To this end, he regularly attended Chancery Court sessions in addition to studying the details of the case. Consequently, he often saw Miss Flite, which to Esther held a sense of foreboding for Richard's ultimate fate.

Richard's disappointment and a new idea — For all his usual lightheartedness, Richard's inability to settle made him unhappy because he felt he had failed Ada. Even worse, he was in debt. But he had a new idea — he would join the Army! This would give him a chance to repay his debt, and the discipline of not seeing Ada for a while would be a sort of penance. He only needed to purchase an officer's commission and save money. That plan brought back his cheerfulness, and the two of them having arrived at Esther's destination, Richard went his separate way.

Caddy asks Esther for a favor — Earlier in the story, Esther advised Caddy to not hide her engagement from her mother, nor did Esther think Prince should hide it from his father. Caddy — who dearly loved and admired Esther — had taken this advice to heart. So far, she had mentioned it to Prince, who also valued Esther a great deal. Prince was not against the idea except for his concern that his father would misunderstand. It occurred to him that having Esther there when they announced their engagement would be a great help. Caddy would also love it if Esther would accompany her when she broke the news to her mother. Esther was only too happy to help, so off they went to the dance studio.

Caddy and Prince announce their engagement to Mr. Turveydrop — Prince was teaching a lesson when they arrived, but once he finished, the three of them went into his father's private room, where they found the older Mr. Turveydrop practicing his deportment. Prince's father received the ladies with pleasure, and then Prince, with Caddy by his side, made the announcement with the utmost consideration for his father's needs. At first Mr. Turveydrop went into shock, but after many assurances from his son, he finally gave the young couple his heartfelt blessing. Prince promised that Mr. Turveydrop would always be their first consideration in life, so the father granted them co-ownership of the house on the understanding that they would take care of his needs, which he considered minimal. Esther couldn't help noticing that what would normally pass for an imposition by a parent was in this case understood as a generous gift. Even so, everyone seemed happy, so with Prince still having four lessons to teach, Caddy and Esther headed towards the Jellyby home.

Back at the Jellybys' — Esther found the Jellyby house in even greater disarray than usual. Mr. Jellyby had gone bankrupt by now, so the dining room was taken up with his papers, and there were constant visits from two men who were helping him sort out his accounts. The servants had all been dismissed, so the children were left to their own devices and were making a ruckus in the kitchen.

Caddy tells her mother of the engagement — Upstairs in her room, Mrs. Jellyby was sorting letters related to the African cause, and although she took a moment to acknowledge Esther and Caddy, her reception of her daughter was cool. To her, Caddy was trivial, the news of her engagement was "nonsense," and she had no time for it. If Caddy wanted to introduce her new fiancé (a mere dance teacher with no humanitarian interests), then she would have to come on an evening when there were no philanthropic meetings. Yet for all her disdain and lack of interest, Mrs. Jellyby communicated her message with a pleasant smile and composed exterior. Her solution to such trivialities as her daughter's engagement and her husband's bankruptcy was to focus on bigger, more important things, for which purpose she now excused herself.

A depressing outcome — This cool reception from her mother left Caddy sobbing and Esther unable to respond, except that it was clearly depressing. To cheer themselves up, the two young women spent some time telling the children fairy tales, which helped, though it was impossible to ignore the sound of crashing furniture upstairs whenever Mr. Jellyby attempted to throw himself out the window — or so Esther interpreted the noises.

A warm welcome at Bleak House — Esther's welcome home was the opposite of the cold disdain that had greeted Caddy, who had only wanted some sign of affection and blessing. Esther had only been gone a day, yet everyone at Bleak House was excited and happy to see her. And Ada and Mr. Jarndyce took such an interest in Caddy's story that Esther was embarrassed at all the talking they had gotten out of her.

A little surprise — Finally, Esther retired for the night, and as she was settling in, she heard a quiet knock at the door. It was Charley Neckett, who now politely introduced herself as Esther's new maid, a gift of love from Mr. Jarndyce. There was an instant affection between them as Charley told Esther how Mr. Jarndyce had provided for her and her siblings: Tom was in school, and little Emma was being cared for by Mrs. Blinder. The siblings were to see each other once a month, and Mr. Jarndyce had kindly given them time to get used to the idea of not being together. Deeply moved, Esther told her to never forget that Mr. Jarndyce was the source of all this benevolence, but Charley attributed it to Esther, emphasizing that it had been done out of love for her. Charley added it was also Mr. Jarndyce's hope that Esther would teach her from time to time, and meanwhile, she promised to be the best maid she could be—and she proved it by immediately setting about straightening things up. The chapter ends with both Esther and Charley weeping for joy.

Chapter 24 — An Appeal Case

Mr. Jarndyce helps Richard sort things out — Richard was quick to communicate his new plan to Mr. Jarndyce, who spent a lot of time working out the details with him. The upshot was that Richard finally submitted an application for the position of ensign with the royal cavalry. As usual, he then threw himself into learning the necessary skills.

Richard receives a commission in Ireland — Within a few months, Richard was living with a professor in London and seldom visited Bleak House. Eventually, he received a commission as a regiment officer in Ireland and immediately set out to inform his guardian.

Mr. Jarndyce advises Richard and Ada to break off their engagement — At Bleak House, Mr. Jarndyce and Richard spent considerable time discussing the new situation in private. Finally, Jarndyce called in Ada and Esther. It was obvious by Richard's angry demeanor that he and his guardian were not in agreement. The main source of that was Jarndyce's opinion that Richard and Ada should call off their engagement for the moment. They were still young, and now was not the best time to make such a commitment. In general, Mr. Jarndyce remained cheerful and calm throughout, but at one point he became vehement as he tried to impress upon Richard the futility of placing his hopes in the Jarndyce case. Unlike Richard, Ada trusted her guardian's advice, so she gently informed Richard that they would only be cousins for the time being.

Richard prepares to go to Ireland — After that, Esther noticed a change in Richard toward Mr. Jarndyce, a lack of trust and openness that hadn't been there before — and this, too, in spite of the fact that Richard agreed with his guardian in his more honest private moments with Esther. But there was much to do to get ready for his upcoming trip, so despite his occasional emotional outbursts, Richard busied himself with more practical things, and he had Mr. Jarndyce and Esther to help him.

Mr. George feels he's seen Esther before — Richard had also been practicing his fencing skills with the help of a former member of the cavalry — Mr. George. Esther had grown curious about him, having heard much, so she positioned herself to be in the same room when he arrived at Bleak House. Mr. George, for his part, was immediately struck by Esther. He felt he had seen her before and kept glancing at her to try to determine where. Esther finally assured him that they had not met, since she never forgot a face — yet he claimed the same thing.

Mr. George tells of his encounter with Gridley — On questioning Mr. George about his business, Mr. Jarndyce discovered that he knew Gridley. Gridley had been among those who came to practice their skills at Mr. George's shooting gallery, and Mr. George remembered him because of his unusual vehemence after all he'd been through with the Chancery Court. In fact, he was so concerned about Gridley's overheated state that he advised him to quit shooting and try some other outlet for his frustrations. The result was a friendship, even though Mr. George had half expected a punch in the face. On Richard's arrival, Mr. George paid his respects and left.

A final day in court — Richard was scheduled to depart that evening, so, all other preparations being done, he invited Esther to join him at the Chancery Court that afternoon. It would be dealing with the

Jarndyce suit, and this was his last chance to hear it for a while. Arriving at the court, Esther was impressed at how sedate and comfortable everything was, in contrast to the torment, chaos, and misery the court had produced in people's lives. Her impressions worsened the more she witnessed the proceedings, and it seemed to her that virtually everyone acknowledged the suit to be a monstrous joke.

Old acquaintances — While Esther and Richard sat there, they were greeted by both Miss Flite and Mr. Kenge, who explained some of the details of the court to them. Later, as they were leaving, Mr. Guppy also appeared on the scene to inform them that someone wished to speak to Esther. It was Mrs. Rachael, the servant from Esther's childhood with Miss Barbary. She was now Mrs. Chadband, and she still retained her former coldness, though she had come to wish Esther well.

Mr. George brings a request for Miss Flite — Following that, Esther happened to spy Mr. George, who had come to retrieve Miss Flite and needed help identifying her. Gridley, whom Mr. George was hiding in his gallery, was on his last legs and had asked for her. Since Miss Flite had been following Esther around, it was easy for Esther to introduce them, and the four of them set off by coach for the shooting gallery.

Mr. Bucket arrives to do his duty — As they were entering the gallery, they were met by a man who introduced himself as a physician, saying he had been sent for just five minutes earlier. Almost immediately, however, the doctor disappeared and was replaced by Mr. Bucket, the detective, who had disguised himself as a doctor. He had discovered that Gridley was hiding out at Mr. George's and had come to apprehend him. Mr. Bucket had great respect for Mr. George, though, being a fellow military man, and would therefore avoid causing trouble for him and go easy on Gridley.

Mr. Jarndyce and his wards go to see Gridley — At Gridley's request, Mr. George and Miss Flite went in to see him first. Meanwhile Mr. Bucket chatted with Richard, Esther, and Phil, Mr. George's eccentric assistant. As Esther and Richard were about to leave, Mr. George returned with a request from Gridley, who wanted to see them. Right at that moment, Mr. Jarndyce also showed up and joined them, his motive being to help a fellow sufferer because of the Chancery Court.

Gridley's dying words — As they entered the sparse room, they saw Gridley lying on a couch, with Miss Flite by his side and his hand in hers. Gridley was a mere shadow of himself, but he was happy to see Mr. Jarndyce and shook his hand. Drawing a tearful Miss Flite closer, he acknowledged her as the one constant in his life, bound as they were by the deep suffering caused by the Chancery Court. He told them how, after many years of fighting the court, his strength had suddenly broken down, and he felt he no longer had much time to live. He hoped the Chancery Court would never find out—that he would live on in its memory has the defiant man from Shropshire.

Mr. Bucket's attempts at encouragement — Mr. Bucket, who by now was also in the room, encouraged Mr. Gridley to not give up so soon. He good-naturedly reminded him of all the times he had arrested him for threatening the Lord Chancellor and his colleagues, and that there would be many more such times. He even tried to rouse him by threatening him with the warrant he had from Mr. Tulkinghorn— anything to shake him out of his weakened state.

Gridley dies; Richard sets sail for Ireland — The problem was solved when Miss Flite suddenly let out a scream. Night had fallen in the meantime. That evening, as Richard set sail for Ireland, Gridley's dying words about Miss Flite as his only unbroken tie resounded in Esther's heart.

Chapter 25 — Mrs. Snagsby Sees All

The change in Mr. Snagsby — Mr. Snagsby was no longer is old peaceful self. Since his visit to Tom-all-Alone's, a change had set in that even he didn't understand. The recent events he had witnessed seemed to hide some dark mystery that had begun to color his life. A simple question as to his availability evoked feelings of guilt and apprehension, sometimes even eliciting more violent reactions — like ear flipping — when the questioner was a boy. The feelings had even penetrated his dreams, making it impossible for them to escape the notice of his wife.

Mrs. Snagsby's suspicions — Being ill at ease, Mr. Snagsby was unable to look his wife in the face, and because of that, she had all types of suspicions about the situation. She began snooping around in his belongings, watching for signs of mischief, and she drew ill-founded conclusions from different facts and events.

Mrs. Snagsby seeks a solution — In fact, Mrs. Snagsby's brain was working overtime trying to find a solution, and she finally lighted on Jo as her best bet. After all, "Nimrod" (her name for Nemo) was dead and the mysterious lady's whereabouts were unknown. To her, it seemed strange and disrespectful that Jo never responded to Mr. Chadband's invitation. The thought had even grown in her mind that Jo was Mr. Snagsby's illegitimate child. To determine this, she watched them both carefully, so it was convenient when Mr. Chadband ran into Jo on the street and coerced him into coming to one of his meetings by threatening to take him to the police.

Jo's reluctant attendance — Jo was not thrilled with the idea of being Mr. Chadband's project, so his attendance was hardly enthusiastic. But he did shuffle in once tea was over and Mr. Chadband, who saw himself as a "vessel," had filled his "ship" with oil — the metaphor used by Dickens for food in relation to Mr. Chadband, whom he describes as fat and oily. Meanwhile, Mrs. Snagsby had become hyper-alert to any sign that might corroborate her suspicion that her husband was Jo's father. So when Jo first entered and exchanged glances with Mr. Snagsby, Mrs. Snagsby built it into something more than what it is.

During the Reverend Chadband's introductory speeches, he got the resistant Jo into position, explaining that it was his duty to edify and improve him. He saw himself as a heavenly reaper working in the fields of the Lord, and he delivered these ideas with his usual pretentious eloquence. Today his target listener (since he liked to focus on one person during his speeches) was poor Mr. Snagsby, who was already befuddled enough and now became the hapless victim of the self-satisfied Mr. Chadband.

Effects of Mr. Chadband's speechifying — During Mr. Chadband's speeches, Mrs. Snagsby continued watching her husband for the slightest hint of guilt. At one point, when Mr. Chadband mentioned the word "parents" in reference to Jo, Mrs. Snagsby gave her husband a disconcerting look when he confessed to having no idea who Jo's parents were. That look made him so uncomfortable that he refrained from saying anything else throughout the meeting. Meanwhile, Jo had fallen asleep, which to Mr. Chadband was just another proof of his degenerate state. Dickens remarks here that if Chadband had only removed his own self-conceit and allowed the story of the Christ light to speak for itself, Jo might have recognized its worth. But Mr. Chadband was not about to remove his ego from the picture, and Jo remained ignorant of the truth. By contrast, Mrs. Snagsby became increasingly affected, sobbing and finally throwing a screaming fit that knocked her out, so that she had to be carried upstairs. With all the commotion, Guster was having a hard time fighting off her own epileptic fit, though she managed it for the time being.

Guster and Mr. Snagsby meet Jo on his way out—Having had enough and figuring that Mr. Snagsby wouldn't be communicating with him that day, Jo finally left the room. Downstairs, Guster—who had taken pity on him in the meantime—offered him her own simple dinner. She told him that she, too, had never known her parents and then promptly ran off, unable to resist the oncoming seizure any longer. Meanwhile, Mr. Snagsby had also come downstairs and, placing a half crown in Jo's hand, commended him for saying nothing about the mysterious lady and urged him to maintain his silence for the general good.

Mrs. Snagsby continues haunting her husband—The evening ends as Jo goes back to his forlorn but honest life. Mr. Snagsby, too, returns to things as usual—except that the ghost of his suspicious wife now follows him around everywhere.

Chapter 26 — Sharpshooters

Mr. George's morning routine — Most of the residents around George's Shooting Gallery had shady occupations. They were gamblers, card sharks, ex-cons, spies, traitors, and gangsters, so it made sense that they kept a nighttime schedule. Mr. George, however, was still a trooper at heart, and both he and Phil rose early. In true trooper fashion, George's morning routine included braving the winter weather to hose himself down outside with cold water, scrub himself dry with a rough towel, and tame his curly hair with two hard-bristled brushes. While Phil swept the floor and prepared their breakfast, Mr. George smoked his pipe as he walked back and forth.

Phil's dream — But today Mr. George broke away from his thoughts to ask Phil about his dream. Earlier, Phil had mentioned that he'd dreamt about the countryside. This was strange because Phil had never been to the countryside except once, to the marshes, though he didn't know where. But in his dream, he saw swans feeding upon the grass, an image unknown to him from his own life, which had been restricted to the city.

Phil talks about his life — Mr. George then told Phil that he had been born and raised in the country. In fact, his mother still lived there. But returning to Phil, George asked whether he was interested in seeing the country. Phil didn't think he was up for anything new at his age, though he had no idea what that was, having lost track somewhere around eighteen. He only knew he was eight when he ran off with a tinker on April Fool's Day, and since he could only count to ten, he figured everything from eight plus however many years had passed since that first April Fool's Day. Once he hit eighteen, though, he couldn't figure any higher. Eventually, the tinker's alcoholism did him in, and Phil inherited his tinkering business, although most of the tinker's income had come from lodging wandering tinkers. That worked in part because the original tinker could sing and play music, something Phil couldn't do. So between his lack of musical talent and his ugly looks — made worse by a rough life and several industrial accidents — Phil was unable to maintain his client base.

Phil's gratitude to Mr. George — It was after one of those accidents that Phil (full name, Phil Squod) met Mr. George. Phil had been working at a fireworks factory and was blown out the window. When Mr. George found him, he was crawling alongside a wall with the aid of two sticks. He was flabbergasted when Mr. George, brimming with health and strength, stopped to ask about him. Speaking about the incident made Phil more and more excited as he expressed his gratitude to Mr. George for taking him in. He would do anything for Mr. George, including act as a shooting target for his customers. Besides, he had been kicked around so much in life that it didn't matter. Those statements left Mr. George laughing as he rose to help Phil get the shop in order for the day's business.

A visit from Grandfather Smallweed — At one point, Mr. George heard some curious footsteps approaching. It was Grandfather Smallweed, who was carried in on a chair by two men (who were practically choked in the process) and followed by his granddaughter Judy. The two men having been dismissed, Grandfather Smallweed asked to be taken closer to the fire, which Phil did so forcefully that it left the old man reeling and panting. Grandfather Smallweed then expressed his discomfort at the fact that Phil always seemed to have a weapon in his hands (part of his everyday tasks, since he cleaned them). He was concerned that something might happen by accident, so after a nod from Mr. George, Phil put down the gun he was holding.

Grandfather Smallweed hems and haws — All that being settled, Grandfather Smallweed still wasn't forthcoming about his real purpose. He hemmed and hawed and made small talk to such an extent that even Judy was becoming impatient. Finally, Mr. George insisted that he get to the point. He knew that Smallweed hadn't come to socialize and that he wasn't the "good friend" he kept pretending to be.

Grandfather Smallweed wants to procure a sample of Nemo's writing — Eventually, it came out that a well-known lawyer was looking for a writing sample from the late Captain Hawdon, and he had come to Smallweed on the chance that he might have one. Grandfather Smallweed, however, only had signatures, but it occurred to him that Mr. George might have a more pertinent sample. Mr. George did indeed have something, but he refused to make any promises until he knew more about the lawyer's reasons. Grandfather Smallweed had promised to meet the lawyer that day within the hour, so he now pressured Mr. George to come with him. Agreeing, Mr. George retrieved the paper, and stashing it in his breast pocket, he had Phil carry the old man out to the coach — another grueling experience for Grandfather Smallweed. And so, with the Smallweeds in the cab and Mr. George in the box seat up front, the coach drove off to the lawyer's.

Chapter 27 — More Old Soldiers Than One

At Mr. Tulkinghorn's — The coach soon arrived at Lincoln's Inn Fields, where Mr. George was quick to recognize Mr. Tulkinghorn's name. After bringing Grandfather Smallweed upstairs to Mr. Tulkinghorn's apartment, Mr. George took the liberty of looking around, as Mr. Tulkinghorn hadn't yet arrived. One box in particular stood out to Mr. George — the one labeled with Sir Leicester's name, title, and estate. That, of course, was where George's mother, Mrs. Rouncewell, was employed, but Mr. George said nothing about that.

Mr. Tulkinghorn questions Mr. George about the writing — Grandfather Smallweed was more interested in Mr. Tulkinghorn's wealth, which was apparently considerable. But before he could go into much detail, Mr. Tulkinghorn arrived, sporting his usual indifferent look. After a cordial greeting, Mr. Tulkinghorn (unlike Mr. Smallweed) got right to the point: he would be willing to pay good money for the sample of Captain Hawdon's handwriting. Mr. George, however, was not Grandfather Smallweed, and it was not so easy to wrest the paper from him for any amount of money. The whole thing made him uneasy, and he preferred not to be involved.

Mr. George agrees to consult with an "old soldier" friend — Mr. Smallweed, who evidently stood to gain from the transaction, became more and more perturbed at Mr. George's reluctance. Mr. Tulkinghorn, on the other hand, despite his obvious interest in the paper, displayed his usual calm indifference. However, Mr. George agreed to consult with a friend of his, an "old soldier" with a clearer understanding of these matters, and he promised that once he had done that, he would give his final decision.

Grandfather Smallweed's vehemence — With that, Mr. George was ready to go, but Mr. Smallweed first needed to confer privately with Mr. Tulkinghorn. His feelings on the matter were so strong that he fell off his chair relaying them, bringing Mr. Tulkinghorn down with him. He was ready to practically rip the buttons off Mr. George's shirt to get the piece of paper, but Mr. Tulkinghorn was not in favor using violence. Even with Mr. Smallweed finally downstairs and in the carriage, it was all Mr. George could do to get the old man to release his grip on his shirt button.

Mrs. Bagnet — Mr. George then strode southward across the Thames to the major junction called the Elephant and Castle, and finally to a little music shop. On arriving there, he noticed a strong, healthy-looking woman emerging from the shop with a basin. It was Mrs. Bagnet, the wife of his friend, the "old soldier." She was washing greens, a perpetual activity of hers. When she noticed George, she greeted him with the unwelcoming statement that she wished he were far away. He was too much of a vagabond for her taste, likely to pull Matthew, her husband, away from her. Why hadn't George become a family man when he had the chance? George agreed that it might have done him good, but in the end, he couldn't wrap his head around it.

The rest of the Bagnet family — Now inside with Mrs. Bagnet, Mr. George greeted her two young daughters with their nicknames, Quebec and Malta, which stood for the barracks where they were born. In fact, the whole place had the atmosphere of a barrack — sparse, orderly, immaculate, with everyone dutifully employed. Quebec and Malta knew George and were happy to see him. As he sat there talking to them, Mr. Bagnet and his son came home. The son, nicknamed Woolwich, had come from the theater, where he played the fiddle beside his father's bassoon. Woolwich was Mr. George's godson, and George was happy to see he was thriving.

Mr. George asks for advice — Mr. George didn't mince words: he had come seeking advice. Bagnet replied that that was fine, but not a shred of advice would be given if he didn't join them for dinner first. Since Mrs. Bagnet was still preparing the dinner, the two men went for a walk. Mat, George's friend, informed him that the real advice-giver was his wife. She had built up their shop from next to nothing, and it was she, too, who had advised Mat to switch from his previous instruments to the bassoon, which had since managed to earn him a living. However, they had to keep up the appearance of a proper family hierarchy — what Mat called "maintaining discipline." It shouldn't therefore be obvious that his wife was giving the advice. Somehow, he had to make it look like she was simply voicing his opinion.

Voicing her husband's "opinion" — That being understood, they all enjoyed their dinner, and afterwards the two men sat down with their pipes, while the wife, having cleaned everything, did her needlework. Everyone now being settled and Mrs. Bagnet's head clear of greens and other pressing matters, Mr. George stated his case. The husband then transferred the responsibility of voicing "his" opinion to his wife. Luckily, it confirmed George's own: to avoid people and matters he did not understand and to have nothing to do with mysterious affairs.

Mr. George gets an earful from Mr. Tulkinghorn — Relieved at this wise piece of advice, Mr. George smoked another pipe, took his leave of the family, and made his way toward Lincoln's Inn Fields. Arriving at Mr. Tulkinghorn's, he found the door locked, though he hadn't seen this at first in the darkness, for by now it was already evening. He promptly heard the angry voice of Mr. Tulkinghorn behind him, demanding to know why he hadn't noticed the locked door and whether he had changed his mind. In response, Mr. George confirmed what Mr. Tulkinghorn instinctively already knew — that George wasn't interested in the exchange.

Mr. Tulkinghorn condemns Mr. George for harboring Gridley — Having no more use for Mr. George, Mr. Tulkinghorn dismissed him, but not without first mentioning his disapproval of George's harboring the "murderous" Gridley. Had Tulkinghorn known that, he would not have invited Mr. George in earlier. Mr. Tulkinghorn then slammed the door, leaving Mr. George indignant at his remark, made worse by the look from the clerk who passed him on the stairs, evidently thinking he was the "murderer." All this left Mr. George in a bad mood, but that lasted only a few minutes as he headed home, whistling himself back to his normal state.

Chapter 28 — The Ironmaster

Back at Chesney Wold — Chesney Wold was cold and damp again in spite of all attempts to make it comfortable, so though Sir Leicester had by now recovered from his arthritis, the weather was still seeping into his bones. That meant that Sir Leicester and his lady would soon be deserting Chesney Wold for their place in London.

Sir Leicester's cousins — Of less fashionable interest than the Dedlocks but included in their society were Sir Leicester's poorer relatives, of which he seemed to have many. Of course, he also had many well-situated cousins, and he bore both situations gracefully, with dignity on the one hand and generosity on the other.

Volumnia Dedlock — This was fortunate for the poorer cousins, who despite their lack of means were not allowed to do any real work, forcing them to rely on the good graces of their more affluent relations. The most prominent of these was Volumnia Dedlock, a lady of about sixty with a predilection for too much rouge and an overused pearl necklace. Her talents for making paper ornaments and singing Spanish songs to the guitar had lost the interest of the rest of society, so she depended on Sir Leicester for her meager living and spent most of her time in Bath, where she lived. She was almost lucky enough to receive a pension from the government, but that fell through, leading Sir Leicester to conclude that England was going downhill.

Bob Stables — Something similar happened to the Honorable Bob Stables, whose talents extended to shooting game and making livestock feed. He had wished for a comfortable government post — not normally an unusual request or difficult to resolve. But again it proved impossible, so again Sir Leicester concluded that the country was going to seed.

Entertaining the impoverished cousins — There were many such cousins whose aristocratic status had prevented them from having any real success or useful purpose. Their great function was to act as a backdrop to Lady Dedlock's magnificence, which was exactly what they did on this damp and dreary night at Chesney Wold as they engaged in various entertainments throughout the drawing room.

Talk of Rosa and Watt's father, the industrialist — It was in this setting that Volumnia sat by the hearth between Sir Leicester and Lady Dedlock, much to the dismay of both — to Sir Leicester, because he found her aesthetically offensive, and to Lady Dedlock, because Volumnia only exacerbated her boredom. Volumnia had noticed Rosa, though, and now she remarked on her special beauty. Lady Dedlock was quick to give Mrs. Rouncewell the credit for spotting her, and that led to talk of Mrs. Rouncewell's sons, specifically, the ironmaster. That son, Sir Leicester informed them, had received an invitation to join the Parliament — yet another sign that England was in disarray. Mr. Rouncewell had declined the offer, but Sir Leicester was still clearly perturbed by the idea that a non-aristocrat, however successful, should be invited.

Mr. Rouncewell's audience — Sir Leicester then informed Lady Dedlock that Mr. Rouncewell had requested an audience with them and would be stopping by shortly. Finding this too much for her delicate sensibilities, Volumnia excused herself for the night and was soon followed by the rest of the cousins.

Mr. Rouncewell discusses Rosa future — Once the guests had retired, Sir Leicester had the servants call in Mr. Rouncewell, a strong, focused man in his fifties, who had a clear idea of his status as a successful industrialist but who also maintained a degree humility and respect in the company of the aristocratic Dedlocks. That did not stop him, however, from clearly voicing his intentions. He had come with regard to his son's interest in Rosa, but he had his own stipulations and wanted to make sure the engagement made sense for all involved, rather than simply being a foolish move on the part of two young people. The main issue was that Rosa, in order to be a suitable match for his son, would have to be educated in an appropriate school, which would mean leaving Chesney Wold. Sir Leicester reminded Mr. Rouncewell that she had attended the village school, but while Mr. Rouncewell acknowledged this, he informed Sir Leicester as respectfully as possible that he did not consider that an adequate education.

A metaphor for larger changes — Between that comment and Mr. Rouncewell's partial comparison of Rosa's current station to that of a factory worker, Sir Leicester was offended and was having difficulty believing his ears. The whole progress of the meeting had been disconcerting to him, as it yet again signified the downfall of England. He therefore informed Mr. Rouncewell with great clarity and restraint that the mutual opposition of their opinions would not stand in the way of Rosa's leaving, should she choose to go, nor would it have any effect on her standing, should she remain. However, he no longer wished to continue the conversation. By the end of the meeting, Mr. Rouncewell had determined that it would be best if he dissuaded his son from courting Rosa.

Despite their differences, the Dedlocks extended Mr. Rouncewell an invitation to spend the night, since it was already late. But Mr. Rouncewell declined: he needed to travel that night to make sure he arrived on time at a meeting the next morning. The scene — in fact, the whole chapter — is a metaphor for the greater change alluded to in Sir Leicester's observations: the decline of the aristocracy and the rise of the powerful and wealthy industrialist class.

Lady Dedlock questions Rosa about her feelings — The chapter ends on a more personal note as Lady Dedlock, now retired to her private quarters, affectionately addresses the lovely and innocent Rosa, asking her whether she's in love. Rosa hesitates — she's not sure, but it's clear that she's deeply attached to Lady Dedlock. For her part, Lady Dedlock's only desire is to see her happy. Her evening ends as she sits by herself looking thoughtfully into the fire, and though she says nothing, she seems to be thinking of her own lost love and hoping to prevent that in another life.

Back to normal — The next day, the cousins and their servants disperse (Dickens quips that they had to have servants, no matter how meager their means), and Chesney Wold is once again its normal, dreary self.

Chapter 29 — The Young Man

The Dedlocks move to London for the winter — With the Dedlocks moved to London for the winter, Chesney Wold was shut down, with almost nothing in sight but leaves, rain, fog, and the few people who tended the house and grounds. By contrast, the London residence was well-lit and warm, and Sir Leicester sat content in his library, surrounded by his art and his books.

Mr. Tulkinghorn's frequent visits — Sir Leicester received frequent visits from Mr. Tulkinghorn, who consulted with him about estate matters. Mr. Tulkinghorn and Lady Dedlock also saw each other often, though they barely acknowledged each other's presence. Dickens spends an entire long paragraph wondering what Mr. Tulkinghorn might have up his sleeve with regard to Lady Dedlock — what secrets he kept buried that might not be to her advantage — and whether it was safe for her to be around him.

Mr. Guppy calls on Lady Dedlock — On this particular day, Lady Dedlock was sitting in her room looking at the fire, while Sir Leicester read to her from the paper. The subject that held his interest — though it bored her terribly — was, as usual, the decline of England. The Dedlocks were interrupted when their bewigged and powdered attendant announced the arrival of "the young man" named Mr. Guppy. Sir Leicester, unimpressed by both Mr. Guppy and his name, seemed indignant at this arrival, but Lady Dedlock informed him that she had approved the visit. Sir Leicester thus acquiesced to her wishes and left them in private.

Despite her approval, Lady Dedlock was also cold toward Mr. Guppy. Mr. Guppy had been sending her regular letters, and she wondered why he couldn't have continued doing so — why seeing her personally seemed such an urgent matter. Unconvinced that his visit had anything to do with her, she resumed looking at the fire and asked him to get on with his message.

Mr. Guppy gets Lady Dedlock's attention — Mr. Guppy's first point was that he was employed at Kenge and Carboy, known for their involvement with the Jarndyce case. That got Lady Dedlock's attention. Nevertheless, Mr. Guppy continued, his mission was not strictly related to Jarndyce and Jarndyce. Had it been, he would have consulted Mr. Tulkinghorn.

Mr. Guppy brings Esther Summerson — Until that moment, Lady Dedlock had left Mr. Guppy standing by the doorway. But realizing now that something was afoot, she invited him to sit, though it came across as more of an order, without the usual graciousness. At this point, Mr. Guppy asked Lady Dedlock for full confidentiality. He also became flustered and needed to consult his scribbled notes in the light, so he momentarily went to the window, crashing into the birdcage on the way. Somewhat reoriented, he now brought up Esther Summerson as his next topic. Had Lady Dedlock ever met Esther, and had she noticed any striking resemblance between the two of them? Lady Dedlock was definitely attentive now, though she remained as composed as ever and denied noticing any family resemblance. Mr. Guppy, however, continued to insist on a resemblance and confessed to watching Lady Dedlock more closely ever since he saw her portrait at Chesney Wold. He even admitted that his main motivation in all this was to gain Esther's favor, which had been non-existent so far. If he could prove to her that she was a rightful heir in the Jarndyce case, perhaps she would cease to spurn him.

Esther's real surname — Dickens comments here that Mr. Guppy was lucky to still have his head at this point. Mr. Guppy, however, was not aware of this, and he now began to go for the jugular. Through the former Mrs. Rachael, now Mrs. Chadband, he had learned of Miss Barbary. And Miss Barbary, who usually kept silent about everything, once admitted to Mrs. Rachael that Esther's real last name was Hawdon. This elicited a "My God!" from Lady Dedlock, who momentarily lost her composure, though she quickly forced herself to regain it. Mr. Guppy had wondered whether the name Barbary rang a bell, and he asked the same about the name Hawdon. Lady Dedlock was too honest to deny knowing the names, though she didn't confess direct knowledge of their bearers and repeatedly asked what any of it had to do with her. But by now she had shown clear signs of distress.

Mr. Guppy's offer — Mr. Guppy continued playing his cards one by one. The name Hawdon had been the name of the dead law writer, and Jo, the sweeper boy, had reported being in touch with a mysterious lady who asked to see the law writer's grave. In fact, Mr. Guppy could bring Jo there and have him corroborate the story. No — Lady Dedlock was not interested in that. Mr. Guppy further revealed that certain letters had been discovered among the law writer's belongings and that he would be obtaining them the following evening. So far, he knew nothing about their details other than that they were old. He would bring them to Lady Dedlock if she thought it worth her while. He finished by repeating the importance of confidentiality — otherwise, if she lodged a complaint, he could be in a lot of trouble.

Lady Dedlock agrees to the offer — Lady Dedlock was still uncertain of Mr. Guppy's full motive, but she agreed that he could bring the letters. She then offered him money, but he refused, saying that his motives did not involve that. With that, Mr. Guppy left as unceremoniously as he had come.

Lady Dedlock's deep distress — There, in her room by herself, unbeknownst to the rest of the household, Lady Dedlock fell to her knees and cried out for the child she thought had died at birth. Her "cruel" sister had rejected her and lied to her, and now all she had was the knowledge that both she and her child had been ripped from each other and from the natural love between them.

Chapter 30 — Esther's Narrative

Mrs. Woodcourt confides in Esther — Some time after Richard's departure for Ireland, Mrs. Woodcourt, the young surgeon's mother, came to stay at Bleak House for three weeks, having been invited by Mr. Jarndyce after she wrote to inform them that her son was well and sent his regards from India. During this time, she took to confiding in Esther, which made Esther a bit nervous, mainly because of Mrs. Woodcourt's obvious vigilance. Mrs. Woodcourt also loved to go on about her exalted Welsh ancestry, often inviting Esther into her room at night to listen to stories about their great ancestor, the hero Morgan ap Kerrig, or her recitations from what appeared to be Welsh epic literature. She would finish by saying that though her son lacked money, he came from an impressive lineage, which limited his marriage choices.

Mrs. Woodcourt asks for Esther's opinion of her son — For all her infatuation with lineage, Mrs. Woodcourt had a high opinion of Esther's character, especially considering her age, and she wanted to know what Esther thought of her son. Esther hedged at first, as she always did when she had a half-conscious emotional block concerning anything. But her innately observant and objective nature usually came to the rescue, and it did in this case, too. She had noticed that Allan Woodcourt was not only a good surgeon but that he had been remarkably compassionate toward Miss Flite. Of course, this pleased his mother, but she was more interested in his casual courtesies toward young ladies, which might give them the idea that he was seriously interested in them, when he wasn't — even by his own admission. He was merely being polite and kind. It seemed as though she was hinting something to Esther, especially when she added that her son's being so far away had made the subject obsolete.

Mrs. Woodcourt predicts Esther's happy marriage to an older man — Mrs. Woodcourt also had the notion that Esther's steady and diligent character suggested she would be happily and auspiciously married to a much older man in the future. She switched to this subject so deftly as to make it seem as if it bore no relationship to the previous topic. Esther could not understand why Mrs. Woodcourt's statement made her so uncomfortable, but it did — to the point of insomnia. Esther's reaction was something of a mystery to herself, as were her mixed feelings towards Mrs. Woodcourt, so when the lady finally left, her departure left Esther with an equal sense of relief and regret.

Caddy announces her impending marriage — The hole was soon filled by Caddy Jellyby, who brought with her the happy news of her upcoming marriage and, along with it, the request for Ada and Esther to be her bridesmaids.

Mr. Jellyby resolves his bankruptcy issues; fatherly advice on the upcoming marriage —

Meanwhile, Mr. Jellyby had settled his bankruptcy issues with his creditors, who had proved sympathetic to his financial woes. He had also gotten a job at the Customs House, and the family had moved to a furnished residence. The children were still as wild as ever, but on the good side of things, Mr. Jellyby was on favorable terms with the elder Mr. Turveydrop. Unfortunately, the news of Caddy's marriage did little to comfort her own father. He hoped that things would turn out better for her than they had in his own marriage. But in his opinion, if she didn't mean it with all her heart, she would be kinder to just kill her husband now. That statement left her distressed, but she assured her father that she hoped her home would be a comfort to him and the Jellyby children.

Preparations for the wedding dress — As for Mrs. Jellyby, she didn't care — to her, the whole subject of the wedding was still trivial nonsense, and to try to get her opinion or help with the wedding dress was futile. Esther and Ada, however, were all too willing to help, and they enlisted the aid of a seamstress and Charley in addition to their own and Caddy's efforts. As much as possible, they relied on their own and Caddy's meager resources, including a £10 note from her father, though Mr. Jarndyce would have been happy to provide more.

Caddy learns housekeeping from Esther — Caddy ended up staying at Bleak House for three weeks, and during that time, aside from working on her wedding dress, she was determined to learn housekeeping from Esther. The idea was amusing to Esther, since she didn't think too highly of her own skills, but she taught Caddy what she knew, and so, between their daily activities and evening entertainments, the time flew by.

The challenge of beautifying the Jellybys and their new home — Then there was the matter of making the Jellybys' new residence presentable for the wedding breakfast. Given Mrs. Jellyby's indifference, this was not easy, but Esther managed to get her cooperation to some degree. The multitude of papers that were strewn all over Mrs. Jellyby's work room would have to be put away — a great inconvenience, especially with a meeting the same day as the wedding. There was also the challenge of making Mrs. Jellyby and the children presentable. Caddy and Esther agreed to wait till the last minute to deal with the children, since any other approach seemed hopeless. As for Caddy's mother, her dresses were in a state of total disarray, and as usual, she didn't care. They managed to pull something together, though, and Mrs. Jellyby, who had grown outward by several sizes, let herself be fitted by the seamstress.

Cleaning house and Mr. Jellyby's admonition — Cleaning the home was more of a challenge than anticipated. So much junk fell out of the closets — including food scraps of all types — that Mr. Jellyby, who had volunteered his help, immediately backed off and resumed leaning on the wall. This was his daily habit while the two young women worked. At one point, though it took all he had, he admonished Caddy to never adopt a mission. As if to confirm his words, Mrs. Jellyby persistently ignored the preparations and kept at her African work until midnight, after which Caddy and Esther finally had a chance to prepare the sitting room for breakfast the next morning. Exhausted, Caddy broke down and cried at one point, but she recovered, and the two of them together worked a little miracle.

The wedding day — The following day, all went well. The room was presentable, the breakfast was adequate, and the children had their own separate breakfast nook upstairs. They cheered on seeing Caddy in her wedding dress, and they all hugged her before she left with Prince, who — to Esther's dismay — was bitten by Peepy. Downstairs, the adults enjoyed themselves to the extent they could. Mr. Turveydrop had accustomed himself to the general lack of deportment in Caddy's family, and aside from Mr. Jarndyce and Ada, there were also the Pardiggles, Mr. Quale and his fiancée Miss Wisk, and a few other philanthropic types in attendance — all of them with a mission of some sort, and none of them favorable to each other's missions, except for Mr. Quale, who saw that sort of supportiveness as his own mission.

The wedding — It was only natural that these all-consuming missions should attend the wedding along with their bearers. Thus, Mr. Turveydrop, whose mission was perfect deportment, deported himself accordingly. Miss Wisk, a confirmed feminist, saw the wedding as yet another demonstration of male tyranny. And Mrs. Jellyby, unconcerned with such trivia, maintained her indifferent composure.

The wedding breakfast — The wedding breakfast was no different. Most of the guests could think of nothing but their missions, while Peepy, who had thrown a tantrum on learning Caddy's new last name, kept dipping his toy into everyone's wine. Had Mr. Jarndyce not been there to ease the conversation and had Esther not held Peepy in her lap, the breakfast would not have been half as civilized as it was.

Caddy and Prince say goodbye — When the time came for Caddy and Prince to leave on their honeymoon, Caddy asked for assurances that her mother had forgiven her. Her mother confirmed that they were great friends and wished her all happiness. Caddy then gave her father a poignant but silent farewell hug. Next it came time for both Prince and Caddy to say goodbye to Mr. Turveydrop, who addressed them with great eloquence and assured them of a welcoming dinner on their return. He added that he would never desert them and expected that they would do their duty, to which they both agreed wholeheartedly. That duty would begin by their prompt return from their honeymoon a week from that day so that the school wouldn't suffer any disruption.

Mr. Jellyby silently thanks Esther — One other goodbye seems worth mentioning. Before Esther left, Mr. Jellyby came to thank her in his silent way. Taking both her hands, he tried to say something but couldn't. She, however, knew what he meant, and though she was flustered, she graciously told him he was welcome.

Conclusion to the wedding day — It was unclear to Mr. Jarndyce and his wards whether things would turn out well for the young couple. As Mr. Jarndyce noted, time would tell. When Esther asked him whether the east wind had attended any part of the day, both Mr. Jarndyce and Ada denied it, adding that no east wind could ever be where Esther was, for fresh air and sunlight accompanied her everywhere.

Chapter 31 — Nurse and Patient

Charley tells Esther of a sick poor boy — Things reverted to normal, but on this day, Charley informed Esther that a woman named Jenny, Liz's friend, had come by looking for her, but Esther had been out at the time. Charley had met Jenny while the latter was buying medicine for a sick poor boy who had once done the same for her. Esther did remember Jenny and Liz, and hearing that, she decided they should visit the poor boy.

A cold, eerie night and a strange premonition — The two of them left without informing anyone at the house. It was nighttime, and the weather was cold and windy. For the first time in days, it had stopped raining, and though it was partly cloudy, there was an eerie glow in the sky that was not the usual glow of city lights in the distance. Esther had the fleeting but definite feeling that something in her life was about to change and that things would no longer be as they were.

They find Jo at the cottage — Arriving at the cottage where Jenny stayed, they found Jenny and Jo, who was huddled on the floor by the fireplace. The place had a strange smell, and the atmosphere seemed unhealthy. Jo was startled when he saw Esther, who hadn't yet lifted her veil, and mistaking her for Lady Dedlock, he kept repeating that he wouldn't go back to the graveyard. He was afraid she might bury him. According to Jenny, he had been delirious and talking about similar things all day.

Ill and delirious, Jo still has to move on — It was Charley who took things in hand and calmed Jo down, in part because Esther felt uncomfortable moving closer because of the shock she produced in Jo. Charley explained to Jo that Esther was not the mysterious lady, and Esther added that she had come to help. They discovered that Jo, who had smallpox, was experiencing alternating chills and fever and that Jenny had found him on the street that morning and taken him in. By his own account, he had just left London the day before, having been told to move on yet again, though he never knew where he should go next. Jenny had done what she could for him, but she was afraid that her drunken husband wouldn't tolerate the situation and would hurt Jo. Meanwhile, Liz had returned and told how she had gone looking for alternate lodging for him, since it was clear he was in no condition to travel. Liz had tried all the official channels, but her efforts were blocked by bureaucracy, and now that the women's husbands were on their way home, things were getting too dangerous for Jo, and Liz herself needed to take her baby and go to her own place. So the women gave him a few pennies, and poor little Jo moved on again.

Esther convinces Jo to stay at Bleak House — Esther and Charley had heard that Jo was staying by a brick kiln, so they headed in that direction and soon found him. When Esther first offered him a place to stay, Jo declined, saying that he would stay among the bricks. Esther was worried that he would die, but Jo had seen so much death already that he seemed unconcerned. Finally, however, he followed Esther and Charley to Bleak House, even though he had his doubts about Esther's connection to the mysterious lady.

Mr. Skimpole's opinion — On arriving at Bleak House, Mr. Jarndyce and Mr. Skimpole, who happened to be there, came right away to see the boy. Mr. Jarndyce was compassionate, as usual, but Mr. Skimpole, using his childishness as an excuse and his medical background as his reasoning, was convinced that they should put the boy back out on the street immediately. The boy was too feverish to stay there, and besides, he was used to being on the street. It occurred to Mr. Jarndyce that prisoners were better taken care of than the poor, which led Mr. Skimpole to wonder why Jo hadn't had the "poetry" to land himself in jail. Jo would have been more interesting to him as a desperate thief or something similar, but Esther finally interrupted his musings to remind everyone that Jo's illness was getting worse and he needed help. That, in Mr. Skimpole's opinion, was ample justification for throwing him out.

A generally compassionate reception — Fortunately, Mr. Jarndyce had more compassion as well as clout with the authorities. But tonight it was too late to help Jo in any other way than to give him a bed, so that was what Mr. Jarndyce ordered. He had shown signs of anger and indignation toward Mr. Skimpole's self-centered opinions, but Esther noticed that her guardian was never fully angry with Mr. Skimpole, since he regarded him as inherently irresponsible. Mr. Skimpole did, however, manage to make a few helpful recommendations based on his medical experience.

The Bleak House household comes to Jo's aid — Everyone else took great compassion on Jo and set about preparing his room in a loft above the stables and making sure he was comfortable. All the servants pitched in, and Esther noticed that Charley was particularly solicitous. Mr. Jarndyce even took the time that night to write a letter on Jo's behalf, and they all slept better knowing that everything that could be done for the boy had been done.

All to no avail — Jo himself, who had been sitting in the hall until being transferred to the loft, seemed strangely removed and unimpressed by the comforts of Bleak House and the arrangements being made on his behalf. The next day, things got even stranger. Already by dawn, there was a general commotion. Jo was gone, and no one knew how or where to. There were limited possibilities as to how he got out, yet he had left without a trace.

Charley falls ill; Esther quarantines them both in her room — While the search for Jo still continued almost a week later, Esther became aware of another, more immediately urgent issue. Charley had become ill, and Esther's instant reaction was to quarantine both Charley and herself in her room. Upset, Ada would come to the door and knock for entrance, but Esther refused to transmit the disease to anyone else — least of all, Ada — so she denied her requests for entrance. That was hard for both of them, but Esther made up it for by communicating daily from the window when Ada was down in the garden.

Esther nurses Charley back to health; Charley's hope — Charley had caught Jo's disease. It began with a shivering coldness and worsened so quickly that Esther gave up her own bed for Charley's comfort and recovery. Esther nursed Charley regularly, often holding her head in her arms. Charley had lost so much of her bloom that Esther worried that she would die or be permanently disfigured from the disease. Throughout that time, though, Esther had noticed Charley's hope, inspired by her deep faith and the inspiration she drew from the gospel stories of resurrection — the story of Lazarus and of the young ruler's daughter whom Jesus raised from the dead. Between that hope and Esther's tender care, Charley recovered both her health and her youthful looks.

Esther catches the disease — There was a price, though. Shortly afterwards, Esther herself fell ill, and now it was Charley's turn to comfort and care for her. The two of them still remained quarantined, and in order to contain the disease, Esther arranged to have only one household servant minister to her needs. For a few days, she was still able to communicate with Ada from the window, but soon Charley had to take over, and Esther instructed her to spare Ada's feelings by telling her that she was sleeping rather than revealing the truth that she was too weak to come to the window. The chapter ends as Esther asks Charley to hold her hand and informs her that she is blind.

Chapter 32 — The Appointed Time

A typical evening at Cook's Court — At first glance, all seemed to be business as usual at Cook's Court and its nearby surroundings. Lincoln's Inn Fields had closed down except for the few remaining lawyers who were working overtime. Strains of piano music and Little Swills's singing wafted over from Sol's Arms pub to Cook's Court, where the ladies stood in the doorway gossiping about Mr. Krook's drinking and Mr. Weevle, the promising young man who had taken over the second-floor room in Krook's building.

A strange burning smell in the air — Mr. Weevle was also out that night. He was particularly restless this evening as he repeatedly came out and went back in. On one of his ventures outside, he was met by Mr. Snagsby, who was taking his evening stroll and felt drawn toward Krook's shop because of the recent events associated with it. Mr. Snagsby pointed out a strange greasy smell in the air, like something burning. Mr. Weevle agreed and guessed that the pub had burnt some chops, to which Mr. Snagsby added that they must have lost their freshness even before being burnt. Somehow the smell evoked horror in Mr. Weevle, and Mr. Snagsby guessed it had something to do with his apartment and the previous tenant's death. He found it strange that Mr. Weevle and Nemo both worked for him as law writers and lived in the same room. Mr. Weevle kept looking around nervously, and the topic of conversation was not helping his uneasiness. However, it was time for Mr. Snagsby to go, since he was concerned that his wife would come looking for him.

A mysterious meeting adds to the unease — Mrs. Snagsby had been following her husband the whole time, and Mr. Weevle now noticed her — though he didn't know her — as she walked by, poorly disguised in a handkerchief she had wrapped around her head. But he had other things on his mind. He had been waiting for someone who was clearly late, and that added to his nervousness. Just at that moment, the person arrived. It was Mr. Guppy, and the two of them immediately went up to Jobling's (Weevle's) room. Where had Guppy been? Guppy protested that he'd said he would meet Jobling at around ten o'clock, and he couldn't help noticing his friend's uneasy mood. In truth, Jobling was depressed and couldn't shake it, attributing his feelings to the room and its history. It had an atmosphere of death, further symbolized by the burning candle with the winding sheet (wax dripped down to form a shroudlike sheet, symbolizing death), a symbol Dickens used earlier in the novel when Nemo died. Guppy added that his lateness had partly been caused by Mr. Snagsby's presence, which he had tried to avoid, but that information only added to Jobling's uneasiness because it emphasized the mystery that seemed to continuously surround Guppy's movements.

Mr. Guppy tries to explain his motives — To lighten things up, Mr. Guppy diverted the conversation to the pictures hanging on Jobling's walls. One in particular stood out to him — the picture of Lady Dedlock over the mantelpiece. Guppy explained that much of what he did surrounded his desire to ease the pain of the strong imprint on his "art" (heart) caused by his love for Esther Summerson (though he never mentioned her name). He was not pleased that Jobling had been so insensitive to his feelings, but he finally dropped the subject after Jobling apologized twice and ordered him to let it go.

Jobling's agreement — In any case, this delicate subject was Mr. Guppy's reason for wanting the letters that Krook had taken from Nemo's suitcase and secreted away, even though he couldn't read them himself. At midnight tonight, on his birthday, Krook had agreed to give them to Jobling (to him, Mr. Weevle), who would then go through them on his own so that he could later interpret them for Mr. Krook. In fact, Jobling had secretly agreed to hand them over to Mr. Guppy, and Guppy had no intention of returning them, claiming that Krook never owned them. Guppy's plot to fool Krook by giving him a fake substitute did not ease Jobling's mind. Krook had too sharp an eye for letter shapes, even if he couldn't read.

Mysterious circumstances — Both Jobling and Guppy found it strange that Krook had chosen midnight as the meeting time. Jobling had last seen Krook at about eight, when he helped him close up the shop, and he'd noticed how Krook had placed his cap on the chair. A short while later, after Jobling had left the room, he had heard Krook humming a tune, but after that, he had heard nothing at all. Ironically, the tune, which he said was the only one Krook knew, was about drinking and death.

More mysterious questions — Waiting out the few hours left proved difficult that evening. Guppy was as nervous as his friend, and he kept biting his nails and crossing his legs. He wondered how Krook, being unable to read, had managed to write the name "Hawdon." Jobling explained that he'd copied it from a letter, and Guppy asked whether Jobling thought the original hand that wrote that name in the letters was a man's or a woman's. Without hesitation, Jobling replied that it was woman's.

Something strange in the air — Right around then, Guppy noticed odd bits of greasy soot that seemed to fall from nowhere and stick to his clothing. The two men guessed there must have been a chimney fire. They continued their half-whispered conversation, but Jobling still felt uncomfortable. The whole thing seemed too strange to him. There was no good reason for it, and living in a room associated with death was taking its toll on him. Around that time, the clocks in the city struck eleven, and as Jobling stirred the fire, Guppy suddenly exclaimed that more of the disgusting soot was falling on him and sticking to his clothing. They decided to open the window to get some air, and that brought them a sense of relief for a while. But as they were leaning out the window, Guppy noticed an even more repulsive yellow substance. He had been tapping the window sill, and now this disgusting greasy substance was on his fingers. Looking around, they could see it dripping down the sides of the wall. Mr. Guppy shut the window and quickly washed it off his hand as best he could. By the time he was done, it was midnight.

A horrifying explanation — The time had come for Jobling to head down to retrieve the letters from Mr. Krook. But he soon came running back up — Krook was nowhere to be found. This time, Guppy and Jobling went down together. Still, there was no sign of either Krook or the letters. There were various hints here and there that he had been there. His hat and coat still lay on the chair, the bottle of alcohol he always drank stood on the table, and the string that had tied the bundle of letters together lay on the floor. But the real clue came from the cat, which stood there hissing at a smoking pile of something on the floor. Horrified, Guppy and Jobling realized they were looking at the remains of Mr. Krook, a victim of spontaneous combustion.

Chapter 33 — Interlopers

An immediate investigation — As soon as Guppy and Jobling figured out what had happened, they immediately cried for help, which came right away in the form of the same two policemen who had been at Nemo' inquest. The beadle had brought them, and now they were busy asking questions and taking notes.

Excitement at Cook's Court — In fact, all of Cook's Court was up that night, unable to sleep because of the commotion. Sol's Arms also gave Miss Flite a bed for the night to get her out of Krook's building. Of course, this sort of thing was big business for the pub, which kept its doors open all night. The policemen and fireman benefited, too, with a large number of Cook's Court residents offering to buy them drinks. They weren't the only ones being treated. The owner of the pub gave Weevle (aka Jobling) and Guppy all the drinks they wanted, because their presence drew more business. They ended up spending all night at the bar, telling their story even through their growing drunkenness.

Mr. Snagsby's "guilt" — By morning, much of Cook's Court still hadn't gone home but had fallen asleep at the pub. Now the rest of the neighbors came to see what had happened, and Mr. Snagsby was among them. One of the policemen had directed him there, and Snagsby now found the exhausted Weevle and Guppy switched from alcohol to tea and breakfast. As he was exclaiming about the whole affair, he was surprised to see his wife walk into the pub, sporting her usual accusing look. Being a kind and courteous gentleman, he offered her something to drink and tried to ease her into the conversation, but Mrs. Snagsby's attitude remained the same.

Mr. Snagsby's confusion — Mr. Snagsby was so perturbed and confused by his wife's expression that he took her aside and asked her about it. Unfortunately, it didn't do much good. His wife was so convinced of his guilt that she was ready to accuse him of being involved in Krook's death. By the end of the conversation, Snagsby had still not managed to dispel his wife's doubts. He meekly accompanied her back home, but even that didn't help. Her look was so accusing that he began to believe in his own guilt.

Jobling wants out — Guppy and Weevle finally emerged from the pub and took a little walk to shake off their drowsiness. Exhausted and upset by recent events, Weevle said he'd had enough of mystery and conspiracy. After the two of them had argued a while, Guppy made it clear that he wanted to come to an agreement about what they had witnessed the previous night. He then tried to convince his friend that it would be worthwhile to stay in his current apartment so he could explore Krook's belongings, especially since Krook had no known relations. But Jobling was so upset by the place that he wanted nothing more to do with it, even if it meant giving up the possibility of striking gold among Krook's junk.

Krook's surprise relatives — The conversation was interrupted when a coach pulled up with the entire Smallweed family in it, and Guppy and Weevle soon learned from Grandfather Smallweed that Mr. Krook had indeed had a relation — Grandmother Smallweed, who was Krook's sister. Mr. Guppy wondered why young Smallweed had never mentioned Krook as his uncle, but Bart had never even met him, and besides, the family wasn't proud of that connection. However, that was irrelevant now.

Assuming there was no will, Grandfather Smallweed had come to take over the administration of the estate with the help of Mr. Tulkinghorn. His claim was soon corroborated by Mr. Tulkinghorn's clerk, so there was no more arguing the fact. That was a relief to Jobling, though Mr. Guppy was disappointed.

Krook's death draws widespread attention — Interest in Krook's death wasn't confined to the immediate neighborhood. Scientists and philosophers came from great distances to inspect the phenomenon, and there was much argument about its validity. Between that, the newspaper coverage, the coroner's inquest, and the continuous presence of the two policemen, Cook's Court and its neighboring pub stayed busy and entertained.

Guppy informs Lady Dedlock of the letters' destruction — Now locked out Krook's building and a mere footnote at the inquest, Mr. Guppy was disappointed. However, he still had to inform Lady Dedlock of the outcome — that the letters had been destroyed along with Mr. Krook. Lady Dedlock made it clear that this would be the last time she would receive Mr. Guppy, so if he had anything to add, he should say it now. He didn't, so he excused himself, but as he was leaving, Mr. Tulkinghorn came into the room. Seeing Lady Dedlock, he apologized, claiming he hadn't expected to encounter her. In the meantime, though, he had recognized Mr. Guppy as being from Kenge and Carboy. The chapter ends as Mr. Tulkinghorn escorts Lady Dedlock to her coach, but the incident left him perplexed and wondering what it meant.

Chapter 34 — A Turn of the Screw

Mr. George receives a letter — Mr. George was trying to figure out whether the letter he had received was a bluff or an actual threat, so he called Phil over to help him. The letter was from Grandfather Smallweed, who was now demanding full payment of a loan by the next day. That confused Mr. George. He had already paid one and a half times the principal in interest and miscellaneous payments, and the loan was supposed to be renewable and indeed had been renewed many times.

Phil's assessment; George's dilemma — As far as Phil was concerned, there was no great mystery to it. Old Smallweed was a greedy parasite and not to be trusted. He was simply putting on the screws, which was perfectly in character. That still seemed odd to Mr. George because until now he had always had time to pay off the bill. But Phil's answer to that was that the time had simply run out. Unfortunately, Mr. George didn't have the money. Phil suggested bankruptcy, but Mr. George quickly dismissed the idea. His friend, Mat Bagnet, had co-signed, and that would make him liable, which would be unfair to him and his family.

The Bagnets learn about the problem — As they were talking, Mat Bagnet and his wife appeared at the shop. They had come to co-sign the new loan agreement, not realizing that things had changed. Mr. George then read them the letter, which he'd only gotten fifteen minutes before, and he explained that he had no intention of jeopardizing their family. If he thought it would pay the bill, he would sell everything he had. Mr. Bagnet and George therefore determined to go then and there to see old Smallweed.

Grandfather Smallweed smashes the pipe — When the two men arrived at the Smallweeds' that morning, they found Judy in a contemptuous mood. Old man Smallweed pretended to be welcoming at first, but there was something sinister in his attitude. He insisted that Judy bring the pipe, even after Mr. George informed him that he didn't feel like smoking it that day. He had come to resolve the matter of the letter and make sure that the Bagnets did not end up in a financial mess. Grandfather Smallweed was not too cooperative. In the end, he smashed the pipe, instructed the two troopers to take up the issue with his lawyer, and threw them out of his home, telling them both to go to hell.

The two troopers briefly cross paths with Mrs. Rouncewell at Mr. Tulkinghorn's — When the two men arrived at Mr. Tulkinghorn's office, they learned that Tulkinghorn wanted nothing to do with them. They decided to wait anyway and had been there an hour when Mrs. Rouncewell emerged from Mr. Tulkinghorn's inner room. Seeing the two troopers, she gave Mr. Bagnet her compliments, telling him how she, too, had a son who had joined the military. But Mr. George was busy studying an almanac, so it seemed he didn't see or recognize his mother.

Mr. George makes a bargain with Mr. Tulkinghorn — The two troopers' persistence paid off, and Mr. Tulkinghorn finally gave them an audience, though without much hospitality. Mr. George explained that his motive was to save his friend from being liable for his debt, but that also failed to gain Mr. Tulkinghorn's sympathy. Finally, George got his attention when he told him privately that he would hand over the paper he had refused to give him at his last visit. He was willing to do this to save his friend. In return, Mr. Tulkinghorn offered to restore the former loan agreement and take measures to make sure that Mr. Bagnet and his family would never be liable for the debt. He did not normally deal in such matters, but he would make an exception in this case. Mr. George therefore reluctantly pulled out the paper and gave it to Mr. Tulkinghorn to review, stating that it was nothing but Captain Hawdon's final instructions to him. As usual, Mr. Tulkinghorn's expression betrayed nothing as he read it.

Mr. George's serious mood — Having concluded their business, the two men headed for Mr. Bagnet's house. Mr. George was to have dinner with them, but it was clear to the whole family that he was not his usual self. He was usually lighthearted, but that day he seemed serious. Even after dinner, when he normally sat before the fire with Mr. Bagnet and smoked, he took no interest in his pipe. The family tried to cheer him up, but his seriousness wasn't related to anything they had done. In fact, he was deeply appreciative of them, and he showed his special appreciation for Mrs. Bagnet when he instructed her son to mind the look of a good and honest face like his mother's. He was to remember it in her old age and be kind to her both now and then, so he would have no regrets. Mr. George then excused himself to go smoke his pipe outside.

Chapter 35 — Esther's Narrative

Esther's visions during her illness — Esther's sickness lasted a number of weeks, and the change in her routine was so complete that her previous life soon seemed like a distant dream compressed into a much shorter time frame than actual. During this time, she had visions of endless stairs leading up to the sky and endless toil climbing those stairs. Sometimes she would forget she was in her bed, though on another level she never lost sight of that fact. Another more frightening vision was of being part of a fiery circle in a black void. This was agonizing for Esther, and she prayed to be removed from the circle.

Esther's unselfishness under all conditions — Esther's motive in mentioning these things was not to ramble but to benefit others by improving the understanding of such things. Similarly, when she felt she was dying, her sole thought was not for herself but for those she was leaving behind.

Esther's sight is gradually restored — By that point, she was in a completely restful state, and it was then that she began to see again. And while she still kept Ada at bay with Charley's help, she could now begin to read the letters her friend had sent her twice a day. She could also see the care that Charley put into keeping their private apartment neat and clean, and she was deeply moved by the love expressed by all on her behalf.

Esther loses her good looks but finds an even greater love — Finally, Esther began to strengthen and regain a sense of involvement in life. Eventually, she was able to sit up and take tea, and it was then that she broached the subject of her looks with Charley. Charley had hidden the mirror out of compassion, but Esther explained that she could handle the change. She was comforted by the fact that her guardian, who could now finally visit her, felt the greatest compassion for her and seemed to love her even more despite the change. He told her that the whole household and all her close friends had been fretting over her. Even Miss Flite, on hearing she was ill, had made the twenty-mile walk just to see her.

The poisonous effect of Jarndyce and Jarndyce — Richard had even written to Mr. Jarndyce while Esther was unable to respond, though he did so with a cold resentment. But her guardian understood: it was the effect of the Jarndyce and Jarndyce case, which would ruin even the angels. Esther pointed out that it hadn't marred his own character, but her guardian protested — the east wind had shown itself too many times for that to be true. In any case, it had destroyed the character and peace of many a good man, and now Richard had come under its spell. They needed to be patient and forgiving with him in the hope that he would free himself soon enough.

A prayer of love fulfilled — Now, however, there were other things to think about. Ada would love to see Esther, but Esther felt she needed a little more time — perhaps a week in the country alone with Charley. As though on cue, Mr. Boythorn's unsolicited invitation to take over his country home stood ready for her. But before she left for the country, Esther agreed to receive Miss Flite on the understanding that it would mean a great deal to that lady. Esther was so moved by the general outpouring of love in her direction that she couldn't help thinking back to her old prayer, long ago, when she had asked to be a good and true person who might be of some benefit to others and earn a little love in life. Now she prayed the same thing with renewed humility.

Miss Flite's visit; the veiled lady visits Jenny and asks about Esther—Miss Flite's visit did not disappoint, with its outpouring of tears and compassion for Esther's suffering. But she had also come to relay information. On their way to Bleak House, Miss Flite and Charley had learned from Jenny that a veiled lady had come to see her at the cottage during Esther's illness. The lady had asked about Esther and had taken a handkerchief left by Esther on a previous visit. In return, she left some money, but no one knew who she was.

Miss Flite's story—Perceiving that Miss Flite needed food and warmth, Esther decided it was time for dinner. Afterwards, Miss Flite began talking about her favorite subject, the Jarndyce case. She told how her whole family—all dead now—had been drawn into its evil hold. She knew the signs, and she had watched others, too, like Gridley and Richard, drawn in and ruined one by one. Her father had died, bitter and angry, in debtor's prison; her brother became an alcoholic; her sister had gotten into something unmentionable—yet all of them had once been respectable. She herself had felt the pull early on and now was simply waiting for a judgment, though she knew better. She hoped that someone would be able to convince Richard to change his mind before too late.

Mr. Woodcourt's heroism—But there was good news, too. Mr. Woodcourt had proven himself a hero during a shipwreck somewhere near India, and now he was practically worshipped by the people. The news report, which Miss Flite pulled out of her bag and gave to Esther, told of his tireless efforts helping the victims.

Esther's admission of Woodcourt's love—Esther was so moved that she cried, and as the narrator, she finally admitted to the reader her sense that Mr. Woodcourt loved her—or had loved before her face became disfigured by the illness. She believed he would have admitted his love to her if he had been more prosperous. Now, though, she was glad it hadn't come to that. It would have been one more burden on her conscience now that her appearance had changed. Things were simpler as they were, and she was glad to honor him without any interfering complications.

Chapter 36 — Chesney Wold

Esther in Lincolnshire — John Jarndyce accompanied Esther and Charley to Boythorn's Lincolnshire home, which, to Esther's delight, had been meticulously prepared for her. Boythorn had already left, so Esther wrote him a thank you note for his hospitality. With Charley off to bed and the letter mailed, Esther now felt it was time to face herself in the mirror, something she hadn't done yet.

Confronting her new face in the mirror — Before doing so, Esther sat down and gave herself a pep talk. If she was to keep the promise she had made in her youth — to be true and good — then she needed to do so no matter what her appearance. The first step was to count her blessings, and one of these was her hair, which she now let down. And so, armed with what remaining good looks she had — though she never considered herself a great beauty — Esther confronted her now scarred face. Mostly, she was happy that she was calm and able to let go of her past appearance with relative ease and no bitterness.

Esther's unselfish attitude — The one thing that still troubled Esther with regard to this issue was the thought of dishonoring Allan Woodcourt. She had cherished the flowers he left her on his departure, drying them and keeping them in a favorite book. No one knew about this, but she wondered now if continuing to keep them did him justice. She concluded it would be all right as long as she kept the matter to herself. He should not be required to respond to her disfigured face as though it was the same face he left behind.

A healthy country routine — Having resolved these questions, Esther now set about her daily country routine with Charley. They took walks and horseback rides together, and Boythorn's housekeeper made sure they got plenty of nourishment. Through regular trips to the village, they also got to know the kind villagers, who welcomed Esther with open arms. With all the fresh air, walking, rest, sunshine, nourishment, and friendly relations, both Esther and Charley quickly assumed a healthy look and a sense of cheer and comfort.

A surprise visit — Throughout this time, Esther had only admired Chesney Wold from a distance. There was a bench under a tree in a clearing where she and Charley would go, and Esther would sit there while Charley picked wildflowers. As far as Esther knew, the Dedlocks were not at the estate, so she was surprised one day to see a female figure coming toward her. It was Lady Dedlock, though without her usual reserve and indifference. There was an expression on her face that Esther had never seen before on any face — one she had yearned for when she was a young girl, though seeing it now created a state of confusion and panic within her. It was only when Esther called Charley that Lady Dedlock's expression reverted to something closer to its usual haughty indifference. Even so, Lady Dedlock remained kind and concerned, though she asked Esther to send Charley back to the house. Once Charley was gone, she sat down next to Esther and produced the handkerchief that Esther had left with Jenny. The sight of it sent Esther into an even greater panic, but before she knew it, Lady Dedlock had shed all remaining restraint and was holding her in a loving embrace and kissing her. Afterwards, she fell to her knees, begging Esther to forgive her for her ignorance and negligence, having been led to believe that her child had died in infancy.

Mother and child embrace — Mother and child were now kneeling on the ground, embracing each other, with Esther assuring her mother that she loved her and had forgiven her long ago. But though they had just found each other, this would also be the last time they would be together. In order to not shame her husband, Lady Dedlock would have to preserve the mask of cold indifference she had built up over the years. There was no going back, and it was a path she would have to tread alone. The existence of her beloved child would have to remain a secret. She confessed that on hearing Esther was sick, she had felt a terrible panic, which confirmed to her that Esther was indeed her child. In her usual unselfish way, Esther was relieved that her disfigured face now left no clue as to the nearness of their blood relationship.

Lady Dedlock gives Esther a letter—Esther's mother now handed her a letter, with the instructions to burn it once she was done reading it. There was still a danger that this secret could be discovered, primarily by Mr. Tulkinghorn, who was ever watchful of Lady Dedlock's movements and who had no shred of human compassion. Esther suggested that Mr. Jarndyce might be able to help. Her mother wondered whether he knew at all, and when Esther assured her that he didn't, Lady Dedlock gave her permission to tell him but to keep the knowledge of that from her. She still had some pride, and she would also have to reject the offer for help.

A final farewell—The time had come to part, and as Lady Dedlock held her child for the final time, she implored Esther to remember that under that brilliant veneer lay the poor, suffering heart of an anguished mother who had to tread her silent, tortured path alone. She begged Esther to forgive her and to pray to heaven for her, though she doubted heaven could ever forgive her.

Destroying the letter; a wave of guilt and shame—It took Esther an hour to regain her composure after her mother's departure, and on arriving home, she went straight to her room and read the letter. After reading it, Esther immediately burnt the letter, but even with that act, she felt the weight of shame and guilt, and she wondered in her confusion and grief whether it might not have been better if she had died at birth after all. Wasn't her existence the last remaining piece of evidence that spoke against her mother?

Thoughts of guilt and terror—These were Esther's thoughts as she fell asleep, and the next day was no better. As though in imitation of her mental state, the weather was cloudy and gray, and that evening Esther walked to Chesney Wold mansion for the first time since her arrival in Lincolnshire. As she went along the perimeter of the house, she took in its sights, sounds, and scents—the gardens, lime trees, fountains, turrets, walkways, statues, stables—and in the evening's darkness, she noticed one lighted window that she thought might be her mother's. When she reached the Ghost's Walk, her footsteps echoed so on the terrace that the legend suddenly seemed true to her—and she the reason for it. That thought terrified her so much that she ran back as fast as she could.

The power of love over fear—On arriving back in her room, Esther found two letters—one from Ada and one from John Jarndyce, both so full of love and faith in her that she knew her feelings of fear and guilt had no real basis. She had had so much love and so many blessings in her life, and heaven itself would certainly not fault her for her parents' past mistakes. By the next morning, she was completely free of the previous days' fears.

A happy reunion with Ada—That was a good thing, because Ada was arriving that afternoon, and Esther wanted to be at her best. The house and garden had been fully prepared, and even Mr.

Boythorn's bird, which he had left behind for them, stood ready as part of the welcoming committee. Esther was still concerned about the impact of her new look on Ada, and there were several hours left to mull it over before her arrival. But before she knew it, Ada had come, and though Esther hid from her at first, there was no reason for her fretting. Ada loved her just as she always had, and their reunion was one of pure affection and happiness.

Chapter 37 — Jarndyce and Jarndyce

Esther keeps her secret to herself — Esther resisted the temptation to tell Ada the truth about Lady Dedlock, even when Ada mentioned the coldness of her veneer and Esther thought of her mother's true anguish. In general, however, she managed to leave such thoughts for those moments when she was alone and there was no danger of revealing the truth.

A surprise meeting with Richard — A week after Ada arrived, Esther got a message that she was wanted at the local pub by an unknown gentleman. It was already evening when she arrived, and the landlord took her into a private room where, to her delight, she found herself facing Richard. She had removed her veil in stages, but the change in her looks made no impact on him, and his reception of her was warm and joyous. Esther expressed her gratitude but then turned serious, adding that she wished to reconcile Richard with John Jarndyce. This was a subject Richard also wanted to discuss, though not at that moment. Right now, he wanted to cast all that aside and surprise his lovely cousin Ada. Was he welcome where they were staying? Esther assured him that he was even welcome at Bleak House.

Esther's private doubts, Skimpole's bad influence — Esther then asked how Richard liked his new career. His answer was non-committal: it was an adequate temporary occupation. He still placed his hopes in a favorable unfoldment of the Jarndyce suit, but when Esther saw a shadow pass across his face, she thought of Miss Flite, though she kept that to herself. But on to happier subjects … Richard was pleased to announce that Mr. Skimpole had come along at his (Skimpole's) request, all expenses paid by Richard, of course. Expenses aside, he found Skimpole's childlike, unworldly presence entertaining and refreshing. Esther's view of Skimpole was more cynical. Somehow the notion of unworldliness did not mesh with Mr. Skimpole's opportunism, though she again kept this opinion to herself. Even worse, Skimpole's flighty, careless imaginings and his irresponsible philosophy were the last thing Richard needed right now. Someone like her guardian, who was already grounded in what Esther called "right principle and purpose" and needed relief from dealing with difficult worldly matters, could benefit from Skimpole's lightheartedness. But Richard needed balancing in the other direction, and Esther suspected that the real motives of the "dear old infant" — as Richard called Skimpole — were not what they seemed.

Richard's obsessiveness — Even Richard's reunion with Ada rubbed Esther the wrong way. It was obvious that Ada loved him dearly, even now with their new relationship as merely cousins. But Richard's own thoughts seemed to gravitate mostly toward Jarndyce and Jarndyce, and everything else in his life, including Ada, took second place. His excuse was that he could not settle until the Jarndyce suit was settled, though he didn't say this directly to Ada but reserved it for his private conversation with Esther the next morning.

Richard is caught in the web of Jarndyce and Jarndyce — The next morning, Esther and Richard met at around seven and went to the park together. Richard was immediately taken in by the beauty of the woods, especially with the glorious weather that day, but when Esther suggested that he take some rest in the area before returning to Jarndyce and Jarndyce, he refused. Nothing could distract him from what had become a complete obsession. Again, Esther saw shades of the same dark insanity that had gripped others. It was a rare soul, like her guardian's, that did not succumb to its hold, though Richard claimed that it had changed even John Jarndyce.

Richard suspects John Jarndyce of selfish ulterior motives — After studying the case, Richard had concluded that Mr. Jarndyce's noble exterior harbored a lurking self-interest. Apparently, the case included several wills that were under review, and in one instance, Richard and Ada stood to gain much more than their guardian. That fact made Jarndyce's motives and behavior suspect to him. Jarndyce's apparent lack of interest in the suit, his insistence that Ada and Richard break off their engagement, his constant attempts to dissuade Richard from his fascination with the case — all this seemed like a cover for more materialistic motives. Esther was appalled that Richard could come to these conclusions, having lived with Jarndyce and known him closely. But her shock soon turned to pity. So far gone did Richard seem with his obsession that she felt it was pointless to say much more. It was then that he told her of the letter he had written to Mr. Jarndyce, in which he suggested they air their differences openly.

Esther tries again to reason with Richard — None of this surprised Esther. She had already heard of it from Jarndyce, who had relayed it to her without any resentment. Richard was relieved to hear that. He believed Mr. Jarndyce to be a man of honor — he just suspected that things were more complex and that the case affected anyone who came near it. That notion, in his opinion, justified his obsession with bringing the case to a conclusion. Hearing this, Esther tried again to reason with him. Hadn't many others before him tried to do that, only to finally be overwhelmed and destroyed by the lawsuit? Richard believed he had the wit, youth, and determination to succeed where others had failed, especially since he had made it his life's mission. That, to Esther, was disheartening news, but Richard seemed to feel that while others were overwhelmed by the case, he had taken control of it. Esther did not agree. It seemed to her that he was postponing every good judgment and decision until after the case was resolved, which she sadly acknowledged to herself might never happen. An entire life on hold! It seemed a great waste to her. And while she kept these thoughts to herself, she made every reasonable effort to be as honest and direct as she could with Richard.

Richard asks Esther to communicate his views to Ada — One of Richard's requests to Esther was to have her relay his views on Mr. Jarndyce to Ada, hopefully softening them in the process and showing Richard in his best light. He wanted her to know that Mr. Jarndyce had not changed his stance when responding to his letter, that he (Richard) was working on her behalf as well as his own, and that when she came of age — as he already had — perhaps they could becoming engaged again. In the meantime, he would not see her much but would focus his attentions on the lawsuit.

Richard is in debt again — Esther then asked him whether he was in debt again. Richard seemed surprised at the question — of course, he was. Anyone pursuing a goal, he argued, had to invest in it. But whichever will won out, he and Ada stood to gain, and that would cover his debts. This seemed a huge mistake to Esther, but none of her admonitions had any effect.

Ada's letter to Richard — On arriving home, Esther spoke to Ada about Richard's decisions. In response, Ada wrote Richard a concerned letter stating that she was sure he would someday see John Jarndyce as he truly was, a good and honorable man. She also wanted Richard to know that nothing would make her happier than if he gave up the Jarndyce case forever. To her, it was clear that nothing would ever come of it, and it made her unhappy to think that the efforts he was making and the misery he would suffer were partly on her behalf. Lastly, she made it clear that she would much rather see him free and happy with someone else than postponing a promising life because of some dim prospect of becoming wealthy with her. Despite her youth, she knew that she was just his first love and that young love often faded later in life. No amount of inexperience on her part could diminish her certainty on these points. Unfortunately, Ada's loving note had no effect on Richard's attitudes. Her obvious love boosted his mood, but he remained convinced that he was right.

A futile appeal to Skimpole for help — Esther next appealed to Howard Skimpole for help. She tried to impress upon him that they all had a responsibility to steer Richard in a healthier direction. "Responsibility," however, was not a word Skimpole could connect with — certainly not in relation to himself. Nor did he have any common sense and should not be expected to demonstrate it. Esther expressed her dismay over the fact that his lack of sense did Richard no favors. This took Mr. Skimpole by surprise for a moment, and he tried to argue his way out of it, claiming the superiority of "poetry" over practicality. In the end, it was clear that Skimpole remained unconcerned with anyone's fate but his own, and Esther realized that enlisting his help was a pointless exercise.

Mr. Vholes — Esther and Skimpole had been walking outside, and now they joined Richard and Ada, who were walking ahead of them. A stranger approached from the opposite direction, and both Richard and Skimpole recognized him. It was Mr. Vholes, Richard's new legal counsel after Richard left Kenge and Carboy. According to Skimpole, Vholes was the epitome of responsibility.

Mr. Vholes's reason for coming — Esther's impression of Vholes was of a stiff, introverted, unhealthy man. He explained that his reason for coming was to alert Richard that his case would be "in the Chancellor's paper" the next day, which appeared to mean that it was up for review. This created a great deal of excitement for Richard, who subsequently ran off to make arrangements to leave that night with Vholes. It proved to him that their new, faster way of doing things was working.

After Richard left, Esther asked Mr. Vholes whether Richard's presence in court would make a difference. Mr. Vholes replied no but added that Richard was his client and that he was therefore obliged to carry out his wishes. He further explained that he had three daughters and an elderly father to provide for.

Richard drives off to his fate — That evening, the group saw Richard and Mr. Vholes off as their coach drove away to London and the Chancery Court. It was a scene Esther would never forget — of two contrasting figures, the young, excited gentleman and his tense companion with the predatory gaze. Ada later confided in Esther that no matter what Richard's fate was, she would always be there to love him. And according to Esther, she kept her promise.

Chapter 38 — A Struggle

Life returns to normal — When their stay at Boythorn's was up, Esther, Charley, and Ada returned to Bleak House, where Esther, her health now fully restored, resumed her normal duties. That kept her busy for a while as she got all the accounts and other household things back in order. Once she was done with that, she decided to go to London, inspired by something Lady Dedlock had written in her letter — though she didn't say what.

Esther visits Caddy as a cover — Esther's excuse for visiting London was to see Caddy, and Caddy, who loved Esther dearly, was only too happy to oblige. So off Esther went, arriving at the Turveydrops' early in the day. Caddy and Prince had settled in nicely with the elder Mr. Turveydrop and seemed happily oblivious to his tendency to take advantage of their willingness to serve him and sacrifice for him.

News of Caddy's parents and Peepy — Esther next asked how Caddy's parents were doing. She and her mother were on good terms, though she rarely saw her. Mrs. Jellyby seemed afraid of catching Caddy's "absurd" behavior patterns. Mr. Jellyby, on the other hand, came by every evening and, seated in his favorite chair, would take snuff with the elder Mr. Turveydrop — something Mr. Jellyby had never done before — and listen to his stories about the Prince Regent. Even Peepy had found a comfortable place there and was welcomed by father Turveydrop, who indulged him in little ways and kept him busy and entertained.

Caddy's new happy, busy life — Caddy was deeply grateful for this acceptance of her family, and in addition to her involvement with them, she kept herself busy helping Prince. Aside from her household chores and service to the elder Turveydrop, she was learning music and dance to the best of her ability. That way she could help her already overburdened husband, whose health had suffered from the constant workload and long hours involved in running a dance school. She could now play the piano and the kit (a small violin), and she was helping Prince train and manage his four young apprentices.

Esther's intention to meet Mr. Guppy — The topic then switched to Esther's business in London. Her intention was to visit Mr. Guppy in private to straighten out some issues that still bothered her. Since she had met Caddy through Mr. Guppy, it seemed natural to take her along.

Esther meets Mr. Guppy at his mother's home — Mr. Guppy was living with his mother, so they headed over to her home. Old Mrs. Guppy had a perpetual grin on her face, which made her look silly. On top of that, she liked to roll her head and also elbow Caddy, apparently to express her enjoyment. Her son, who was her pride and joy, was sitting at a table reading law papers when the two young ladies arrived. Since Esther wanted to speak to Mr. Guppy privately, Caddy and Mrs. Guppy left the room. So far, Esther had not yet removed her veil, and as she spoke to Mr. Guppy, she still noticed clear signs of his earlier infatuation with her. When asked, for example, whether he had received her note, he removed it from his breast and kissed it.

Mr. Guppy's change of heart — That all changed when Esther lifted her veil. Suddenly, Mr. Guppy turned red and had a hard time speaking because of some unexpected obstruction in his throat. It became extremely important to him to ensure that his earlier marriage proposal was a thing of the past. To this, Esther agreed wholeheartedly. She added that she needed no proof from him that she was not, in fact, the orphan girl she formerly believed she was, and she would appreciate it if he let the subject of her background — of which she was now aware — to rest once and for all. Still blushing, hemming, and hawing, Guppy agreed to her wishes; and Esther, having completed her business, now left with Caddy. The chapter ends with a confused Mr. Guppy running after them several times, his unkempt hair blown by the wind, begging Esther for more assurances — especially now that they had a witness in Caddy — that his previous proposal was no longer valid. And through it all, Esther, who had never had any intention of accepting Guppy's proposal, remained calm, clear, and a little amused.

Chapter 39 — Attorney and Client

Mr. Vholes's business — Mr. Vholes's office was a dark, dirty, dingy, cramped little place, just like the inn that housed it in Chancery Lane. In spite of its name and location, this desolate place, called Symond's Inn, was not one of the Inns of Chancery. It was, however, home to Mr. Vholes's modest business, which, though not spectacular, had helped to gain him respectability. Mr. Vholes was an avid practitioner of that basic rule that the English legal career existed mainly to produce income for its practitioners. If the public had understood this simple rule and dispensed with the notion that legal bureaucracy had anything to do with law and order, it would have been far less likely to question the endless parade of mysterious procedures. Regardless, Mr. Vholes had three daughters and an elderly father to support, so his priorities were clear.

The importance of preserving the status quo — Fortunately for Mr. Vholes, the other lawyers understood that the system had to take precedence at all costs, especially since those costs came out of the clients' pockets. That didn't make the clients happy, but the lawyers managed to keep them confused enough that it didn't matter. If nothing else, they could make their clients feel guilty for threatening the livelihood of respectable men like Mr. Vholes, not to mention the socioeconomic stability of England.

Richard's impatience and Vholes's professional indifference — In this atmosphere of perpetual red tape and redundancy, Richard grew increasingly impatient and frustrated over how little got done on a normal day in Chancery. Of course, that same inefficiency worked in Mr. Vholes's favor, so he naturally counseled Richard to be patient. He explained that things *were* progressing, albeit slowly. On the other hand, Mr. Vholes never made promises and never encouraged his clients' hopes. Still, he was a "rock" of dependability who worked even during the long vacation.

Richard becomes a victim of the Jarndyce suit — So Richard went from the dark, dismal office back out into the street, where the sun was shining. But his own state of mind made no such dramatic change. He had allowed himself to become a victim of the Jarndyce suit.

Guppy and Weevle's conversation — Richard was unaware that he was being watched by Weevle and Guppy. Weevle noticed his brooding attitude, which Guppy explained as resulting from his involvement with the Jarndyce case. He added that he was glad Richard had left Kenge and Carboy, since he never liked him. Richard wasn't the only one who had quit. Young Smallweed had also left to take care of his grandfather's business. Since Weevle's arrival, Smallweed's relationship with Guppy had grown more distant, but Guppy managed to fix that situation. Guppy was therefore still able to get information out of Smallweed about his family's activities. After all, Guppy preferred not to go into the old rag and bottle shop himself. He then revealed to Weevle that his prior motive for retrieving Lady Dedlock's letters (impressing Esther) had been dashed to pieces. Now his only concern was to make sure that the letters were truly gone.

The mystery surrounding Krook's legacy — Meanwhile, the gossip surrounding the Smallweed case and Krook's death was the worst ever. Since the house had been opened by the police to the Smallweeds, the family had been there every day from eight in the morning till nine at night looking through Krook's belongings. No one, including the Chancery Court, had any idea what they'd found, but the conjecture was that there was money falling out of every object, and the Smallweeds' secrecy was driving the Court mad. The lawyers themselves would even go through the boxes of trash occasionally sent out by the Smallweeds, and the two scribes who earlier had worked together at the scene now sneaked around separately looking for hidden treasure. No one in the whole neighborhood could get enough on the subject. So when the Smallweeds let Weevle and Guppy into the house, it was yet another cause for jealousy and malicious gossip.

The Smallweeds' dark, dingy inheritance — The gossipers might have changed their minds had they been admitted themselves. Being shut off from the public, the house was dark and dingier than ever. Once Weevle and Guppy adjusted their vision, they could see the Smallweeds positioned in various places amid the paper and junk. The two young men's eyes scanned the room several times, and by the second time, Guppy's vision had adjusted enough that he noticed Mr. Tulkinghorn standing in the background looking on. After chatting a bit with Grandfather Smallweed, who claimed that Krook had left mostly junk and trash, Weevle and Guppy excused themselves and went upstairs to pack Weevle's things.

Mr. Tulkinghorn asks to speak with Guppy — The room was still sooty from the night of Krook's combustion, so the two young men tried to minimize what they touched. As they were packing, the Krook's devilish cat appeared at the door and wouldn't leave until Mr. Tulkinghorn tripped over her. Tulkinghorn wanted to speak privately with Mr. Guppy and hinted that it had something to do with Guppy's earlier meeting with Lady Dedlock. As respectfully as possible, Mr. Guppy informed Mr. Tulkinghorn that whatever they discussed could be discussed in front of his friend and that he did not feel obliged to tell him anything about the situation with Lady Dedlock, whose name they never actually mentioned.

Guppy gets nervous — Genteel and unruffled as ever, Mr. Tulkinghorn took note of the situation, excused himself, and went his way. But his inquiry made Mr. Guppy even more uncomfortable than he already was, and hinting to Weevle that he had had some dealings with Lady Dedlock, he urged his confused friend to hurry with the packing so they could finally leave and put the whole incident behind them.

Chapter 40 — National and Domestic

England's government falters — For a while, England's political system was in a uproar because of a conflict between Lord Coodle and Sir Doodle, as Dickens calls them. So pivotal were they in their roles that the government was considered non-existent without them, so it came as a relief to those who cared that the two men mended their differences with words rather than guns. Not that most of England did care. The greater part of the population went right on doing whatever it normally did, blissfully oblivious to the fact that its government was leaderless for a while. However, once Sir Doodle did return, he brought all his cousins and nephews with him. This naturally had an effect on the elite English social scene, and so, Mrs. Rouncewell, anticipating a burst of social activity at Chesney Wold, set about making the necessary preparations.

The shadow on the portrait — But until the guests arrived, only the ancestral Dedlock portraits graced the empty drawing room, which now transformed itself in the glowing light of the summer sunset that virtually brought the dull pictures to life. But as the sun set further below the horizon, an ancient tree began to cast a strange shadow across Lady Dedlock's portrait, in its central place above the mantelpiece. Even nightfall could not disperse it but made it more threatening, for the glow of the sun was replaced by the moonlight, which added a haunting aspect to the surrounding landscape and the shapes within the house.

Lady Dedlock's ill health — As though to confirm the shadow's omen, a groom reported to Mrs. Rouncewell that Lady Dedlock had not been feeling well and that she had been spending most of her time in town in her room. Mrs. Rouncewell replied that the fresh air and healthy soil at Chesney Wold would do her good.

The "value" of political campaigns — The Dedlocks arrived the following evening, along with a great many guests. All this social activity now ties into the political activity mentioned in the first paragraph, and the general impression is that the domestic and political activities are more or less equally useless except as a means to extend political influence. Earlier, Dickens mentioned that Sir Doodle was disseminating his influence through gold coins (sovereigns) and beer, both staples of English life and therefore a good way to reach one's fellow countrymen. Such campaigns had the added benefit of keeping the relatives busy. Now, at least, they could ride around to the different campaign speeches and polling sites. Even Volumnia could be put to good use on these occasions, which made the most of her ability to dance, dine, and converse.

Lady Dedlock remains aloof — Through all the comings and goings of the guests, Lady Dedlock did indeed keep mostly to herself. Her health was still poor, so she restricted her appearances till the afternoons or evenings and remained more aloof than usual. Yet she was such a luminary that all she had to do to improve the dull events was to show up. Sir Leicester, too, in his own way outshone the dullness of the many relatives who now surrounded him.

Sir Leicester discusses their campaign with Volumnia — By now it was clear that Sir Leicester considered himself on the side of "England," also known as "the Government." Whoever was on the other side — namely, the "people" — belonged to that part of England that had lost its mind. This all came out in Sir Leicester's talk with Volumnia, who, though naive, had proven herself a more thoughtful conversationalist than Sir Leicester initially believed. She understood enough to affirm that Sir Leicester's side had no opposition, in spite of his assertion that they were only doing "tolerably," which he explained was a gentleman's version of "tolerably" and therefore several cuts above the average. But her naiveté showed itself more distinctly when Sir Leicester had to explain that their side had had to expend large sums of money on "necessary" costs to ensure its position even in its own strongholds. The people simply were not being as supportive as they ought to be. At first, he refused to explain these costs, though here he looked resentfully at some of the cousins and mentioned that Volumnia might hear of rumors accusing their side of bribery. Some people had even suggested that the money that normally went to the Church had been diverted to Parliament.

Volumnia brings up the topic of Mr. Tulkinghorn — Volumnia next brought of the subject of Mr. Tulkinghorn, though Sir Leicester didn't know why: he was neither a candidate, nor was he employed by one. It turned out that Volumnia admired him and wondered where he was. One of the cousins informed them that Tulkinghorn had been called to consult in the ironworks area and that it would be wonderful if he returned soon to give them news of Lord Coodle's defeat there.

Mr. Tulkinghorn arrives — Just at that moment, the servant announced that Mr. Tulkinghorn had arrived and would be staying for dinner. This was delightful news for Volumnia, but Lady Dedlock, who had been sitting by the window the whole time, had a less welcoming reaction. And when the cannon boomed just prior to his entrance and everyone wondered what it was about, she announced that a rat had been shot dead. Sir Leicester gently corrected her and then quickly changed the subject.

Tulkinghorn relays the latest election news — It was a good thing, too, because Tulkinghorn had by now fully entered and seated himself near Sir Leicester. The news from the election front was not good: their party was losing at a ratio of 3 to 1. Furthermore, Mr. Rouncewell, the ironmaster, had been active as a speechmaker in the election against them, and his straightforward simplicity was effective with the people. Even his son, Watt, Rosa's would-be suitor, had helped out a great deal. This was all horrifying to Sir Leicester, who was sure that the floodgates of civilization had broken down altogether. In his mind, it was a good thing for Rosa that she had not gone along with these people to be miseducated by them, when she could do so much better at Chesney Wold. Mr. Tulkinghorn, however, countered that the ironmaster and his people would probably not see it that way — that they, too, had their pride.

Mr. Tulkinghorn reveals Lady Dedlock's secret without mentioning names — Supposedly to illustrate a point, Mr. Tulkinghorn then asked Lady Dedlock's permission to tell a real-life story, though he would not name any names for now. Sitting by the window in the moonlight, Lady Dedlock silently agreed.

Mr. Tulkinghorn's story was of a young girl whom a great lady took under her wing. That same lady had once been in love with an army captain, who became the father of her child. But this captain was associated with poor results in life, and he and the lady never married. She had kept their relationship secret, and when he died, she thought that was the end of it. But through a series of coincidences that Tulkinghorn did not mention, certain parties got wind of it, and ultimately the father of the young girl also learned of it and removed his daughter from the service of the great lady. This was Tulkinghorn's point — that these people could not see the difference between themselves and the most accomplished members of the aristocracy. Having finished, Mr. Tulkinghorn begged Lady Dedlock's pardon for any pain the story might have caused.

Lady Dedlock retires in silence — Afterwards, there was some conjecture by the listeners as to what the story meant, though people had different ideas. Then, the evening being late, Lady Dedlock finally stirred from her stillness and, accompanied by Volumnia, retired to her room.

Chapter 41 — In Mr. Tulkinghorn's Room

An unexpected meeting — Mr. Tulkinghorn had now retired to his turret room at Chesney Wold, and to the extent that he was capable of any emotion, he was content, having accomplished his aim. Still, his mind was not completely settled as he paced the floor of his room and then went out onto the roof to pace further and look up at the stars. As he walked back and forth on the roof, he suddenly realized that he was not alone. Lady Dedlock had come upstairs to his room and was now staring back at him through the glass doors and French window through which he exited onto the roof.

Lady Dedlock's expression — Lady Dedlock's presence created a disturbance in Tulkinghorn, and he found himself trying to define the passion she was restraining despite her outward composure. Eventually he realized he was seeing a combination of anger, fear, and shame. Yet Lady Dedlock's capacity for restraint earned Tulkinghorn's immediate respect. To him, it signified immense personal power.

Tulkinghorn explains why he divulged her secret story — Having now taken note of each other, the two of them entered the room, Mr. Tulkinghorn from the roof and Lady Dedlock from the hallway. Her first question was why he had related her story before so many people. Tulkinghorn answered that it was his way of informing her that he was aware of it. This certainty was new — only days old — though he had harbored suspicions for some time. The part about the young girl, however, was made up, though based on his conjecture of what might actually happen if Rosa's friends and relatives knew.

Lady Dedlock's concern for Rosa and Sir Leicester — Lady Dedlock's next concern was Rosa. What could she do to spare the girl the possibility of such a scenario? Mr. Tulkinghorn was no help here. Following that, she thought only of her husband's welfare. She had expected that she would one day be exposed, and now she was prepared to do whatever was necessary to ameliorate the situation for her husband. Was there something for her to sign or write? She was ready. Mr. Tulkinghorn did not want to trouble her in any regard, but as he continued to study her reactions, he was amazed at her power as an individual.

Mr. Tulkinghorn reasoning about the situation — Lady Dedlock's solution to the evening's events was to leave for good. Her valuables and things were all in order, she had set aside a little money for herself, and she had disguised herself in someone else's dress. Her sole intention now was to disappear, and she had come to tell Mr. Tulkinghorn to convey that she would henceforth be lost to the world. But Mr. Tulkinghorn wouldn't hear of it. He hadn't yet made up his mind as to his next step, and the most important thing to consider now was Sir Leicester. Furthermore, there was no separation between Sir Leicester's feelings and the family honor. Lady Dedlock did not want to continue her age-old charade, but Mr. Tulkinghorn made the strong point that for her to leave would not only put Sir Leicester in a state of shock but also spread the news with great speed that something was dreadfully wrong at Chesney Wold. He had thought carefully about the situation, and it was clear to him that Sir Leicester was deeply in love with her, and the information Mr. Tulkinghorn and Lady Dedlock now shared about her secret past might not change that. In that case, Mr. Tulkinghorn was absolutely convinced that it would be better for Sir Leicester and himself if nothing were said. He wanted to take

Lady Dedlock's needs into account as well, but he flatly stated that he could not make her his primary consideration.

Lady Dedlock understands that she is at Mr. Tulkinghorn's mercy — Being as intelligent and strong as she was, Lady Dedlock immediately knew what that meant. Dickens says that she seemed frozen by the starlight as she confirmed the implications of Mr. Tulkinghorn's statements. She was to remain there and continue the masquerade. If she left, it would be by Mr. Tulkinghorn's determination and timing. He promised to notify her in advance. Otherwise, things would continue as they always had.

Lady Dedlock spends the rest of the night in private agony — Lady Dedlock did not say much more. Having verified that she had understood and that this path was necessary, and having assured Mr. Tulkinghorn that she would vouch for his faithfulness to Sir Leicester should the issue ever arise, she retired to her room. But she did not sleep that night. The controlled presence that had manifested itself in Mr. Tulkinghorn's room was now shed for the agonized woman who paced the floor, her figure contorted, her hands holding the back of her head, her hair wild — all while others slept, and only the sound of footsteps on the Ghost's Walk kept her company.

Things return to almost normal — As the moon faded and the sun rose again over the landscape, Chesney Wold came back to life. All seemed as it had always been, though today Mr. Tulkinghorn looked much older than before — and much closer to the grave.

Chapter 42 — In Mr. Tulkinghorn's Chambers

Mr. Tulkinghorn returns to London to find Mr. Snagsby waiting by his door — Mr. Tulkinghorn's business at Chesney Wold now accomplished, he returned from the fresh countryside to his dusty London chambers. It was evening as he arrived, and the lamplighter was just lighting the street lamps. As he got to the top of the dark stairway, he noticed Mr. Snagsby waiting for him by the door. Mr. Tulkinghorn encouraged him to speak his mind right there, so Mr. Snagsby explained in his longwinded way that Mlle. Hortense had repeatedly showed up at Cook's Court, specifically at Mr. Snagsby's shop. She was looking for Mr. Tulkinghorn, but being refused admittance by his clerk, she resorted to Mr. Snagsby, and that was causing problems with both his naturally jealous wife and his weak-minded, epileptic servant Guster, who had already had one bad fit because of Hortense's fierce looks. Mr. Tulkinghorn promised to resolve the issue, telling Snagsby that he should send her his way if she ever bothered him again.

Hortense arrives right after Mr. Snagsby leaves — That statement was hardly necessary. Mr. Snagsby having just left, Mr. Tulkinghorn had barely let himself into his apartment and retrieved the key to his wine cellar when he noticed Hortense herself at his door. He had just finished grumbling to himself about how women were put on the earth to make trouble, but now he showed his usual imperturbable exterior as he urged her to state her purpose.

Hortense's complaint — Hortense was first of all incensed that she had had such a hard time gaining access to Mr. Tulkinghorn. She felt used and mistreated by him and had come to return the two gold sovereigns he had paid her to obtain information about Lady Dedlock. Actually, she threw them down on the floor to show her contempt. Unruffled, as usual, Mr. Tulkinghorn commented that she must be wealthy if she could afford to fling money around. She replied that she had a wealth of hatred for Lady Dedlock and that it was her rage that motivated her. She was sure Mr. Tulkinghorn knew that and had used her. He, on the other hand, was not so sure, and he now asked her whether she was done.

Mlle. Hortense's demand and Mr. Tulkinghorn's reply — She was not. Her added demand was that Mr. Tulkinghorn either find her a job or hire her to pursue and defame Lady Dedlock, a service Hortense would perform with the utmost enthusiasm. She was convinced that that was his goal as well. Mr. Tulkinghorn contemplated her with his usual indifference and then addressed the situation as he saw it: Mademoiselle Hortense had stated her case and made her demands, and if she didn't get them, she would return again and again until she got what she wanted, if not to him, then to Mr. Snagsby. Having assessed the situation correctly, he advised her to take her money and go. When she refused, he informed her that there was a simple solution for such situations — jail. The wine-cellar key he now held in his head was just a small example of a much larger key that could be used to imprison women like her, who insisted on harassing their neighbors. If she visited either him or Mr. Snagsby again, he would make good on his threat and call the police immediately. They would not be so polite.

Hortense leaves, and life goes on at Mr. Tulkinghorn's — Hortense's fury had switched at one point to polite sarcasm, but with such a clear message from Mr. Tulkinghorn, she now turned and left without another word or look. That wasn't about to disturb his evening, and after retrieving his bottle of expensive aged port, he spent the rest of the evening enjoying it.

Chapter 43 — Esther's Narrative

Esther's efforts to protect Lady Dedlock — True to her promise, Esther went out of her way to protect Lady Dedlock's secret. If the topic of Lady Dedlock came up, she did her best to ignore it, even leaving the room to avoid the conversation. Not wanting to create any new problems for her mother, she focused on the abundant good in her life and evaded the least hint of any contact between them.

Richard's continued poor judgment — That was not difficult at Bleak House, where the main topic was Richard. Nothing had changed. Richard still mistrusted his former guardian and placed his faith in the Jarndyce suit. John Jarndyce still chose to be patient while making every effort to get Richard to change course. Ada continued loving Richard, as only she could, even though she disagreed with his approach. And Esther quietly watched and tried to influence things for the better.

Misgivings about Skimpole; Jarndyce determines to fix things — Neither Esther nor Ada approved of Skimpole's careless influence and his misuse of Richard's money, so one day they mentioned their misgivings to their guardian. At first, Jarndyce simply laughed at the idea. How could Skimpole have a serious influence on anyone? He was such a child, entirely clueless about the world. Esther was unconvinced. In her view, he encouraged Richard in a bad direction. But it was Ada who, in her gracious way, asked the pointed question that obviously disturbed Mr. Jarndyce. She wanted to know how Skimpole had become such a child to begin with. Jarndyce guessed that Skimpole's childhood training had been unbalanced, that he had received too much praise for his impractical, imaginative qualities and had therefore learned to emphasize them. Yet he seemed unsure. Ada, again graciously but pointedly, mentioned that it was a shame he took advantage of Richard financially. There Mr. Jarndyce wholeheartedly agreed and determined at once to change things. Esther tactfully added that Skimpole had accepted a gift of £5 from Mr. Vholes for introducing Vholes to Richard. Again, John Jarndyce began making excuses. He was sure Skimpole had no idea that there was anything wrong with his action. Hadn't he confessed it to her himself? However, they would pay him a visit and straighten things out, and then the young ladies would understand once they saw Skimpole on his own turf.

Mr. Skimpole on his own turf — Mr. Skimpole's rental house — evidently paid for by someone else, if at all — was in a poor section of town inhabited by many Spanish immigrants. Both the house and its fixtures were in a state of disrepair. Esther's impression was of dinginess and dirt with touches of leisurely living: pillows, cushions, a couch, an armchair, a piano, sketching materials, newspapers, and other items related to leisurely pursuits. What food and drink there was made the same impression. Instead of the standard breakfast fare of mutton chops, there was fruit, cake, coffee, and a light wine. Mr. Skimpole, who had been lying on the couch in his morning robe (even though it was noon) got up to greet his guests and show them around. In his usual poetic way, he saw himself as a bird, and this was where he sang … To Jarndyce, this seemed proof of his friend's hopeless impracticality.

Jarndyce tries reasoning with Skimpole — Indeed, Mr. Skimpole's entire family shared that trait. He was about to retrieve his three daughters to introduce them, but Mr. Jarndyce wanted to first discuss his relationship with Richard, or rather, Richard's wallet. He did not think Richard should be paying for both Skimpole and himself. Here Skimpole begged off in his usual way: how could he pay for himself if he had no money? Besides, he didn't understand money and couldn't be held responsible for what happened to it, so his friend Jarndyce's suggestion that he borrow from him instead of taking from Richard seemed nonsensical. Anyway, he hadn't realized that Richard was poor. Mr. Jarndyce added that Richard's faith in the Jarndyce suit was no help in that department and that Skimpole should not encourage it. But Skimpole protested that he didn't know enough about it to encourage anything, his sole motive being to play along with Richard's own enthusiasm. Jarndyce seemed satisfied.

Skimpole introduces his family — Happy the investigation was over, Skimpole now went to fetch his family. His sons had all left by now, but he still had his wife and three daughters, whom he had nicknamed Beauty, Sentiment, and Comedy, according to their strengths — with hairstyles and clothing to match. Each had a real name, too. Beauty was Arethusa, Sentiment was Laura, and Comedy was Kitty. Esther noticed that Skimpole's wife must have once been beautiful but had since become frail and sickly. All were talented in music and art, and not one understood anything about money or time, which distressed Skimpole's wife. The daughters, however, enjoyed and indulged their father's personality, which he described as the least worldly and practical of all. He explained that none of them could cook or sew, but they still had their place in life as admirers of other people's accomplishments. The family didn't know how it survived, but it did, and his daughter Beauty had already propagated the family line by marrying another impractical child and giving birth to two more children. She and her family lived upstairs, and Skimpole had no doubt that his other daughters would someday follow her example.

Obvious evasion and quiet provision — While Ada and Esther were chatting with the girls, they noticed that Mr. Jarndyce was quietly giving Mrs. Skimpole some money. Meanwhile, Harold Skimpole was getting ready to accompany his friends to Bleak House. He had angered the baker, their neighbor, who had kindly loaned the family some armchairs and was unhappy when he found them in dilapidated condition. This made no sense to Skimpole or his daughters, who thought the baker was a "bad" man for being angry. After all, chairs were meant to be used. Skimpole's solution was to disappear for a few days to maintain his good mood. As usual, Esther observed what escaped him — that his family would be left dealing with the baker. But that didn't matter to Skimpole. He was as happy as ever, playing the piano, singing, and drawing as soon as they all arrived at Bleak House.

A visit from Sir Leicester — But that evening the home would be graced by the presence of another unexpected guest — Sir Leicester Dedlock. Esther was too bewildered on hearing of his arrival to escape in time, and she soon found herself being introduced to him by Mr. Jarndyce. Sir Leicester had been passing by on his way from Chesney Wold and wanted to express his regrets that any members of refined society should have been prevented from visiting Chesney Wold or should have received the wrong impression of his family, who had a tradition of hospitality. He wanted to be sure that they understood that any lack of hospitality on his part was reserved only for Mr. Boythorn, and that was due only to external circumstances, which he implied were created by Boythorn. Having made himself clear, Sir Leicester departed as graciously as he came.

Esther feels the need to reveal her secret to her guardian — All this time, Esther had avoided engaging in the conversation or even looking at Sir Leicester, and after he left, she fled to her room to regain her composure. Fortunately, she discovered later that the general opinion was just that she had been shy in the presence of someone of Sir Leicester's stature. But the situation presented a new problem: there was now a high probability that Esther could no longer avoid seeing her mother. She needed her guardian's advice and would therefore have to tell him her secret. There was also a strong likelihood that Mr. Skimpole would try to make himself the beneficiary of Sir Leicester's generosity, and this troubled Esther. She therefore determined to speak to her guardian that evening after everyone had retired.

Surprising revelations and Esther's deep gratitude — Mr. Jarndyce was in his reading room when Esther asked to enter. He received her warmly and gave her his full attention, though with an unusual expression she had noticed only one other time, when he had declined to explain his thoughts. Now, however, she needed his counsel more than ever. Mr. Jarndyce looked startled and confused, unsure why Esther was being so serious. When she mentioned Sir Leicester's visit as the impetus, Jarndyce seemed even more surprised. He could see no relationship between them. But one topic led to another, and he revealed that Boythorn's great disappointment in love earlier in his life had been none other than Lady Dedlock's sister. In her severe way, she had cut off the relationship, insisting that she would henceforth be dead to Boythorn. Still plagued with a sense of guilt at being the supposed cause of others' pain, Esther burst out with the news that Lady Dedlock was her mother and that Lady Dedlock's sister, Miss Barbary, was the godmother she grew up with. Even though Esther understood her own innocence, she would have continued blaming herself had Jarndyce not sent her to bed with gentle, comforting words of wisdom. As Esther fell asleep that night, she felt more grateful than ever, and she wondered how she could ever fully repay him for all he had done.

Chapter 44 — The Letter and the Answer

Mr. Jarndyce's advice — Mr. Jarndyce agreed that Esther should avoid contact with Lady Dedlock, and he would do his best to prevent Skimpole from making things more difficult. Unfortunately, he did not feel competent to advise Lady Dedlock, whose name he preferred not to mention, but if he could ever help her, he certainly would. He had no doubt that she was right in her distrust of Mr. Tulkinghorn, whom he considered "dangerous," and he thought they would be wise to keep their secret to themselves.

Additional concerns — But Mr. Tulkinghorn wasn't Esther's only concern. She had had her doubts about Mr. Guppy and Hortense, the French maid. Fortunately, whatever danger may have existed with Mr. Guppy seemed past. As for Hortense, Mr. Jarndyce chose to see her unusually determined approach to Esther as nothing more than the typical action of an unemployed woman looking for a job. Esther thought her behavior seemed excessive even in that context, but her guardian pointed out that Hortense was prone to rash behavior. The best thing Esther could do was to simply continue being her good, sweet self, and meanwhile, her guardian would watch the situation with the Dedlocks to the degree that he could.

A special letter — At that moment, Esther thought she perceived the unusual look she had noticed before on her guardian's face, and she had the feeling she was beginning to grasp its meaning. Mr. Jarndyce confirmed her thoughts when he mentioned that there was something he had been meaning to speak to her about. He hadn't known how to say it, so he decided he would write it. Esther had produced great changes in him, and for that he was deeply grateful. They agreed that a week from then she should send Charley to pick up the letter, but only if Esther could be absolutely certain that John Jarndyce would remain the same to her regardless of how she responded. If she had the slightest doubt about the integrity of that promise, she should not send Charley. Esther already knew how she felt, and she found it strange that her guardian should claim that she had changed him after all he had done for her.

A marriage proposal — The evening came when Esther was to send Charley to retrieve the letter, and after Charley had deposited the letter and left, Esther sat looking at it for a while. She was thinking of the different phases of her life — how she had evolved from a forlorn little orphan girl to a beloved, happy, useful young woman. She had already guessed the letter's contents, but when she did finally read it, she had trouble processing it and had to reread it several times. Strangely, she found herself crying, not because the letter was lacking in love — in fact, it was full of love and consideration. But as she took in what was essentially a marriage proposal from a man who was all too aware of the vast difference in their ages, she felt that something in her life had died. It was not that she wasn't happy. This was, after all, the opportunity she had been looking for — the chance to do good and express her deepest gratitude to one who had done nothing but good to her, a man whose character she loved and admired deeply and who loved her in spite of the changes in appearance. It was an offer made with tenderness, foresight, and unselfish consideration for Esther's future. To be the mistress of Bleak House was certainly a privilege, and there was no doubt that she was happy, but there seemed to be some loss that went along with it. She tried to encourage herself with her usual self-talk before the mirror, and she thought of Mrs. Woodcourt and how she had predicted this marriage. That thought turned her mind to the flowers left by Allan Woodcourt, and she now took the flowers — since dried — and brought them into Ada's room, where she stood crying over her beautiful sleeping friend. She then returned to her own bedroom to forever burn them and their memory in the candle's flame.

Esther gives her answer — A week went by before Esther said anything to John Jarndyce, but in the meantime, he was his usual cheerful, honest, open self, never prodding her for an answer or even a hint of what she was thinking. The week now over, Esther approached Jarndyce alone. Timid and shaking, she embraced and kissed the man who till now had been her guardian. When he asked her whether that meant that she had accepted his offer, she replied yes. But neither of them said anything to anyone else, and true to Jarndyce's promise, nothing changed.

Chapter 45 — In Trust

Mr. Vholes visits Bleak House — Things went along as usual until one day, when Mr. Vholes paid a visit to Bleak House. His mission was to tell them that Richard was in dire financial straits, yet unlikely to ask for help from such sources as Mr. Jarndyce, who could lighten his burden or at least provide useful advice. Mr. Vholes hadn't come in a professional capacity but as a concerned human being who was at a loss about what to do. Unfortunately, Mr. Jarndyce was in the same position, which was why he summoned Esther, thinking that her friendship with Richard might provide a solution.

Esther proposes to visit Richard — He was right. Esther did have an idea: she could go visit Richard, who was stationed in Deal, near Dover. At first, her guardian objected because of the length of the trip, but Esther insisted, and that same day they all rode to London. By nighttime, both Esther and Charley, who had been sent with her, were on the Kent mail train. As the train rolled along through the night, Esther wondered whether her visit would pay off.

The seaport of Deal — The train arrived in Deal in the early morning, when the fog still lay thick, giving the seaside town a dismal look. But Esther's dreary first impressions improved once she and Charley checked into the hotel. Charley was thrilled that the room was decorated like a ship's cabin, and with the two of them having now freshened up and feeling warm and cozy, they chose to have an early breakfast instead of sleeping. By now, the fog was lifting to reveal a crowd of boats in the harbor, including one newly arrived East India Company ship. That gave Charley plenty to think about as she asked Esther about India, and between the changing light and the bustling seaport, the two of them began to enjoy their surroundings.

Meeting Richard — The next step was to meet with Richard, so Esther and Charley headed over to the barracks. Richard answered immediately, embracing Esther enthusiastically. He had been writing her a letter, which he now crumpled. As Esther looked around, she noticed Richard's messy room and his tired, unkempt look.

Richard foolish dedication to the Jarndyce suit — Esther soon learned that Richard had made the same decision for his Army career as for all his previous careers. His only interest in life still lay with the Jarndyce case, yet he refused to discuss either the case or John Jarndyce. Seeing his stubbornness, she decided not to argue and instead delivered the letter Ada had sent, which Richard now agreed to read.

Ada's offer — Richard moved to the window to read Ada's letter, and when he turned around again, Esther could see that he had been crying. Ada had offered him her entire small inheritance, due to be hers as soon as she came of age. The stipulation was that he would stay with the Army and get his life together. Suddenly, his tears turned to anger as he accused John Jarndyce of trying to separate him from such a loving, noble heart. But Esther wouldn't stand for it, and to her surprise, she reprimanded Richard so forcefully that he immediately relented.

Richard's Army career is over — But Richard didn't feel he could agree to Ada's offer as stated. His time with the Army was up. Aside from his relentless focus on the Jarndyce case, his superiors were fed up with him, and the feeling that he should leave was mutual. Still, with the help of Mr. Vholes, he could invest Ada's gift and live off the interest while pursuing the Jarndyce case.

Esther's disappointment — Esther was dismayed to see a look of false hope brightening Richard's face, but it was no use trying to talk him out of his plans. She then asked for proof that leaving the Army was not just Richard's idea, so he showed her the documents. Disappointed at being unable to help, Esther decided to return to the hotel, where she and Charley would wait until Richard was ready to leave with them for London.

Esther spots Allan Woodcourt — Esther and Charley walked back along the beach, where they saw a crowd gathering around some Navy officers from the East India ship. There was a cheerfulness about the gentlemen and the crowd that met them, and it caught Esther and Charley's attention. Suddenly, Esther grabbed Charley and rushed her to the hotel. She had seen Allan Woodcourt among the recent arrivals and was embarrassed by the change in her looks. But realizing that was an unacceptable reaction, she encouraged herself to take a different attitude. After all, what reason did she have to feel that way?

Esther meets Allan Woodcourt — Her courage now better, Esther adjusted her veil to reveal half her face and then sent Mr. Woodcourt a note. By now, he and his party had arrived in the hotel, and on receiving her message, he came right away to see her. She immediately noticed the pity in his face for her scarred condition, but casting her veil aside, she did her best to keep the conversation lighthearted. They talked about Miss Flite and about Mr. Woodcourt's service in India, which had left him no richer or better off than before, though Esther told him how they had heard of his heroic deeds. He mentioned that he was unlikely to return to India, and he also told her he had been saddened to hear about her illness. However, Esther assured him that she had fully recovered and was happy. Even so, he kept looking at her with great sympathy.

Woodcourt's perceptiveness about Richard — By now, Richard had arrived, and he and Woodcourt greeted each other heartily. As the conversation progressed, it was clear to Esther that Richard's career difficulties had not escaped Mr. Woodcourt. Following an early dinner together, Woodcourt asked about Richard as he retrieved his luggage. He had never seen such a desolate, desperate expression on a young person's face. Esther explained the bare facts and then asked Woodcourt if, once he returned to London, he would keep Richard company as a friend. Her gratitude for that would be boundless, and she blessed him when he readily accepted her trust. When Richard returned and mentioned meeting in London, Woodcourt showed a natural spontaneous enthusiasm for the idea. As the coach drove off, Esther once again observed a look of pity for her on his face, and she was thankful that someone remembered her past self.

Chapter 46 — Stop Him!

Allan Woodcourt wanders into Tom-all-Alone's — It was the wee hours of the morning in Tom-all-Alone's, long after darkness had engulfed its filthy, diseased streets and air. No one was awake at this time of night except Allan Woodcourt, who now wandered the streets from insomnia. His interest as he passed Tom-all-Alone's was not idle curiosity but the genuine compassion of one accustomed to helping those afflicted by squalor, disease, and need.

Woodcourt dresses Jenny's wounded forehead — Wandering down its polluted, muddy central street, Woodcourt found a woman sleeping by a door. He saw that she had had a long, hard journey and that her forehead was wounded. His easygoing, humble, and charitable manner quickly put her at ease as he examined and dressed her wound. While he was doing this, he observed from different clues that she must be married to a brickmaker. He knew from experience that brickmakers were abusive, and it came as no surprise that her husband had gotten himself in trouble. He asked her whether she had children, but she — Jenny — only mentioned Liz's baby, and Woodcourt deduced from this that her own child had died. When he found out that she lived twenty-three miles away, he asked her if she had enough money for a place to stay, which she affirmed. Having finished dressing the wound, he kindly took his leave of her.

Woodcourt notices Jo — As Woodcourt continued down the street, he suddenly noticed something moving in the shadows by the walls of the houses. It was a young boy furtively trying to escape notice. He was haggard and desperate-looking, and he was going out of his way to remain hidden. Something about him looked familiar to Woodcourt, but he couldn't place him.

The chase — Suddenly, both the boy and woman reappeared. She was chasing him and yelling at Woodcourt to stop him. Not knowing whom he was chasing or why but assuming it was for a good reason, he ran after Jo, who escaped his grasp multiple times until Woodcourt finally cornered him. At that point, Jenny arrived, and as soon as she mentioned Jo's name, Woodcourt remembered seeing him at the coroner's inquest.

Woodcourt learns of Jo's disease and Esther's attempt to help — Jo couldn't understand why people wouldn't leave him alone. Hadn't he suffered enough already? Gradually, the story emerged of Jo's illness and how a kind "young lady" had brought him to her home in an attempt to help him. Woodcourt's silent, horrified reaction indicated that he realized the young woman was Esther and that she had contracted her illness from Jo. Jenny expressed a mixture of anger and tears at Jo's ingratitude in running away and at Esther's disfigurement through the disease, though it was unable to mar her lovely figure and her sweetness of character, voice, and demeanor. Jo, too, seemed disturbed by the news of Esther's illness, for he trembled and rubbed his face with the surrounding slime.

Woodcourt questions Jo — Woodcourt's struggle to contain his emotions was so obvious that even Jenny noticed it. Having gotten a hold of himself, however, he began questioning Jo. Where had he been, and why had he come back? Jo replied that he had been gone the whole time, but he was sick and poor, and since no one but Mr. Snagsby ever helped him, he had come back hoping to get some money from him. Woodcourt wanted to know why he had run away from Bleak House after Esther (though none of them directly mentioned her name or the house) tried to help him. This got an upset reaction from Jo, who felt terrible that he had brought harm upon someone else.

Jo tells Woodcourt what happened — As for where he had been, Jo wouldn't answer at first. He seemed afraid that someone was listening and that there would be consequences. He admitted, though, that someone had taken him, and he finally whispered the name in Woodcourt's ear. Woodcourt's response implied that Jo had gotten himself into trouble and was therefore taken by the constable, but he never actually said this. Woodcourt finally learned that Jo had been transported to a hospital, given four half-crowns on his release, and told to never return to London. But now it was a moot point: he was on his way to the grave.

Woodcourt takes Jo away from the slum — Woodcourt assured Jo that he would try to keep that from happening. If Jo would walk with him, he would conceal him until they got to a better hiding place. By now, Jo had learned to trust Woodcourt, and he promised not to run unless he saw "him" (the constable). In the meantime, the sun had risen, so it was important for them to get moving. As they took leave of Jenny, Jo, full of emotion, urged her to tell the "young lady" that he'd never meant her any harm.

Chapter 47 — Jo's Will

Jo follows Woodcourt — The relatively clear air and morning brightness of the city contrasted sharply with the dank, diseased darkness of the slum. As Woodcourt led Jo along the city streets, he occasionally checked to see if the boy was still there but soon realized that it wasn't necessary. Jo was following, though he still watched furtively as he slinked along the walls in case the dreaded Inspector Bucket should appear.

Taking care of Jo's immediate needs — Woodcourt's first concern was to meet Jo's immediate needs — food, medicine, and housing. This was easier said than done. Jo's condition, disgusting and horrifying to many, made him seem neither human nor animal in their eyes. Nor could Woodcourt be sure that Jo would remain in either a hospital or workhouse, the lodging choices that immediately came to mind — so afraid was he of meeting up with Bucket. But first things first. Jo was emaciated and sick, and now a food stand presented itself, so Woodcourt bought the boy some breakfast. At first, Jo, who was on the point of starvation, wolfed the food down, but even food had lost its interest for him, and he eventually set it aside.

"Medicine" for Jo; Woodcourt learns about the veiled lady — Concerned, Woodcourt asked Jo to breathe in, which he did with some difficulty. Likening his body to a heavy cart, he mentioned again that he was "a-moving on," meaning to the grave. Seeing no pharmacy nearby, Woodcourt went into a pub to procure some wine, which he administered to Jo in lieu of medicine. As the doctor considered his next move, he observed that the wine had had a beneficial effect: Jo was eating again and looked brighter. While Jo munched on his food, Woodcourt got him to talk a little, and in that way he learned — to his surprise — about the veiled lady.

Consulting Miss Flite about lodging — By the time Jo had finished, Woodcourt had had the idea of consulting Miss Flite on a possible place for Jo to stay. So they headed over to the old rag and bottle shop, but finding it shut down, they learned from Judy that Miss Flite had moved to nearby Bell Yard.

Miss Flite was thrilled to see her beloved doctor again, and she was just as honored to be asked for advice. She had taken over Gridley's old room, and that reminded her of Mr. George, who was sure to have a solution. So off they went to the Shooting Gallery, luckily nearby, where Miss Flite introduced the doctor to "General George."

Woodcourt explains his mission — Mr. George was pleased to meet Woodcourt, who also had a good impression of the former trooper. Mistaking Woodcourt for a sailor at first, George quickly learned of his role as a ship's doctor and his mission to find Jo a place to stay. That Jo wanted to keep his whereabouts hidden from Bucket was no surprise to George, who acknowledged Bucket's odd behavior. Yet in spite of Jo's insistence on secrecy, Woodcourt wanted Mr. Jarndyce and Esther to know of Jo's return, in case they wanted to see him. That, in part, was why he wanted to find him a place among good people, and Woodcourt wondered if Mr. George knew of anyone nearby.

Mr. George offers to take Jo in — By now, Mr. George had taken note of Jo, who had been waiting in the entranceway. Meanwhile, Phil had also appeared and was winking encouragingly at Mr. George.

Mr. George's response to Woodcourt was that he would be pleased to do anything that was of service to Miss Summerson, and though their place wasn't much, they would take in the boy for free except for meals. However, he added, there was a chance they could be evicted, but as long as they were there, the boy was welcome.

Mr. George asks about Jo's health — Mr. George then asked whether Jo was infectious, since they had had more than their share of illness already. Allan Woodcourt was sure he was not, but he affirmed that the boy himself was gravely ill. Hearing that, Mr. George decided they should waste no time getting him off the street.

Jo as utter outcast — Dickens takes a moment here to note that Jo lacked the interest of an African native or other exotic philanthropic case. The filth, slime, and disease that made him unrecognizable as a human being were born and bred on English soil. There was nothing romantic or exalted about him as a charity case, and Dickens describes him as a kind of untouchable, neither human nor animal — a total outcast. This was also Jo's sense of himself, and being sensitive to other people's cringing reactions, it was with reluctance and discomfort that he now came forward.

Practical compassion: a bed, bath, clothing, medicine — Still, Jo was able to recognize genuine kindness, and now he expressed his thanks and respect to Mr. George. Mr. George, for his part, was intent on getting Jo a comfortable bed. Phil, too, had great empathy for Jo, having himself been found in a gutter as an infant. Mr. George's next idea was to get Jo a bath and some new clothes, so Jo and Phil went off together to take care of that. Mr. Woodcourt happily donated some money to the cause and left to buy more medicine as well. Miss Flite was overjoyed that her original idea had met with such success, but remembering her need to be in court, she excused herself.

Mr. George asks about Woodcourt's attitude toward Esther — When Woodcourt returned, he found Mr. George pacing the floor, so he joined him. Mr. George wanted to know whether Woodcourt's concern for Jo was related to Esther Summerson's earlier interest in the boy. He added that that was certainly true of him, and when Woodcourt agreed, Mr. George glanced at him with apparent approval.

Mr. George's anger over Tulkinghorn's tactics — But Mr. George had other things on his mind as well. He knew where Bucket had taken Jo in Lincoln's Inn Fields, and he revealed the place as Mr. Tulkinghorn's. Jo's connection to Bucket and Tulkinghorn had been a certain dead man. Woodcourt vaguely remembered Mr. Tulkinghorn's name and appearance. When he asked Mr. George for more details, Mr. George went into a tirade about Tulkinghorn's cruel character and manipulative methods. He explained that he was the man who could evict him and that he was constantly playing power games, refusing to deal with Mr. George directly. He was glad they would never meet in combat, because if they did, he knew Tulkinghorn would be struck down in an instant.

Woodcourt informs Mr. Jarndyce about Jo — By this time, Jo and Phil had returned, so Dr. Woodcourt gave Jo some medicine, left instructions, and went home to take care of his own needs. That did not include sleeping, which he skipped in favor of informing of Mr. Jarndyce of Jo's situation. From Jarndyce, he learned that there were strong reasons for keeping the matter to themselves, and the two of them went back to Mr. George's to visit Jo, whose "cart" had grown heavier in the meantime.

Jo asks to have a message delivered to Mr. Snagsby — It had become clear by now that Jo was dying, and he requested that someone tell Mr. Snagsby, which Woodcourt finally did. Snagsby had to first overcome the discomfort he felt at being constantly watched by his wife. Moreover, he was confused about all the secrecy: first, an admonition for secrecy by Mr. Bucket, and now the warning to keep things secret from Mr. Bucket. It made no sense to him, and he was overwhelmed.

Snagsby visits Jo — But Mr. Snagsby's compassion was greater than his confusion, and that evening, he visited Jo. Nothing could have made Jo happier. Grateful that he was warm and comfortable, Jo now confided his deep sorrow at having transmitted his illness to Esther. He was impressed and thankful that she had even come to visit him the day before and that she had shown no trace of anger or resentment. He said he was so moved that he had had to turn away at one point, and he noticed the same reaction in other people. He added that the doctor had also cried over him, and it was clear that Jo was grateful for all the kindness.

Mr. Snagsby promises to write Jo's apology — Mr. Snagsby's compassion had been aroused as soon as he neared Jo's bedside, and he had already deposited three half crowns there as a token of his caring. But Jo had a different request. He wanted Mr. Snagsby to write his apology in large letters for all to see. He never intended to hurt anyone, and he was sorry he had caused anyone harm. He would be grateful if this could be done after he died. He knew Mr. Woodcourt had suffered because of Esther's illness and disfigurement, and he hoped to gain his forgiveness through this apology. Mr. Snagsby agreed, causing Jo to laugh with gratitude and happiness over his kindness. Depositing yet another half crown, Mr. Snagsby left his little friend for the last time.

Jo's final days — Over the next few days, Jo lay under the watchful eyes of Phil, who nursed him; of Mr. George, who shared his energy and cheer; of Mr. Jarndyce, who visited often; and of Dr. Woodcourt, who attended to him regularly. One day, Jo, now on his last legs, dreamt that he was back in Tom-all-Alone's, and he was relieved to see Allan Woodcourt by his side, assuring him that that wasn't the case.

Jo's final moments — When Jo had rested a while, Allan quietly asked him if he had ever prayed. The only prayers Jo had ever heard were Mr. Chadband's or those by other men who sometimes came to Tom-all-Alone's. But Jo's impression had always been that they were praying to themselves. Jo relayed this with difficulty, and it was clear that he was fading fast. Now he told Allan that he wanted to be buried next to Nemo in the graveyard behind the gate where he had swept. Nemo had always been kind to him, and they had had a connection. Allan promised to do so. After Jo thanked him, he told the doctor how everything was turning dark, and he wondered whether a light would soon appear. As Jo's senses faded, Allan leaned over and gently asked him to repeat the "Our Father," phrase by phrase. By "Hallowed be Thy ...," the light Jo had been waiting for had come, and Jo's little earthly life was over.

Chapter 48 — Closing In

Darkness under the glitter — With the stylish elite now back in London, Chesney Wold was once again deserted for the town residence and high-society gatherings. At the center of all this fashionable bustle, Lady Dedlock still maintained her regal position in spite of the recent distressing events in her life. And Mr. Tulkinghorn still lurked in the shadows watching, as he had always done. On the surface, little had changed, and only they were aware of the recent meeting that transformed their relationship forever.

Lady Dedlock dismisses Rosa — Happiness had not been one of Lady Dedlock's constant companions, and now that matters had become even more uncomfortable, there was no chance it would ever enter her life. But it still lay within her power to ensure happiness for a few other people, and right now, the person most strongly on her mind was Rosa — young, beautiful, affectionate Rosa, who loved and believed in Lady Dedlock and had seen a tender side of her few had experienced. Lady Dedlock had determined that it would be best for Rosa to go with Mr. Rouncewell, the ironmaster, and now she informed her in private that the arrangements had already been made — he was to arrive that same day. Rosa protested, but Lady Dedlock explained that it would be better if Rosa did not experience the change about to happen in her.

Lady Dedlock's change in attitude — Earlier in the chapter, a languid male cousin had compared Lady Dedlock's increased appearance of arrogance and indifference to Lady Macbeth (without naming that character directly), and the rest of the chapter plays on that allusion. Now Lady Dedlock wasted no time in creating the shift in her exterior character. Having made her decision about Rosa, she left the unhappy girl to wait in the room by herself, and when Lady Dedlock emerged later, it was clear the shift was complete.

Mr. Tulkinghorn in the shadows — Lady Dedlock's first step regarding her decision was to inform Sir Leicester, who was sitting in his study. Mr. Tulkinghorn was there, too, lurking unobtrusively. He asked whether Lady Dedlock would prefer that he leave, but when she indicated that she would tolerate his presence, he moved to the window and stood there, looking out. The view — a stately yet lifeless street — held no interest for Lady Dedlock as it was. Yet Mr. Tulkinghorn's darkening presence was no improvement, and Lady Dedlock would have been happier with him gone.

Lady Dedlock tells Sir Leicester; Mr. Rouncewell takes Rosa — Lady Dedlock pretended to be tired of the matter with Rosa and informed Sir Leicester of the arrangements she had made and the fact that Mr. Rouncewell had already arrived. Unaware of her real motives, Sir Leicester at first argued against Rosa's leaving. Lady Dedlock had been fond of her company, and Rosa stood to lose many advantages by leaving. By now, Mr. Rouncewell had arrived in the room, and in his presence Lady Dedlock made it clear that Rosa was a good girl and that she had nothing bad to say about her. But if Mr. Rouncewell's son still had any interest in Rosa, then she would be better off going. Mr. Rouncewell had done his best to dissuade his son from that, but he confessed that he had not been wholly successful. That said, the three of them agreed that Rosa should go with him right then and there. Rosa herself was sobbing, which prompted Mr. Tulkinghorn to come out of the shadows and observe that she did not appear to want to go after all. But Mr. Rouncewell quickly came to the rescue, explaining that she lacked breeding and experience. Unable to argue, Mr. Tulkinghorn acquiesced in spite of Rosa's tearful protests, and Rosa went off with Mr. Rouncewell.

Tulkinghorn breaks his agreement with Lady Dedlock — Lady Dedlock seemed paler than before, in spite of now having taken care of the issue on her mind. That evening, Sir Leicester had to attend to some Parliamentary business, so Lady Dedlock planned to eat alone. On asking whether Mr. Tulkinghorn had left yet, she discovered that he wanted to meet with her, so she agreed to see him during her dinner hour. Mr. Tulkinghorn got right to the point. In his view, she had broken their agreement to keep everything as usual, and she was therefore not trustworthy. That meant that he could also break his side of the agreement. Lady Dedlock quickly surmised that this was the short notice he had mentioned in their meeting in the turret room. She asked whether he intended to tell Sir Leicester that night. No, but there was a chance that it could happen the next day, however, he would not tell her anything definite. One thing Lady Dedlock knew — Tulkinghorn would have no mercy on her. But she remained silent on this, though she gave him a harsh look at one point. In their final exchange, she asked him whether he was going home or staying. He answered that he was going home.

A silent world fails to warn Mr. Tulkinghorn — Mr. Tulkinghorn checked his watch against the great clock, yet the clock, though it told time perfectly, could not warn Tulkinghorn to not go home. The grand houses that held the secrets he knew so well also stood mute, unable to warn him. Nothing in his surroundings was able to speak the words he needed to hear.

Lady Dedlock goes for a walk; the sound of gunshot disturbs the silence — Meanwhile, Lady Dedlock took the keys from her servant and went out into the moonlit, star-studded night to take a walk, presumably to relieve her headache. Mr. Tulkinghorn, too, having arrived home, proceeded down to his cellar to retrieve his wine, and as he crossed the courtyard, he noticed how bright and still the night was.

The narrator then spends an entire long paragraph describing the beauty and quiet of the nighttime country and cityscape, as though surveyed from above. The effect is of a deepening stillness — until a sudden shot rings out. There is a momentary disturbance as people open their windows or come out of their homes. Animals react — running, howling, and barking. And then, everything goes back to normal.

A mysterious end — Mr. Tulkinghorn's own rooms were dark, but the pointing Roman Allegory figure on his ceiling now takes on new significance as it seems to hint at the crime committed. The next morning, the horrified cleaners discover Tulkinghorn's body, with a bullet wound to the heart. The shades are drawn, the body is removed, and the investigators arrive to take down the details — the suddenly snuffed candles, the stain on the rug, the unconsumed wine. But for now, the crime remains a mystery, and the pointing Roman can only keep pointing.

The metaphor of light and darkness — From the beginning of the chapter, there is a continuous play on the imagery of light and darkness that has been a theme throughout the book. The first few paragraphs contrast the superficial glitter of upper-crust society with the dark shadows that lurk in its corners, most notably in the figure of Mr. Tulkinghorn but also within Lady Dedlock's unhappy soul. The chapter's main action takes place over the course of one day, beginning in the morning and ending at night under the light of a full moon and numberless stars. Earlier, when Lady Dedlock is informing Sir Leicester of her intentions, as the evening descends and the outside lamps are lit, the view from the window is further obscured by Mr. Tulkinghorn's figure casting its ever lengthening shadow on Lady Dedlock. The imagery of shadow appears again under the trees at night, when Lady Dedlock goes out for a walk to relieve her headache. And they make their final statement in this chapter in Mr. Tulkinghorn's darkened room, though by now the sun has risen. Earlier it had been lit by two candles, but those were quickly snuffed out, along with Mr. Tulkinghorn's life, and only the moonlight remained to light the space. Now, in the daytime, the shades are drawn, and darkness and death fill the room.

Chapter 49 — Dutiful Friendship

Mrs. Bagnet's birthday — Today is Mrs. Bagnet's birthday. No other family member's birthday inspires the same level of celebration and effort, at least not for Mr. Bagnet. That means giving "the old girl" the day off while he does the shopping, cooking, and serving. Mrs. Bagnet plays along in her good-natured way. She even knows what the "surprise" dinner will be, so when her husband asks her what she wants, she simply says "Fowls." She knows he's "secretly" already bought them and will show them off as soon as she says the word. That they're the toughest birds available and that he's not known for his cooking is less important than his enthusiasm. The three children also help out, setting the table and working in the kitchen, while the "old girl" has to stop herself from interfering whenever she sees something about to go dreadfully wrong — like the fowls about to burn on the spit. Luckily, one of the girls recognizes the problem in time, so Mrs. Bagnet can pretend to relax again and enjoy her leisurely birthday.

Talk of Mr. George — Dinner is to be followed by a prompt afternoon visit from Mr. George. Mr. George's company on the old girl's birthday has been a tradition since Mrs. Bagnet was a young woman, and the mention of his name makes her speculate that their friend has the travel bug again. She's convinced that if he resolved his money issues, he would leave. She has noticed a restlessness and anger about him lately, though her husband explains this as the result of George's unhappy association with Mr. Tulkinghorn.

The birthday dinner — The dinner finally makes it to the table, though not as successfully as could have been wished. The poultry is tough, the gravy is flavorless, and the potatoes are falling apart. Still, Mrs. Bagnet would never hurt her husband's feelings, so she cheerfully lets him fill her plate with stringy poultry meat, while she watches him and her son happily eating, oblivious that the food is substandard.

The girls do their best to clean up; Mr. George arrives — Next it was the young daughters' turn to show off their cleaning ability, which they did to the best of their ability. But it wasn't till they were done that Mrs. Bagnet could finally relax, now that the danger of disaster was over. By then, it was time for Mr. George to arrive, which he did right on time in good soldierly fashion. Mrs. Bagnet noticed immediately that he looked pale and distraught. George himself hadn't realized this, and he explained that Jo's death the day before had affected him.

A birthday present from Mr. George; Mr. George's distress — But George wanted to talk about more cheerful things, especially on Mrs. Bagnet's birthday. First, he produced a brooch he'd brought her as a birthday present. There was a lot of ooohing and aahing as Mrs. Bagnet proclaimed it the "beautifullest" thing she had ever seen. For luck, she wanted George to pin it on her, but his hand was shaking, and he nearly dropped it. That upset him, since this was an easy task and one he had no problem with normally. Jo's death obviously still bothered him, and to make matters worse, it reminded him of Gridley, which in turn reminded him of Tulkinghorn's unnatural grip on both of them. Mrs. Bagnet's remedy for all this was to get out the pipe.

Pipes, drinks, toasts, and ... Mr. Bucket? — With both George and Mr. Bagnet smoking their evening pipes and the two girls being ready with the "mixtur" (a festive drink), it was time for the birthday toast. As the party proceeded with speeches and toasts (fortunately short), in came an unexpected guest—Mr. Bucket. He had stopped to look at the musical instruments in the shop window, then noticed the party in the background and recognized Mr. George. He greeted everyone in a warm, friendly manner and even had the two girls sitting on his lap giving him kisses. That won everyone over, and Mrs. Bagnet soon included him in the drinks and pipe smoking. She was especially happy that a friend of George's had stopped by, since that might raise his spirits.

Mr. Bucket ingratiates himself—Bucket was surprised that Mr. George was in low spirits, but the conversation soon turned to other things. Bucket seemed especially interested in whether or not there was a way out of the backyard, even inspecting it personally. Satisfied that there was not, he sat down next to Mr. George and asked him again how he was doing. When George said he was better, Bucket seemed encouraging—after all, what could a strong, healthy man like George have on his mind that would bother him? He emphasized this a couple of times and then turned to Woolwich, soon discovering that he was George's godson and that he played the fife. What a coincidence! He, too, had played the fife as a boy. In no time, he had Woolwich playing as he sang along, and before the evening was over, he got himself invited to Mrs. Bagnet's next birthday party and expressed his hope that she and his wife would become friends.

Bucket and George leave arm in arm—All this time, he never forgot Mr. George, whom he had carefully observed all evening. He even waited to leave until the trooper was ready. After some final socializing and friendly business talk about possibly buying a cello from Mr. Bagnet, Bucket exchanged warm goodbyes with the family and headed out with Mr. George.

Bucket pulls George into a pub—Heading out with George meant taking his arm as they walked down the street, prompting Mrs. Bagnet to comment to her husband on how much Bucket seemed to like George. Eventually, though, the roads became uncomfortably narrow, so George mentioned walking single file as a better option. But Bucket had other things on his mind. After telling George that he needed to talk to him about something, he directed him into a pub and then barred the door with his back.

Bucket arrests George—Suddenly, friendly camaraderie switched to all business as George was taken into custody. Mr. George was surprised. On what charge? After reminding George of his rights and cautioning him to watch what he said, Bucket asked him whether he was aware that there had been a murder. That surprised George, too, and when he learned that Tulkinghorn had been shot, he turned pale and broke into a sweat. Still, he couldn't understand why Bucket suspected him. The whole thing seemed incredible. But Bucket persisted. Where was George the night before? Suddenly, it dawned on Mr. George. It was true—he had been at Lincoln's Inn Fields. Moreover, Bucket knew that he had been there a lot recently and that his relationship with Tulkinghorn had been strained. Next he informed George that Sir Leicester was offering 100 guineas to find the killer, and Bucket figured he might as well get the reward.

Bucket leads George away in handcuffs—Momentarily dumbstruck, Mr. George collected himself and agreed to go. It angered him, though, when Bucket produced handcuffs, but George cooperated. Out of consideration for the trooper's feelings, Bucket had also brought a mantle to cover George. George's last request before they left was for Bucket to pull his hat down so that no one would recognize him. To make things as comfortable as possible for George, Bucket obliged, and together they headed back out into the night.

Chapter 50 — Esther's Narrative

Esther visits a sick Caddy — When Esther returned, she discovered that Caddy was ill. By now, Caddy had given birth to an infant girl named after Esther, her godmother. Little Esther was herself unhealthy, with low energy, dark veins in her face, and shadows under her eyes. But Caddy was used to it and didn't let it prevent her from planning for her little girl's future.

A temporary transfer to London — But now Caddy was sick, too, so Esther visited her daily. These constant visits prompted John Jarndyce to transfer the whole Bleak House family to their London residence, partly to reduce Esther's traveling but also because the following day was Ada's 21st birthday, and London seemed a better setting.

Allan Woodcourt examines Caddy — Jarndyce's next concern was for Caddy's health. Esther guessed it would be a matter of weeks before she recovered, so Jarndyce suggested getting a second opinion from Woodcourt. Esther had no objections, but the suggestion surprised and confused her, and she thought she sensed Ada's thoughts returning to when Woodcourt left Esther a farewell gift of flowers.

Esther tells Ada about her engagement — That night, at midnight, Esther was the first to wish Ada happy birthday, and she then broke the news of her engagement to Jarndyce. Ada was thrilled, and Esther felt relieved at eliminating her own doubts about her association with Woodcourt. Later that day, they all quickly settled into their London residence, and even with Richard absent, they had an enjoyable birthday dinner with Allan Woodcourt.

Caddy's unselfishness and Esther's kindness — Caddy's illness dragged on for several months, and in that time, Esther came to appreciate her even more as she learned the extent of her thoughtfulness. In spite of her own weakness, Caddy still thought mostly of her family's needs. During that time, Esther made things as cheerful and comfortable as possible for Caddy, improving the room, reading to her, talking to her, or working next to her.

Caddy's visitors — Among Caddy's frequent visitors were Ada and, of course, Prince, who looked in on her throughout the day. To make him feel better, Caddy would lie about her real condition. Mrs. Jellyby also visited once in a while, though she was easily distracted by Borrioboola-Gha. Then there was Caddy's father-in-law, whose long eloquent speeches granting her every desire during her illness contrasted with her own real consideration for his needs at all times. But he had his "Deportment" to keep up, and he managed to move Caddy, though Esther wasn't convinced. Finally, there was Caddy's father, Mr. Jellyby, who did little more than sit in silence, leaning his head against the wall after asking Caddy how she was.

Woodcourt becomes Caddy's doctor — Allan Woodcourt was now Caddy's regular doctor, and Caddy soon began to recover under his constant expert care. That gave Esther a little more time to herself. She usually left as Woodcourt was arriving, though they still saw each other a fair amount. By now, she was comfortable around him, having settled her future in her mind. As for Woodcourt's own future, it was still undecided. He helped his former teacher, Mr. Badger, but he had no permanent job as of yet.

Esther notices that Ada is sad — Around that time, Esther noticed a disturbing change in Ada. Their conversations were no longer as open, and there seemed to be a wall between them. Esther convinced herself that it had to do with her own engagement to John Jarndyce — that Ada felt something was wrong with that situation — so Esther tried to counteract that by acting perpetually cheerful and busy.

Woodcourt might go abroad; Ada sheds tears — Unfortunately, it didn't work, and one night as the three of them were sitting together, John Jarndyce brought up the subject of Woodcourt. Jarndyce had a high regard for the young doctor but thought he had noticed a sense of disappointment in him recently. It didn't seem likely to him that Woodcourt would remain in England. Instead, he believed he would be going abroad again for a long time. Esther, who had acted cheerful throughout the conversation, commented that he would always carry their good wishes with them. Ada had been quiet the whole time, but when Esther looked up at her, she noticed that Ada was crying.

Esther tries speaking with Ada — After trying to comfort Ada, Esther took her upstairs and tried to talk to her, but Ada couldn't bring herself to discuss what was on her mind. Esther tried to reassure her, but Ada did not agree that nothing was wrong, and she seemed surprised that Esther should think so.

Esther wonders about Ada's secret — Esther returned to Ada's room after Ada had fallen asleep. Even in her sleep, Ada seemed grieved about something, and Esther wondered again what it was. Recently, she had noticed Ada working on something, but Ada hadn't been open about that, either. It also seemed significant that Ada slept with one hand beneath her pillow. That night, Esther fell asleep wishing she could restore Ada to her old self, but the new day brought no change.

Chapter 51 — Enlightened

Woodcourt gets Richard's address — True to his promise to befriend Richard, Woodcourt immediately went to Vholes to get Richard's address. That was easier said than done. Vholes spent a considerable amount of time digressing, hinting that he wanted money in return, his main excuse being that Richard was playing high stakes and needed funds. But Woodcourt had a strong focus and determined character, and he eventually learned that Richard lived in the neighboring second-floor apartment.

Richard is dejected — When Woodcourt entered, Richard was staring vacantly, a book in his lap. It was obvious he was depressed. The reason, of course, was the Chancery suit, the only thing Richard could focus on, though it did him no good. At least, Woodcourt accepted him as he was. Richard was adamant, though, that he was working on the suit for both Ada and himself. He did not want to appear selfish to his friend.

Esther and Ada visit Richard — This took place around the time that Esther started caring for Caddy, and hearing about it from Woodcourt, Esther feared again that Ada's inheritance would disappear because of Richard's actions. She therefore suggested to Ada that they both go see Richard, and she was surprised when Ada seemed willing but unenthusiastic.

Richard praises Woodcourt — Off they went to Symond's Inn and poked around until they found Richard's apartment, though somehow Ada always knew which way to go. On entering, they found Richard engrossed in the Jarndyce case, as usual. After greeting them warmly, he informed them that Woodcourt had left just a short while earlier. He went on to tell them how cheerful and faithful Woodcourt was in spite of his heavy work load. The only thing he lacked was Richard and Vholes's optimism about the Jarndyce case, but Richard attributed that to Woodcourt's lack of knowledge.

Richard refuses to take a break — Esther quietly blessed Woodcourt in her mind and then, looking around at the dusty room and Richard's haggard, anxious face, Esther wondered aloud whether the place was good for his health. She suggested a break might be in order, but for Richard, a break was out of the question. The suit would end at some point, if he didn't die first, but he was convinced it would resolve in his and Ada's favor. Esther couldn't see Ada's face as Richard addressed them both with almost military determination and enthusiasm, but Esther had come to distrust such outbursts, which only masked his misery. He must have seen it in her face, because he admitted to sometimes being extremely tired. He found the case exhausting.

Ada reveals that she and Richard are married — Ada had been quiet the whole time. As she lovingly embraced Richard, she informed Esther that she would not be returning to Bleak House. She and Richard had been married for more than two months. Her time at Bleak House was over, and she urged Esther to go home without her.

A light dawns — Esther's reaction was mixed. She mostly felt sorry for them, but she was also happy that they loved each other. As she sat between, just like in the early days, they told her about how they had gotten married one day while Esther was busy caring for Caddy. Ada had tried offering Richard all she owned, but he refused to take it, leaving her no other way of helping but marriage. Her quandary had been how to tell Esther and Jarndyce. For two months, she struggled in silence, only wearing her wedding ring while she slept. Esther had already guessed this from seeing Ada's hand under the pillow. Now the last two months suddenly made sense, and Esther silently chided herself for not thinking of it.

A hole in Esther's life — Esther remained cheerful while there, but as soon as she left, she started sobbing. Suddenly, there was a hole in her life. She tried talking herself out of her unhappiness but then realized it was a natural reaction and gave herself room to cry. Once home, she found her guardian gone, so she decided to go back to Symond's Inn that evening with Charley, not to visit but just to be near her beloved Ada. Charley was the only one who knew about it, and after looking up at the window, Esther quietly went up to the apartment door by herself, kissed it, listened for her friends' voices, and left again.

Jarndyce laments Bleak House's emptiness — By now Mr. Jarndyce was back, having gone out earlier to find out about Jo. Neither of them knew at that point that he had died. Looking at Esther, Jarndyce noticed that she had been crying, and when he saw Ada's empty chair, he immediately guessed that Ada and Richard were married. His reaction was the same as Esther's: he felt sorry for them. Sighing, he added that Bleak House was emptying quickly. But Esther's answer, though shy, was that its mistress was still there and would do everything she could to make it a cheerful place. Jarndyce smiled — he was sure she would succeed. Yet Esther secretly doubted whether she had lived up to her new role since the day she answered his letter several months ago.

Chapter 52 — Obstinacy

News of Tulkinghorn's murder and George's arrest — A day later, Esther and John Jarndyce were shocked to learn from Woodcourt that Mr. George had been arrested for the murder of Mr. Tulkinghorn. Sir Leicester's sizable reward made no sense to Esther until she learned that Tulkinghorn had been his lawyer, and in that moment she remembered how much her mother had feared and disliked him.

The idea that Mr. George could be guilty seemed strange to all. His strength, honesty, and compassion had made such a good impression that it seemed impossible. Yet numerous facts spoke against him: his presence near the murder scene, his obvious dislike of Tulkinghorn, his violent outbursts. However, Jarndyce agreed with Esther that they could not desert Mr. George, no matter what the evidence. Woodcourt added that he would be seeing him at the prison, and Jarndyce offered to join him. Meanwhile, Esther had made it her mission to prevent further suspicion of any innocent individuals, so she too decided to go along.

Mr. George is relieved to see his friends — Considering where he was, Mr. George was in good spirits, true to his trooper nature. He claimed that his unsettled life had made it easy for him to adjust to such places. His main worry had been that his friends might judge him unfairly, but now as he welcomed them to his cell, he felt a wave of gratitude and relief.

Mr. George refuses the help of a lawyer — Mr. Jarndyce's first concern was for Mr. George's comfort, and he urged George to get in touch if he needed anything. Jarndyce's second concern was that George needed a lawyer, since honest evidence was not enough even if the defendant was innocent. But Mr. George wanted nothing to do with lawyers. For the moment, the case had been delayed as Mr. Bucket collected more evidence. Mr. George was sure that his innocence would prove itself, and he preferred to have it determined honestly. He disliked the usual legal methods, claiming that a lawyer might prove him innocent through underhanded means, but he would rather die having been proven guilty through honest evidence. Besides, there was more to it. His name had been disgraced and his home and belongings turned upside down. He also knew that if he had led a more conservative lifestyle in the past, he would not be under suspicion now. It wasn't just a matter of being set free: he wanted his name cleared. He would not change his mind, nor did he want any of his relatives to suffer because of him.

Mrs. Bagnet rants about George's stubbornness — During his speech, George had paused a moment at the sound of his cell door opening. The new visitors were Mr. and Mrs. Bagnet, whom George now greeted warmly, introducing them as good friends. He explained that he had been arrested at their house, a bitter memory for Mr. Bagnet, who felt duped by Mr. Bucket. The Bagnet's had heard part of George's speech just now, and Mrs. Bagnet (at her husband's prompting) started ranting about how stubborn and nonsensical George was to refuse legal help. He had always been like that — insisting on doing things his way and impossible to convince otherwise. Mr. Jarndyce was impressed by Mrs. Bagnet's honesty and common sense, but none of that made a dent in George's stance. Knowing the situation was hopeless, Mrs. Bagnet changed the subject and offered George the food basket she had brought. Hopefully, he wasn't too stubborn to accept that. She continued ranting, but her manner was friendly, too, and George received her scolding good-naturedly.

A sudden recollection — Between rants, Mrs. Bagnet had motioned with her eyes to Esther that she wanted to meet the Jarndyce group outside and that they should leave ahead of the Bagnets. As Esther, Jarndyce, and Woodcourt headed towards the door, Mr. George suddenly noticed Esther's size and shape. She distinctly reminded him of a cloaked figure that had passed him on Mr. Tulkinghorn's stairs the night of the crime. He remembered that the person had a fringed mantle, and the resemblance to Esther was so strong that he almost spoke to the person. But he dismissed the incident as unrelated, though the impression had struck him.

Mrs. Bagnet's plan — It didn't take long for the Bagnets to join the Jarndyce group outside the prison. Mrs. Bagnet looked flustered, and her tears revealed her real feelings. George's past had put him in a difficult position, and she feared a bad outcome. Jarndyce assured her that the right counsel and a wise approach could counteract that. But Mrs. Bagnet was concerned about George's obstinacy — although she had a solution. She would retrieve his mother, and she would do so immediately. Impressed with her honesty and determination, Jarndyce offered her money for the trip, but she claimed she didn't need it. With fond kisses and instructions to her husband to take care of the children, Mrs. Bagnet set out for Chesney Wold, armed only with an old gray cloak and umbrella, her steady companions on all her journeys. Looking after her, Mr. Jarndyce expressed concern. But her husband explained that there was no need: what the old girl said, the old girl did. And she had proved herself many times.

Chapter 53 — The Track

Mr. Bucket gets serious — Mr. Bucket was generally relaxed in his approach to humanity, and he enjoyed spending time with his wife, herself an amateur detective. But lately he had no time to go home as he pursued his investigation of the Tulkinghorn murder.

Tulkinghorn's funeral — The day of Tulkinghorn's funeral drew a huge crowd and an equally huge number of carriages representing the different aristocratic families. For the most part, though, only the coachmen were present, the carriages themselves being empty. Sir Leicester, however, was there, along with a few others. Mr. Bucket was also there, seated in his own carriage, examining the crowd at Lincoln's Inn Fields from behind the coach's blinds. For a while, he was particularly distracted by the sight of his wife, who stood on the steps of Tulkinghorn's former residence, accompanied by their new female lodger. But then his carriage began to move, ultimately depositing him near the Dedlocks' London home, his next stop.

Anonymous letters — Mr. Bucket had his own key, so he let himself in and was immediately informed by the doorman that he had another letter. Mr. Bucket was not a great letter writer, especially since letters were often used as incriminating evidence in court, so the fact that he had received six letters in one day was unusual. This was not the first of its type, either. Both the handwriting and the message were identical, and the anonymous message simply read: Lady Dedlock. On one level, Mr. Bucket was not impressed. As far as the reward was concerned, the information was superfluous. But he filed the letter away along with the others.

The daily progress report — Mr. Bucket then decided to look in the library to see if any other letters sent to the house had the same handwriting. But none did, and he determined to speak to Sir Leicester about it the next morning. Later that evening, he joined Sir Leicester, Volumnia, and the exhausted cousin in the drawing room, in accordance Sir Leicester's wish for a daily progress report. To this end, Sir Leicester was ready to see Mr. Bucket in private, if necessary, at any time of day. And he was willing to spend any amount of money to do right by Mr. Tulkinghorn's memory and repair any incidental damage to his own name and house.

Volumnia is curious, but Mr. Bucket remains silent — For the moment, however, Mr. Bucket refrained from reporting any news. The lack of information aroused the curiosity of Volumnia, who tried to extract more information. But although the case was nearly complete, Mr. Bucket had an official obligation to remain silent on the details. He then set up an appointment with Sir Leicester for the morning and bid them all goodnight, having been dismissed by Sir Leicester. Before leaving, however, he wondered why Sir Leicester had posted the bill of reward in the stairway. Sir Leicester did not hesitate to explain that he wanted all to understand the magnitude of the crime and his determination to solve it and punish the killer. He was willing to take it down if Mr. Bucket objected, but Mr. Bucket agreed that it should remain, having already been posted.

Bucket engages "Mercury" in conversation — Shortly after his conversation with Sir Leicester and his cousins, Mr. Bucket was warming himself by the fire and having a seemingly casual conversation with "Mercury," the doorman. First he asked about his height. According to Mercury, he was 6'3". Mr.

Bucket had developed a method of making flattering remarks or adjusting himself to the interests of whomever he was dealing with. He would then interject stray comments related to what he was trying to find out. In this case, he urged Mercury to model and then inserted various comments and questions about Lady Dedlock. Was she out for the night? Yes, she had gone to dinner. Did she go out often. Every night … and so on.

Mr. Bucket learns a few facts about Lady Dedlock — Just then, Lady Dedlock herself arrived. She briefly addressed Mr. Bucket, asking if he had learned anything new and then proceeded up the stairs and out of sight, noting the reward bill on the way. Mr. Bucket commented to Mercury that she looked lovely but unwell, and through his questioning he discovered that Lady Dedlock regularly had headaches, that she tried to walk them off, and that she had gone on one of her walks the night of the murder. He managed to pin down the exact time she left and the fact that Mercury let her out. Furthermore, he had personally witnessed the moment, having passed the house on his way to see his aunt that night. and he had noticed that Lady Dedlock was wearing a fringed mantle. Wasn't that so? Yes, it was. Mr. Bucket thanked Mercury for the conversation, encouraged him once more to model, and retired to his room in the Dedlock's mansion. But his work was not yet over.

Chapter 54 — Springing a Mine

A private meeting — The next morning, Mr. Bucket met with Sir Leicester in the library. Sir Leicester mentioned that Lady Dedlock would also be interested in hearing Mr. Bucket's findings, but Mr. Bucket stated emphatically that the meeting had to remain strictly private. He even requested permission to lock the door, making sure to block the keyhole for complete privacy.

Mr. Bucket prepares Sir Leicester — Their privacy now guaranteed, Mr. Bucket first informed Sir Leicester that he had completed the case, although it had turned out that the perpetrator was neither the trooper nor even a man, but a woman. This came as a shock to Sir Leicester, who leaned back in his chair and listened, silent and motionless. But Bucket reasoned that Sir Leicester, being a well-bred gentleman, should be able to handle any information, regardless of how shocking. Furthermore, he should not be perturbed by Mr. Bucket's knowledge of his family's private doings.

Sir Leicester defends Lady Dedlock — It was time now for Mr. Bucket to mention Lady Dedlock, and as soon as he did so, Sir Leicester sat forward with an intense look. He would appreciate leaving Lady Dedlock's name out of the conversation. Mr. Bucket wanted to as well, but it wasn't possible — Lady Dedlock was central to the action. By now, Sir Leicester was angry, and he warned Mr. Bucket that he had better watch what he said about a lady of her standing. But Mr. Bucket informed him that he was simply relaying what was necessary, and as Sir Leicester collected himself, Bucket told him about Tulkinghorn's longtime mistrust of Lady Dedlock. Now Sir Leicester was furious. Tulkinghorn would not have been safe from him, had he known.

Mr. Bucket explains Lady Dedlock's involvement — Mr. Bucket remained calm. These last two days he had more than once contemplated Sir Leicester with a look that was both serious and compassionate. Mr. Bucket quietly continued. He had heard from Tulkinghorn of Lady Dedlock's one-time lover, before she married Sir Leicester. In Mr. Bucket's opinion, she and the deceased man should have married, but things turned out differently. He also knew that she visited his grave, disguised as her maid, and that she had gone out the night of the murder and probably exchanged words with Tulkinghorn. There was also the detail of the fringed black mantle that the trooper had seen on the woman on the staircase. Having summed things up, Bucket now encouraged Sir Leicester to question Lady Dedlock in person and to emphasize to her that is was pointless to deny her actions.

Sir Leicester's pain and consternation — Mr. Bucket hinted that there was more, but Sir Leicester needed a break. Lady Dedlock was his great love and the center of his life, and Mr. Bucket's information had struck at his core. His face, which he had buried in his hands, was now as white as his hair, his speech had slowed, and the sounds that broke his silence did not qualify as words. Why had Mr. Tulkinghorn said nothing? To Sir Leicester, it seemed out of character. Bucket ventured that he was probably about to inform Sir Leicester and that he had already warned Lady Dedlock of his intention.

A commotion in the hallway — They were interrupted by the sound of voices in the downstairs hallway, and Bucket guessed that the commotion had to do with Tulkinghorn's death and that he had better deal with it immediately. All he asked from Sir Leicester was that he support him occasionally with a nod of his head. Sir Leicester agreeing, Mr. Bucket promptly returned with two Mercurys carrying Grandfather Smallweed, followed by Mr. Chadband and his wife, and finally, Mrs. Snagsby. After introducing himself to them and learning the names of all the guests, Mr. Bucket asked them to state their business in visiting Sir Leicester.

Mr. Smallweed's business — Mr. Smallweed went first. When his late brother-in-law Krook died, the Smallweeds found some letters stashed away in his belongings. They were love letters, signed by one "Honoria" to Captain Hawdon. Now Honoria was an unusual name, and wasn't it relevant to this household? And what about the child they had together? He claimed to have given the letters to his good friend Mr. Tulkinghorn, though Bucket knew he had sold them for a good price, and he said so. Smallweed wanted to know where they were, and he wanted a more thorough investigation of the murder. Mr. Bucket became threatening as he informed Mr. Smallweed to mind his own business when it came to the murder investigation. As for the letters, he had them in his coat, and now he produced them. Mr. Smallweed's next move was to demand £500 for them, but Bucket countered that he must mean £50. No, Smallweed meant £500, so Bucket came back with £250. When Smallweed wouldn't budge, Bucket moved on to Mr. Chadband.

The Chadbands' business — Mr. Chadband could never express himself simply, so he launched into one of his sanctimonious speeches. For what purpose had he and his wife come to the home of the wealthy and powerful? Mr. Chadband clothed his statement with his usual pretentious eloquence, but in blunt terms, they had come to bribe Sir Leicester. In return, they would keep silent about this dreadful family secret. With that, he summoned his wife, the former Mrs. Rachael, who shoved her husband out of the way to tell how she had brought up Esther, Lady Dedlock's supposedly dead child, and conspired with Lady Dedlock's late sister to keep the disgraceful information secret.

Mrs. Snagsby's business — Mrs. Snagsby's motives were more complex and mired in her delusion that her husband was having an affair. She went on and on about how injured she was; how she had followed Mr. Snagsby everywhere in an effort to unravel the great (non-existent) mystery he was hiding; how Jo must have been his son; how Mr. Tulkinghorn had been one of the few to sympathize with her; and how she had helped him and her present companions piece together the information now being presented. She had no interest in money. In addition to honoring Mr. Tulkinghorn and helping her friends, she wanted a separation from her unfaithful husband.

Bucket dismisses the guests and promises to follow up — Mr. Bucket knew better than to believe Mrs. Snagsby's delusions, but he said nothing directly. After a few orchestrated nods from Sir Leicester, who had kept his promise to remain silent, Mr. Bucket next questioned why the guests had made such a commotion on entering the mansion. It seemed counterproductive to their purpose. If their intention was to receive money in return for their silence, then they should have acted appropriately. In his opinion, it was time for them to leave. Mr. Smallweed would not back down from his demand for £500, so Bucket humored him with a tentative promise. Mrs. Chadband, too, wanted to know when to expect a follow-up to their unconcluded business visit. Bucket confirmed that he would be seeing them in the next few days.

Mr. Bucket prepares Sir Leicester for the next round — The guests now gone, Mr. Bucket assured Sir Leicester that their "business" could probably be taken care of without much expense. He then turned to the matter of the arrest, which immediately awoke Sir Leicester out of his stupor. He tried to reassure Sir Leicester that the matter would be completely resolved in the most discreet manner possible. Sir Leicester was therefore not to fret over what he was about to see, and he was still to maintain silence for now. Mr. Bucket then summoned Mercury, who went off to fetch the person about to be arrested.

Mademoiselle Hortense is taken into custody — When the door opened a short while later, it revealed not Lady Dedlock but Mademoiselle Hortense. As he had done with Mr. George, Bucket immediately shut the door and barred it with his back. Mademoiselle had not expected to see anyone else, and after apologizing to Sir Leicester she started to leave but quickly realized that she was trapped. Mr. Bucket then introduced her as his lodger as of several weeks ago. She wondered why Sir Leicester would be interested in that, but Mr. Bucket merely told her that they would find out. She then wanted to know why she had been fooled into coming there, in part by Bucket's wife. Her manner in all this was contemptuous and sarcastic, with no effort at being tactful. When Bucket instructed her to sit down, she refused and asked why, so he informed her that she was being arrested on a count of murder and that she had better keep quiet. By this time, Hortense had cooperated and sat down on the couch, where she kept muttering that Bucket was a devil.

Hortense's contempt — Mr. Bucket then turned to Sir Leicester. He explained that Hortense had had a passionate hatred of Lady Dedlock after the latter fired her and that Mr. Tulkinghorn had paid her handsomely for her help in solving Lady Dedlock's mysterious visit with Jo. Hortense kept inserting her scornful objections to his statements, calling them lies and spitting on Sir Leicester and all that he represented (figuratively, though she apparently literally spat on the rug, too). Mr. Bucket continued to warn her that her words could be used against her, but she didn't care. So with Hortense's interjections in the background, Mr. Bucket proceeded to explain how he had figured out that she was guilty.

Mr. Bucket's intuition and plan — Mr. Bucket had never truly suspected George, but with a lot of evidence against the trooper, Bucket felt he had to take him into custody while he investigated further. Around that time, Hortense had started lodging with the Buckets, and that night, as Bucket sat with his wife and their lodger at dinner, he noticed Hortense's excessive pleasantness on the one hand and her exaggerated grief over Tulkinghorn's death. Something about the way she was holding her knife that evening gave him a sudden insight that she was the murderess. But she had a good alibi — she had been seen at the theater both before and after the time of the murder, so given the level of her cunning, Bucket devised the most elaborate plan of his career and enlisted his wife's own brilliant detective abilities to help him. He would avoid going home for the time being, and Mrs. Bucket was to watch Hortense like a hawk, distracting her with misleading information about Mr. Bucket's progress with the case. Meanwhile, the two of them would secretly exchange information at the baker's or similar places.

The evidence mounts against Hortense — Hortense's next move was to accuse Lady Dedlock of the murder through her anonymous two-word letters sent to Mr. Bucket at the Dedlock home. Staying with the Dedlocks had been part of Mr. Bucket's trap, and it worked. He then brought out the letters to show to Sir Leicester, including one final one addressed to Sir Leicester himself, which read in capital letters: "Lady Dedlock, Murderess." In this matter, as in everything else, Mrs. Bucket had been a faithful spy and witness to Hortense's activities — both her writing and mailing of the letters. She had even gathered together the relevant paper and ink. Mr. Bucket was obviously proud of his wife.

The final pieces — That wasn't all. The wad of paper used to stuff the gun exactly matched the bits of torn paper Mrs. Bucket had found and pieced together. And then there was the murder weapon. Following the funeral, Hortense had suggested to Mrs. Bucket that they go to a country teahouse some distance away. At one point during tea, Hortense left for a while and returned out of breath. Mrs. Bucket later relayed the information to her husband, along with the fact that there was a body of water nearby. That night, Mr. Bucket and his helpers searched the area and found the gun within six hours.

Hortense's arrest — Having concluded his description of the investigation, Mr. Bucket, who had been holding Hortense by the arm, clapped a couple of handcuffs on her. As they stood to leave, Hortense asked where Mr. Bucket's wife was. She was told that she would shortly be seeing her at the police station, to which she replied, in her typical violent manner, that she would love to dismember her. Mr. Bucket was neither surprised nor upset — he had expected it and even retained a sense of humor. To the last, Hortense could not contain herself, hurling cruelties and insults as they left the room.

Sir Leicester's agony — Now by himself, Sir Leicester remained in his silent attitude for a while. During Mr. Bucket's long explanation, he had risen only once — when he heard that Hortense had tried to pin the murder on his beloved lady. But he contained himself quickly and sat back down. Now in his aloneness, he rose again, and his pain rose with him. It was as if his whole life were under attack — his home, his reputation, his heritage. But most of all, there was his deeply beloved and honored Lady Dedlock, the cherished center of his existence for so many years. And the agony that now forced him to his knees was born of neither anger nor pride but of love and grief for her, as though her suffering was the source of his own.

Chapter 55 — Flight

Mrs. Rouncewell's gratitude and love — Inspector Bucket decided to get some sleep before finalizing his latest twist in the Tulkinghorn murder case. Meanwhile, Mrs. Bagnet had traveled all the way to Chesney Wold, and she and Mrs. Rouncewell were now making their way back to London by night coach. As the coach drove through the dark winter's night, Mrs. Rouncewell kept kissing the "old girl's" hand, grateful she had taken the trouble to fetch her. Her memories of George were only good. He had been a good boy in his youth, and his motives toward his family had also always been good and considerate, even if he got carried away by his wildness and went off to be soldier. But now he was in jail, and Mrs. Rouncewell's love for her son was mixed with anguish.

Mrs. Rouncewell's pledge to help — Mrs. Bagnet had known something was up when George advised her own son Woolwich to treat his mother with consideration. Seeing George particularly low one day, she had asked him about it, and he told her how he had coincidentally seen his mother at Tulkinghorn's office and how that had brought on a slew of memories and regrets. Mrs. Bagnet had already told this story many times during the coach ride, and now she stressed that they needed to get George all the legal help possible, since it wasn't enough to rely on the truth. Mrs. Rouncewell would do all she could. She knew the Dedlocks would also help, and she hinted briefly that she had some information that might aid her plea. Watching her, Mrs. Bagnet could understand her distress, but she could not figure out why she kept repeating "My Lady" under her breath.

The two women arrive at the prison — It was morning by the time the coach arrived in London, and Mrs. Rouncewell had had a wearing night but soon collected herself as they neared the prison. As for Mrs. Bagnet, she never seemed to show any wear, no matter how long or hard the trip. At Mrs. Bagnet's request, the warden let the two women into the cell as quietly as possible, and on entering they saw George seated as his desk, engrossed in his writing. They watched him in silence for a while, with Mrs. Rouncewell remaining as contained as possible. Only her hands kept moving about, expressing years of motherly emotion.

A loving reunion — All this time, George was unaware of them, but now as his mother told her child to turn towards her, he immediately stood, embraced her, and knelt before her, sobbing and pleading for forgiveness. Mother and son were both overcome with emotion and hardly coherent, and Mrs. Bagnet, too, was privately crying off to the side, happy that George and his mother were together again.

No need for forgiveness — George quickly discovered that the forgiveness he had craved had been given long ago and that his mother had never stopped believing in him. He explained that he had wished to develop into something worthy of his family's affection. After leaving home, he had at first written to his mother, hopeful that things would improve. But as the years passed and the career he had hoped for never materialized, he gradually lost his hope of ever being worthy. His mother didn't agree. She only wished he had let her know he was all right.

George tells of his shame and guilt — But George had his own struggle with shame. The contrast between his own life and his family's respectability made him feel it was too late to go back, even though he could imagine his mother's pain. He knew now that many of his feelings were groundless and that his family would have helped him. But he wasn't sure that it would have done any good, and he convinced himself that he had made his mistakes and now needed to pay for them without shaming his family. Even so, he had occasionally snuck down to Chesney Wold to peek at his mother, and he was deeply grateful to Mrs. Bagnet for bringing them back together. All this time, Mrs. Bagnet had been facing the wall to hide her tears of emotion, and periodically she would give George an affectionate poke or two with her umbrella.

George agrees to see the lawyers but prefers to avoid his brother out of shame — Mrs. Rouncewell's next move was to convince her son to let the lawyers take his case. This he promised to do, but when she mentioned bringing in his successful brother, it was more than he could bear. He felt he was a good-for-nothing in comparison, and he didn't want his brother to know he was in prison. His mother hoped his reluctance was temporary. George didn't know. He only knew he couldn't face him just yet. He would, however, cooperate in every other way, and he had already written down all the facts of his case and his relationship with Mr. Tulkinghorn. He hoped he could read the information to the court himself, but he would hand it over to the lawyers if necessary.

A loving farewell — After an emotional farewell between mother and son, George asked where she was headed next. She answered that she had some business at the Dedlock's London residence. On George's request, Mrs. Bagnet promised to make sure his mother arrived safely.

Mrs. Rouncewell pleads with Lady Dedlock — Having deposited Mrs. Rouncewell at the Dedlock's London home, Mrs. Bagnet returned to her family and resumed her daily routine. Meanwhile, Mrs. Rouncewell went up to meet Lady Dedlock. Lady Dedlock was surprised to see her housekeeper, but she soon learned that George was in prison, charged with the murder of Mr. Tulkinghorn. Mrs. Rouncewell pleaded with her to help clear his name, but Lady Dedlock was not sure what she could do. After telling her mistress that the echo on the Ghost's Walk had been especially loud of late, Mrs. Rouncewell presented Lady Dedlock with a letter, to be read after the housekeeper left. Mrs. Rouncewell did not believe what was in the letter, but if Lady Dedlock knew anything that could save George, she begged her to disclose it.

Lady Dedlock reads the letter; Mr. Guppy arrives — After Mrs. Rouncewell left, Lady Dedlock opened the letter to read a description of the murder scene, and at the bottom, her name and the accusation that she was the killer. Confused, she dropped the letter and stood in a daze until she realized that her servant was announcing the arrival of Mr. Guppy.

Mr. Guppy's warning — Mr. Guppy had come to warn Lady Dedlock that the letters they thought had been destroyed had in fact turned up. He had gathered this from young Smallweed and from his own observation of the four visitors who came to the Dedlocks' residence the day before. They had also been there that morning, evidently to capitalize on the letters' existence. Feeling that he had done his duty in relaying this information, Mr. Guppy excused himself, promising to never bother Lady Dedlock again.

Lady Dedlock decides to flee — The news left Lady Dedlock dazed again, and it was some time after Mr. Guppy's departure that she finally called her servant and asked him where Sir Leicester was and whether he had had company that morning. The servant told her that Sir Leicester had in fact had business company earlier and that he was now by himself in the library. Lady Dedlock was then left alone to face the overwhelming torment and irony of it all. Her relief at Tulkinghorn's death had been short-lived, and her shame and agony was now inevitable through the likely spreading of her old secret. There was no escape. She wrote a quick letter to her husband informing him of her innocence with regard to the murder, though she confessed her guilt in all other things he might hear her accused of. She also told him the facts of her own relationship to the murder case: that Tulkinghorn had threatened to disclose her secret and that she had gone to speak with him but had found his door locked and therefore went home. She did not feel that she could burden Sir Leicester any longer with her unworthiness. Having bid her husband a final goodbye, she placed the sealed letter to her husband on her table, dressed, and departed unnoticed, leaving everything behind.

Chapter 56 — Pursuit

Volumnia finds Sir Leicester unconscious — Everything seemed as usual at the Dedlock mansion until Volumnia, bored with her routine, went into Sir Leicester's library in search of entertainment. As she was poking around, she almost tripped over his unconscious body, and her scream quickly got the household in an uproar. Sir Leicester was carried to his bed, where despite the doctors' efforts, he remained unconscious until nighttime. He had aged tremendously in one day, and when he awoke, his speech was whispered and incoherent.

Sir Leicester reads Lady Dedlock's letter — Mrs. Rouncewell was grateful that she was in town to tend to Sir Leicester, and he was grateful to see her by his bedside on awakening. His ability to write was as impaired as his speech, but with the help of a slate, it soon became evident that he desperately wanted to see Lady Dedlock. But Lady Dedlock was gone, and all that remained was her letter, still sealed. After reading the upsetting letter, Sir Leicester fell unconscious again, and when he awoke an hour later, he asked for Mr. Bucket.

Sir Leicester hires Mr. Bucket to find Lady Dedlock — Mr. Bucket happened to be downstairs, having had a previous appointment, and when he arrived in the room, only he and Mrs. Rouncewell were allowed to remain. Having shown Mr. Bucket the letter, Sir Leicester instructed him to spare no expense in finding Lady Dedlock; and once he had done so, he was to communicate Sir Leicester's total forgiveness. To this end, Sir Leicester furnished Mr. Bucket with plenty of money, and the latter wasted no time getting started, promising to take no rest until he had completed his mission. On the way out, he told Mrs. Rouncewell that her son had been fully cleared, that she had nothing to worry about and everything to be proud of, and that her priority right now was to care for Sir Leicester.

The first part of the search — Mr. Bucket stopped first at Lady Dedlock's quarters in the mansion, where he looked through her dainty, costly belongings, impressed that she could leave all that behind. But only one thing interested him enough to take: a small white handkerchief with Esther Summerson's name on it. After visiting George's Shooting Gallery to procure Esther's address, Mr. Bucket continued to Jarndyce's London residence, where he showed Jarndyce the letter and implored Esther's guardian to let him to take Esther along. Bucket was concerned that Lady Dedlock's note was a suicide note, so he felt there was not a moment to waste, and he also needed Esther's help to gain Lady Dedlock's trust. By now, it was almost one in the morning, and Esther had gone to bed, but understanding the urgency of the situation, Jarndyce fetched her, and she quickly got ready to go.

A lonely figure wandering in the night — The chapter ends as Mr. Bucket waits for Esther on the stairs, wondering where Lady Dedlock could be. The scene shifts — first in his mind, then in reality — to a lonely female figure, dressed in shabby clothing and wandering alone through the cold winter's night near the brickmaker's kiln and cottage. The narrator tells us that such miserable clothing never entered or left the wealthy Dedlock home. But we do not find out who it is, and we are left with a question mark in our minds.

Chapter 57 — Esther's Narrative

Esther accompanies Mr. Bucket — Within ten minutes of waking, Esther was dressed, and fully informed, which included reading Lady Dedlock's letter. Seated in the coach next to Mr. Bucket, she tried to collect herself but remained flustered and confused for several hours. Even so, as Mr. Bucket asked her various questions, she could see that he was sharp, unusually focused, and compassionate. He wanted to know when and how often she had spoken with Lady Dedlock, how the lady got her handkerchief, and whether there was anyone Lady Dedlock was likely to trust.

The police station — Their first stop was a police station, where, among other things, the efficient policemen produced an exceptionally accurate missing person's report of Lady Dedlock. Once that was finished and dispatched, Mr. Bucket prepared Esther for the long night ahead, checking to see that she was warm enough and making sure she remained calm and prepared for anything. That way, she could be the most help to everyone, a sentiment that in her mind confirmed his benevolence.

The port area and the drowned body — At a quarter of two, they were on the road again, crossing the river a number of times till arriving in a seaside town. As Mr. Bucket spoke with some sailors and policemen, Esther noticed with dread a sign announcing the recovery of a drowned body. Thankfully, it was not Lady Dedlock. Mr. Bucket had just wanted to be sure.

The search continues — Off they went again, across the dark, dreadful river and down wintry roads, stopping at pubs and inns throughout the night to question people. At about 5:30 in the morning, Mr. Bucket handed Esther a cup of tea. By then, Esther had recognized that they were nearing St. Albans, where Bleak House was. There was good news: they had found Lady Dedlock's trail, and she was somewhere ahead of them. Thrilled, Esther had to contain herself as Mr. Bucket again signaled her to remain calm.

New revelations — Mr. Bucket wanted to know whether anyone matching Lady Dedlock's description had asked for either Mr. Jarndyce or Esther, so they headed toward Bleak House. On the way, Esther learned of Mr. Bucket's involvement with Jo — how he had personally taken him from Bleak House and warned him to stay away from London, since Jo had no discretion. He had found Jo with the help of Mr. Skimpole, who was staying at Bleak House at the time and whose professions of unworldliness didn't fool Mr. Bucket a bit. He saw him as self-centered and hypocritical, especially in matters of money, and he warned Esther to beware of anyone who claimed to be "innocent," for they were generally the opposite and simply trying to shirk their responsibilities.

The brickmakers' house — According to the Bleak House servants, no one had come by, so Esther and Bucket's next stop would be the brickmakers' house. Bucket had learned from an acquaintance of Jenny's husband that Lady Dedlock had been there, and he decided that this time Esther should do the questioning to keep things as natural as possible.

The brickmakers' families had moved to another place nearby, and when Esther and Mr. Bucket arrived, they discovered that Jenny was missing. Only Liz, the baby, and the two men were there. The men were both gruff and only grudgingly answered Esther's questions. Liz herself was too afraid to talk without her abusive husband's permission, which he also gave grudgingly. But Esther and Mr. Bucket did learn that Lady Dedlock—pale, weak, tired, and hoarse—had been there and that she had sat for about an hour and had some water. Jenny had given her some bread, too, but she barely ate it. Before that she had inquired about Esther but learned that Esther was gone. Lady Dedlock had left late at night—either at 11:20 or 12:20, and had taken the northern route. Jenny had also left at that time, except that she had gone in the opposite direction to London.

The search goes on; Mr. Bucket's theory — Having gotten all the information they could, Mr. Bucket and Esther headed out again. Mr. Bucket had deduced that Lady Dedlock had left her watch with the brickmakers, despite their protests that they had no way of telling time. He just didn't believe that such simple men thought in any terms more precise than half hours. The question that ran through his mind was why—what purpose did she have in giving them her watch? He felt they were missing some vital piece of information. For now, his theory was that it was a form of payment for allowing Jenny to leave in order to deliver a message to Esther in London, but he didn't find that explanation completely satisfactory. In the meantime, they would continue onwards, without a minute to lose.

Maintaining the trail despite snow — It was snowing hard now, cutting their visibility and making things hard for the horses as they slogged down the road, at times slipping and falling. The slow rate of travel was upsetting Esther, who could neither eat nor sleep for worry, but Mr. Bucket consistently reminded her to stay calm, sensible, and as cheerful as possible. Fortunately, she enjoyed watching him interview people in his natural, friendly manner, and his steady focus continued to impress her. One thing was certain: Lady Dedlock had been there, still on foot, and Esther's idea that she might be on her way to see Mr. Boythorn seemed plausible. Esther had mentioned Boythorn earlier when Bucket asked her whom Lady Dedlock might trust. His earlier connection with her sister made it seem like a good possibility. Yet to Bucket, Boythorn's place seemed too close to Lady Dedlock's home turf.

The trail is lost — The snow turned to sleet, making the roads even worse, and the trail that had been so hopeful now turned discouraging as they lost any hint of Lady Dedlock's whereabouts. Mr. Bucket maintained his personable veneer when questioning people, but once back at the coach, he seemed uncertain and confused. He would also disappear for fifteen minutes at a time to investigate an area, but he had no luck.

Esther recovers after fainting — Next they stopped to change the horses at a remote but comfortable inn, where the friendly landlady convinced Esther to relax inside. Alone in a warm room, with no sleep and little to eat, Esther fainted. She awoke to find herself surrounded by the kind faces of the landlady and her daughters, who all got her to take a half hour's nap and have a bite to eat afterwards. Like Mr. Bucket, Esther had been reluctant to take a break until her mother was found.

Mr. Bucket suddenly changes direction — The trip had proceeded throughout in stages, defined on each end by a change of horses. The latest phase of the trip was nine miles long, and like the previous phase, it was marked by tough winter roads and a discouraging lack of clues. Once again, they watched the horses being changed, when Mr. Bucket suddenly got an idea. They would not stay on Lady Dedlock's trail—instead, they would turn around, go back to London, and follow Jenny. Bucket had to calm Esther and convince her that he wasn't deserting her mother. In his excitement, he quickly ordered a new set of horses—four this time, instead of just two—and he sent another man galloping ahead. Having gotten Esther's trust, Bucket ordered the coach to move ahead, and off they raced through the snow and sleet.

Chapter 58 — A Wintry Day and Night

The gossip mills churn — By now, the gossip mills were churning in the wealthy London area that was home to the Dedlock mansion. The official word was that Lady Dedlock had repaired to Chesney Wold and would return shortly, but the gossipmongers had their own version of events, including rumors of divorce.

The general gossip about Lady Dedlock was not confined to the wealthy elite: the jeweler, the fabric merchant, the librarian, and even the sheep farmer all knew the latest talk, if only to entertain their clients. Naturally, the politicians had also had their say. But the rumors had extended beyond fashionable circles to include even those not normally bothered with such things.

Sir Leicester's pain; Lady Dedlock's abandoned rooms — Meanwhile, Sir Leicester was lying in bed, unwell, unable to sleep, and half dazed, watching the snow and wondering when his Lady would come home. He still had trouble speaking, but he managed to communicate to his faithful old housekeeper to have Lady Dedlock's rooms made ready for her. Mrs. Rouncewell obliged but not happily: she silently doubted whether they would ever see Lady Dedlock again, here or anywhere. When she told this to George, who was visiting her, he denied it at first. Her premonitions and talk of the Ghost's Walk seemed superstitious to him. But when he saw the desolate look of Lady Dedlock's deserted apartment, he started to comprehend his mother's sentiments. For no matter what the servants did to make Lady Dedlock's rooms warm and comfortable, they could not inject into them the life they once contained.

Volumnia and Mrs. Rouncewell keep Sir Leicester company — In Lady Dedlock's absence, Volumnia — not knowing what had happened — made an inept attempt to distract and console Sir Leicester, much to his annoyance at times. Fortunately, Mrs. Rouncewell soon returned and took her place, but as she sat by the bedside and watched her master gaze out at the constant snow, forever hopeful of his lady's return, she wondered who would break the news to him that Lady Dedlock was not coming back.

Sir Leicester learns of George's return and asks to see him — Mrs. Rouncewell's thoughts were soon interrupted by Volumnia's compliments about George — a fine specimen of a man, in her opinion. At this, Sir Leicester suddenly perked up. Why was he not told that George was back? Mrs. Rouncewell hadn't thought he was up to the news, which had only happened the day before. But Sir Leicester, on learning George was in the house, demanded to see him at once.

Sir Leicester's statement of forgiveness and commitment — Despite Mr. George's personal shame about his own history, he was a comforting sight to Sir Leicester — a reminder of better days. Sir Leicester even let George prop him up for greater comfort, and in the process, he admired the trooper's strength and gentleness. But Sir Leicester had another motive for calling George to his room. With Volumnia, Mrs. Rouncewell, and George all present, Sir Leicester now declared his unaltered position toward Lady Dedlock. He wanted it thoroughly understood by all three that should he ever become verbally incapacitated, nothing had changed — nor ever would — between Lady Dedlock and himself.

Sir Leicester's concern grows as night falls — As night began to fall, Sir Leicester's pain grew more evident. In denial that it was growing late, he refused at first to have the candles lit. But Mrs. Rouncewell finally convinced him in her gentle way that the lateness of the day would make no difference in the actual state of affairs. Besides, Mr. Bucket had been gone for less than twenty-four hours. To Sir Leicester, twenty-four hours was a long time, but at least he consented to more light and took pleasure in the idea that Lady Dedlock's rooms were being kept ready for her return.

A restless night; Volumnia tries to stay up all night — It was a restless night for everyone, though the exhausted servants were finally allowed to go to bed, having been up the entire night before. Mrs. Rouncewell and George remained with Sir Leicester, with George periodically checking on the other rooms and bringing reports of the latest dreadful weather to Sir Leicester. Volumnia, overshadowed by Sir Leicester's portrait and her own fears — including the possible loss of her income — wandered the house, ultimately settling down with her fatigued and unappreciative maid in Lady Dedlock's rooms. Occasionally, Mr. George's entrance would lift their spirits, but whenever Volumnia inquired about whether Sir Leicester had asked for her, the answer was no. She was nevertheless determined to be readily available, though she could not give a clear reason as to why she had chosen to wait farther away in a room not her own. Finally, however, with the arrival of the wee hours of the morning, Volumnia thought better of her approach and realized that a bit of sleep might help prepare her for the coming day, when her devoted efforts would be needed.

Mr. George keeps watch all night — With everyone else now retired to bed, Mr. George patrolled the great house alone. Throughout the night, he thought of the different periods of his life and of how they had come together in the last few weeks. And he wondered if, during his patrols, some helpful clue might present itself, but there was nothing — just the still, empty night and the dreadful weather.

No news is bad news as a bleak day dawns — Back in Sir Leicester's room, Mr. George was unable to give the old gentleman any positive news. The most he could do was to gently prop him up into a comfortable position. He then opened the curtains to let in the first faint hints of morning, but the breaking day was as bleak as the night before, and the message it sent was one of warning and not of hope.

Chapter 59 — Esther's Narrative

The search continues — By the time the coach with Esther and Mr. Bucket arrived in Islington outside of London, it was already four in the morning. Esther had been tormenting herself about why they had left off searching for her mother and were now on Jenny's trail instead. She was worried about the time loss but decided to trust Mr. Bucket, whose unfailing energy and determination had even supported the struggling horses when they stalled, slipped, or were otherwise challenged along the way.

Close on the trail — Having transferred to another coach and made sure that Esther — whose clothes by now were drenched — was warm and comfortable, Mr. Bucket gave her an encouraging talk. He had been deeply impressed by her calmness and fortitude, and he hoped that she retained her confidence in his plan. They then took off on the next part of their search, and Esther couldn't help noticing that in general the streets kept getting worse and worse, though they would at times emerge onto larger, busier roads. At one point, they stopped at a police station, and from then on, the dark roads seemed to regularly produce police officers, who would consult with Mr. Bucket and direct him to his next goal.

Meeting Mr. Woodcourt — Eventually, Mr. Bucket informed Esther that they had found the person they were seeking, and he asked her to get out and walk with him, since her presence would now come in handy. Esther immediately recognized the area as Chancery Lane. By now, it was 5:30 in the morning, and when Esther — tired, disoriented, and slogging through sleet — ran into Allan Woodcourt, it brought tears to her eyes. He immediately wrapped his cloak around her in spite of her protests, and after asking what they were doing, inquired whether he could go with them. Mr. Bucket, who meanwhile had introduced himself, instantly said yes, and the three of them continued on their way.

Onward to Snagsby's — Their next stop was the Snagsbys', where Mr. Bucket needed to question the servant girl, who had been having seizures all night. This information had come from another officer, who, unbeknownst to Esther, had been following right behind them.

Mr. Bucket orchestrates the visit — Mr. Bucket went in by himself at first, but having had problems dealing with Snagby's servant, Guster, and having learned that Allan Woodcourt was a doctor, he soon reappeared and invited both Esther and Woodcourt inside. Bucket needed to find a letter Guster had, but he was having trouble getting anything out of her. They were greeted by a miserable Mr. Snagsby, who directed them to where they needed to go and then explained to his wife — who was wearing her usual suspicious look — that he had no idea why their three visitors were there at this unusually early hour. Seeing that Esther was being severely scrutinized by Mrs. Snagsby, Mr. Bucket quickly instructed Snagsby and Woodcourt to get Guster to come around, while he took Esther over to a corner to dry out by the fire. Mrs. Snagsby's looks, he explained, should not be of too much concern, since they resulted from a misapprehension which he was about to clear up.

Mr. Bucket scolds Mrs. Snagsby — Mr. Bucket then turned to Mrs. Snagsby and informed her that a woman of her social standing, charms, and intellect should have no reason to think as she did. He advised her to go see Shakespeare's *Othello*, hinting that it might help her see the ultimately dark fate of her jealousy. He also explained who Esther was in relation to the recent business that had involved Mrs. Snagsby and so many other people. And he kept repeating — evidently to clear up her misconceptions about Mr. Snagsby's faithfulness—that no other business was involved. Furthermore, someone had been there that night and handed Guster a letter. That person's life now hung by a thread, and Guster's coherence was the key to finding the crucial letter that might save that woman. Guster's seizures had been occasioned by Mrs. Snagsby's aggressive behavior—the result of her usual suspiciousness—following Guster's receipt of the letter.

Woodcourt retrieves the letter; Mrs. Snagsby cooperates—Before Mr. Bucket could finish scolding Mrs. Snagsby, who was surprised and tearful at this unexpected speech, Mr. Woodcourt came out and handed him the letter. Mr. Bucket quickly analyzed it and then concluded his scolding. Mrs. Snagsby was now to be as helpful as possible, which would begin with leaving the room so he could speak privately with Esther.

Esther reads her mother's letter to Mr. Bucket—Alone with Mr. Bucket, who now resumed his kindly, helpful tone, Esther immediately recognized the handwriting as her mother's. The letter had been written in sections, and it told of Lady Dedlock's final hours and thoughts. She had gone to the brickmakers' cottage to catch a final glimpse of her beloved child and to orchestrate her own disappearance. She was grateful to Jenny for her generous help, and she was now on her way to die. Outwardly, she would die of exhaustion, cold, and hunger, but in truth it was her tormented conscience that killed her. She hoped to bring minimal disgrace to Sir Leicester and considered it right that she had lost everything at once. She had managed to thoroughly disguise herself as she headed to her final stopping place, hinting that it was the burial place of her one-time lover. The letter ended with a goodbye and a request for forgiveness.

Guster tells of her encounter with the unknown woman—It only remained for them to ask Guster a few questions about her interaction with Lady Dedlock. Woodcourt informed them that, with gentle treatment, Guster would be up to it. Esther was naturally upset by the contents of the letter, but she tried to keep herself together as she knelt down to comfort and question Guster. Guster told them that she had been coming home from an errand when she encountered what looked like a "common" person, though her speech was refined. The woman had lost her way and wanted to know where the poor person's graveyard was, the one with the iron gate and the archway. Having nothing to give Guster in return for her help, she blessed her and went her way.

The search resumes—At the mention of the graveyard, Esther had noticed a look of alarm on Mr. Bucket's face. Having now acquired the necessary information, Mr. Bucket wasted no time resuming his search with Esther and Woodcourt, too, by his side, since he realized he might need the help of a doctor. By then, the first light was just appearing, and the wet chill and sleet were still everywhere. Dazed and tired, Esther's impressions as they walked through the streets and courts were of half-real and half-imagined sights, with the imagined ones more prominent.

The woman at the iron gate of the graveyard—The graveyard had the same desecrated, diseased atmosphere as when Jo showed it to Lady Dedlock. A woman resembling Jenny lay at the foot of the iron gate, and the two men had to hold Esther back as she started to run toward her. Mr. Bucket now tried to explain that Jenny and her mother had changed clothes and that Jenny had then taken another route to distract the search party. Esther heard their words, but their meaning wasn't sinking in. To her, the woman at the gate was still Jenny, and it had been Jenny who brought her mother's letter to the

Snagbys'. She could see that this woman was in dire condition. But Esther yet retained a glimmer of hope that this woman might be able to help them save her mother.

A grim discovery — To the two men, it was clear who lay by the iron gate, and the looks on their earnest, compassionate faces did not harbor the same hope. They finally decided to let Esther go to the woman, agreeing quietly between them that it was her right to touch her before anyone else. The woman by the gate had been lying face downward, and as Esther now raised her head, she saw that it was not Jenny but her own dead mother.

Chapter 60 — Perspective

Jarndyce chooses London over Bleak House for now — Following her mother's death, Esther became ill for a short while. She didn't think it was worth mentioning except for the amount of compassion that surrounded her from all her friends. When she was well enough, Mr. Jarndyce called a Growlery meeting. He had meanwhile decided to headquarter in London for the time being. Ada needed Esther, and he didn't want to be too deprived of Esther's company if that meant a lot of traveling for her. Besides, Richard was not well, though outwardly healthy, and Jarndyce wanted to be kept up to date.

Jarndyce's patience with Richard — Esther was always astonished at the patience and gentleness her guardian had towards "Rick." Jarndyce knew that Richard's negative attitude towards him was irrational, but what could you expect? Richard was so immersed in the Jarndyce suit, which contained not one shred of rationality. Jarndyce knew that Richard would come around someday, but he was not in a rush. He would prefer that neither Esther nor Woodcourt discuss this with Richard, but Esther informed him that it was already too late.

Woodcourt's mother stays at the Jarndyce London residence — Jarndyce's next subject was Mrs. Woodcourt. How did Esther feel about letting her stay with them for a while? His intention was to make it easy for Allan to visit his mother. Esther was agreeable, but something about it gave her an uneasy feeling. She couldn't pinpoint it, though, so she dismissed it.

A possible career opening for Woodcourt — That brought up the question from Esther of whether Woodcourt still intended to go overseas. No, came the answer — his plans had changed now that he had a possible career opportunity in Yorkshire. If it happened, it would be six months from now in a pleasant area that blended both town and country. It wasn't a high position or a lot of money, but it would be a great service to the people there, and good things might come of it. Besides, Mr. Jarndyce preferred people who approached their career ambitions with humility and patience, and he considered Woodcourt that type, in addition to being known for his good work.

Esther regularly visits Ada and Richard — Esther now visited Ada and Richard once, sometimes twice a day. Both were always happy to see her, but Richard never ceased to have his head in the Jarndyce case. Meanwhile, Ada's meager inheritance, much of which was used to pay off Richard's debts, was dwindling fast. Still, Ada's brightness and beauty had a transforming effect on the otherwise dark, dismal environment, but Ada herself seemed less gregarious than before.

Miss Flite secrets — One day on her way there, Esther met Miss Flite coming out of Richard and Ada's apartment, following one of her habitual Monday visits. She informed Esther that Richard was still in court with Mr. Vholes, whom she was quick to say she did not like at all. She considered him "dangerous." She then whispered to Esther that she had made Richard the executor of her will. He was such a fixture at the court now, she was sure he would take care of things should she ever prove unable. Esther was dismayed to hear of Richard's status as one of the Chancery's most regular suitors. But Miss Flite had another little secret to relay: she had added two birds to her collection and named them the "Wards in Jarndyce."

Mr. Vholes privately disapproves of Richard's marriage — After Miss Flite left, Esther headed up to Richard and Ada's apartment to have dinner with them. Soon afterwards, both Richard and Mr. Vholes arrived. Esther was not thrilled to see Mr. Vholes, so she was less gracious than usual when he came over to chat with her while Richard and Ada were preparing dinner. She thought he had something vampiric about him, with his tall, skinny body, black outfit, unhealthy look, and inward manner. So when Vholes suggested that Richard and Ada's marriage was ill-advised, Esther was not receptive. Her answers to Vholes's wordy opinions of Richard's affairs were blunt and concise, with no attempt to be supportive. Mr. Vholes himself had had plenty to say while Richard was out of the room, but when he returned, he covered up his real intentions in talking to Esther, even though he claimed to do everything above board.

Richard's poor condition — At least, they had agreed privately that Richard looked unwell. Esther noticed over dinner that his eyes no longer sparkled, he seemed restless and distracted, and his energy was low. He seemed uninterested in food and had clearly lost weight, and his temper was often short. Only once in a while did his former cheerfulness shine through, and he was always clearly happy to see Esther.

After dinner — After Vholes was finished eating, he excused himself, saying that he needed to get back to work. Richard saw him out and on returning was extolling Vholes's virtues so much that Esther had her doubts as to whether he meant it. While Ada and Esther cleaned up, Richard lay exhausted on the couch. And later, when Ada played and sang to entertain him, he insisted on keeping the room dark because the light was painful to him. He claimed his eyes hurt, but Esther also sensed a melancholy feeling in the room.

Richard and Allan Woodcourt go for a walk — The evening's entertainment was interrupted by the arrival of Allan Woodcourt, who offered to go for a walk with Richard. The moon was shining, and Woodcourt's manner with Richard was so friendly and easygoing that Richard was quick to agree.

Ada confides in Esther — With the two men gone, Ada had a chance to confide in Esther. Esther sensed that Ada had something important to say, so she tried to just sit and listen. Ada told Esther of her concern for Richard's well-being and her hope that he would someday let go of the Jarndyce case; but barring that, she spoke of her undying love and devotion to him, no matter what. But there was something else. Ada was going to have a baby, and her deepest wish was that the child would open Richard's eyes and save him from the awful cause that was draining his life. Sadly, that happy possibility was tinged with the heartrending realization that her beloved husband might die before his child was born.

Chapter 61 — A Discovery

Esther asks Skimpole to stop visiting Richard and Ada — Esther continued to visit Ada and Richard every day. In doing so, she would sometimes run into Mr. Skimpole, who would wile away the time at their apartment, chatting idly or playing the piano. Knowing that Ada was pregnant and that Skimpole habitually extracted money from Richard, as he did from everyone, Esther resolved to privately try to convince Skimpole to stop his visits. With that in mind, she headed over to the Skimpoles' home.

As determined as she was, Esther doubted she could get through to Skimpole. Her doubts were almost confirmed when he approached her with his usual carefree, lighthearted attitude. But she decided to stick to the point and not allow herself to be distracted.

To Esther's surprise, Mr. Skimpole agrees — Mr. Skimpole caught on quickly. Before Esther was forced to be too blunt, he realized that his visits to Richard and Ada's might not be as welcome as they once were. Skimpole cheerfully explained to Esther that his whole reason for existing was pleasure, so to be associated with pain of any kind would not work. He would therefore stop his visits. Besides, those two were no longer as fun as they used to be, and he thanked Esther for her practicality and tact in bringing up the subject.

Esther brings up the bribe in reference to Jo — Esther found Skimpole's reasoning convoluted but decided to be satisfied that she had attained her goal. There was, however, one other thing that needed mentioning. It bothered her that Skimpole had taken a bribe from Bucket in reference to Jo. She felt that Skimpole had betrayed John Jarndyce, his host at the time, and that he had fallen short of several moral standards.

Skimpole denies any responsibility — Unfortunately, her reasoning didn't work with him. As usual, Skimpole claimed to have no concept of either morals or money and as such considered himself unbribable. To him, Bucket was an intelligent man of the law who rescued people and otherwise made things right for them, and with the government wanting people to trust such men, Skimpole felt that he needed to show his trust by complying with Bucket. So when Bucket offered him money, Skimpole felt he should cooperate and take it.

Esther sees Skimpole for the last time; Skimpole's self-pitying legacy — Esther was incapable of arguing with this. She had done what she could, and Skimpole, cheerful and entertaining as ever, insisted on walking her home. It would be the last she saw him.

Skimpole's diary was published on his death five years later, and though Esther had heard it was an entertaining, if self-pitying, read, the one line she read herself — that John Jarndyce was the epitome of selfishness — put her off from pursuing it any further.

Richard's worsening state; Woodcourt's beneficial influence — Esther continued to visit Richard and Ada, and Richard continued to deteriorate, spending every day at court and becoming increasingly weak and desperate. Only Allan Woodcourt's frequent visits could momentarily distract him from the Jarndyce suit and get him out into the fresh air. It was therefore not unusual for Esther to see

Woodcourt, and one evening when Esther's guardian failed to pick her up, Woodcourt walked Esther home.

A confession of love — On arriving at the London residence, they noticed that both Mr. Jarndyce and Mrs. Woodcourt were out, so Esther and Woodcourt had time to chat alone. Whatever feelings Esther may have once harbored for Woodcourt she had now thoroughly mastered — or so she thought. Both her appearance and her status had changed, and in her mind there was no going back. So it was with some surprise that she learned that Allan Woodcourt loved and honored her above anyone else.

A bittersweet revelation — That revelation brought tears of joy and sorrow to her eyes — joy, because it meant so much to her to be loved by Woodcourt; sorrow, because it was too late. Woodcourt had feared as much, but each of them still took inspiration from the other's love. Esther asked whether he had received the career position up north, to which he said yes, though it wouldn't be for a while. In the meantime, they both hoped they could continue seeing each other in their helpful capacity at Richard and Ada's, but they knew that the door had been closed on something more. She never told him outright that she would be marrying John Jarndyce, but she hinted it broadly enough that her statements were obvious to a gentleman like Woodcourt. At one point, when Esther confessed how much his love meant to her, Woodcourt turned his face away and cried. And Esther, too, cried after he left — though her tears were not tears of sorrow but of joy and gratitude at being loved so deeply by such a good and noble man. His love would be her inspiration to be her best, but her heart also went out to him because of the difficult road he had to travel.

Chapter 62 — Another Discovery

Esther's resolve to marry Jarndyce — Woodcourt's confession of love, precious as it was to Esther, only strengthened her resolve to marry John Jarndyce. The letter Jarndyce had written her expressed the same pure love for her that she felt for him, and that night she fell asleep with the letter by her head and its words in her heart.

The wedding is set for the next month — Esther awoke the next morning resolved to broach the subject of their marriage with her guardian. He and even Mrs. Woodcourt had noticed Esther looking particularly fresh that morning, and as Esther approached her guardian in private, she also observed more than usual of his bright cheerfulness. It had been some time since their exchange of letters, and though they had a comfortable, loving relationship, she was concerned that something was wrong, as she had heard no more on the subject since then. But nothing was wrong, and Jarndyce, who had had the same subject on his mind, was overjoyed to plan the wedding for the next month.

The arrival of Mr. Smallweed and the mysterious will — The joy of this moment was interrupted by the arrival of Mr. Bucket with ornery old Mr. Smallweed in tow. After introducing Mr. Smallweed, Mr. Bucket explained that, amid Krook's former belongings, Smallweed had found a paper resembling a will signed by Mr. Jarndyce. As usual, Smallweed's interest was to extract money in return for the paper. It was clear to Esther from the way Mr. Bucket presented the information that much more was involved than was being said, but Bucket and Smallweed had apparently agreed beforehand on what should be revealed.

Mr. Jarndyce's response — Mr. Jarndyce listened patiently and, having received the slightly burnt paper, informed Bucket and Smallweed that he never dealt directly with the Jarndyce suit but that he would immediately submit the paper to his solicitor, who would then determine its value. Any remuneration would be determined by that alone. Having explained this to Mr. Smallweed (who thought he should receive a reward for merely handing the paper over), Mr. Bucket, who had bolted the door, now unlocked it and departed with his guest.

An apparent will written in Richard and Ada's favor — Jarndyce and Esther immediately left for Kenge and Carboy, where Mr. Jarndyce, still maintaining his habitual indifference to the suit, handed the piece of paper to Mr. Kenge. His succinct, direct manner in explaining his purpose contrasted sharply with the longwinded, comical way in which he had learned about the paper, not to mention anything that ever happened in the Jarndyce suit. In spite of Mr. Jarndyce's lack of interest, Mr. Kenge found the paper remarkable in several ways: it was a will, apparently in Jarndyce's writing; it had a later dating than any comparable piece of evidence; it had been properly completed and signed, making it a valid document; it significantly increased the amount left to Richard and Ada, reducing the amount left to Jarndyce, though he still received plenty. Mr. Jarndyce was not perturbed by the news. It would make him happy to see Richard and Ada well-off as a result of the Jarndyce suit, but so far, only the legal system had gained from it, and he didn't believe it would ever bring anyone any good.

A noteworthy document — In the meantime, Mr. Kenge had had Mr. Guppy call Mr. Vholes, and once Vholes had arrived and read the paper, he and Kenge conferred privately about it. They spoke in low voices over by the window, but Esther was still able to detect that most of the conversation seemed to revolve around various legal terms having to do with money and the estate. Mr. Vholes had not shown any emotion while perusing the document, but as Esther noted, that was normal for him. On returning from their conference, both lawyers agreed that the document was important and would be of great interest when introduced into evidence the following month, when the Court resumed.

Mr. Jarndyce remains uninterested — Mr. Kenge's excitement had no effect on Mr. Jarndyce. Kenge pledged to inform Mr. Jarndyce as things developed, and Jarndyce pledged to continue to pay no attention. The chapter ends as Mr. Kenge escorts Mr. Jarndyce and Esther to the door while singing his praises of the greatness of England and its legal system, despite his honored client's opinion.

Chapter 63 — Steel and Iron

Changes in Mr. George's life — Much had changed since Mr. George's arrest, release, and meeting with Sir Leicester at such an unfortunate time in the latter's life. Mr. George had since moved to Chesney Wold to aid Sir Leicester on his horseback rides and, as we find out later, to make his own mother happy. The shooting gallery was up for rent, its contents had been sold, and now Mr. George had just a few more things to do to finalize the transition to his new life.

Mr. George sets out to find his brother — Those things involved visiting his brother in the iron country up north, something George had resisted doing out of embarrassment over his vagabond past. But goaded by the strong drive to make all things right, he now set out on horseback to find his older brother.

Iron country — Iron country was a far cry from the green woods of Chesney Wold. The effects of the iron industry could be seen everywhere: the coal, fires, soot, smokestacks, brick, and damage to nature. Finding his brother, however, was not hard. The name Rouncewell was well known in those parts, and with good reason: his brother owned both the large, busy factory and the bank. Whether he was in town or not was another question, but at least George would be able to find his son, the younger Rouncewell.

Watt directs George to the older Rouncewell's office — It was in fact Watt, his brother's son, who greeted George as he entered the factory premises, where the trooper took note of the machinery, the iron in different stages, and earlier, on his way there, the muscled, blackened men he had seen going to dinner. George was also immediately struck by the strong resemblance between Watt and himself in his younger days. Luckily, he had come on a good day. According to Watt, his father was in town and was currently in the office. Under what name should he announce George? Still unsure of himself, George asked to be introduced as Mr. "Steel."

A hearty reunion — The office and its view were as bleak as the surrounding area, but it was clear from the items on his brother's desk — the accounts, the diagrams, the iron samples — that George's brother was an important man. George presented himself as a friend of the long-lost soldier brother, but it took no time for his older brother to see right through his story. What came next was a big surprise. Calling him by his real name, George's older brother welcomed him heartily. All George could do was respond in kind, with tears of joy. Indeed, George had come on the best of all possible days. That same night, they would be celebrating Watt and Rosa's marriage a year from that date, and George would be the guest of honor.

A warm celebration at the ironmaster's elegant home — The elegance of George's brother's home matched his current position in life, though it still showed traces of simpler beginnings. It was clear to George that his nieces and nephews had been trained in keeping with their more elevated social standing, and the discrepancy between their lives and his made him uncomfortable. But no one else seemed to notice. They were too busy enjoying themselves, and the prospect of having George give away the bride was pleasing to all.

George's desire to do the "right" thing — The warm welcome from George's brother extended even further, and the next day he informed George of his plans to give him a place in his company. But grateful as George was for his brother's thorough welcome, he could not accept. He was too far gone in the vagabond way. In fact, he wanted to convince his mother to remove him from her will. He would feel more comfortable and justified about his renewed existence in their lives. But George's brother knew that that was the wrong move — their mother would never hear of it. Besides, why break the dear old woman's heart when finding her long-lost son had brought her so much joy? The older brother could see that that option didn't satisfy George, and though he was amused by his younger brother's resistance, to make him feel better, he suggested that George could give his inheritance away.

George's preference for working under Sir Leicester — That was something George could agree to. But now he explained that a position in the factory would not work, in part because he was assisting Sir Leicester. It might not have the same opportunity as working under his brother, but he was used to taking orders and needed the external discipline. Sir Leicester also preferred George as a helper, and George was happy to both help the old gentleman and comfort his own mother with his presence.

The letter to Esther Summerson — His brother was too wise to try to dissuade him, so that left just one more errand to take care of. George had written a letter to Esther explaining his role in the lives of her late father and mother. George wanted his brother to review the letter before he mailed it from the iron country, which he had decided would be better than mailing it from Chesney Wold, since that might evoke sad memories. In essence, the letter stated that George had agreed to act as a messenger for Captain Hawdon (not mentioned by name), who was living overseas at the time. George had had a short note from Hawdon instructing him about delivering a letter to Esther's mother, who was not yet married. It was that note that had been extracted from him by Mr. Tulkinghorn (also not mentioned by name), but that situation had happened only under duress. Furthermore, he had not been aware that Captain Hawdon had been alive, since he was reported drowned many years ago, right around the time his ship would have pulled into the harbor where he was to meet her mother. Had George known he was alive, he would have offered the law writer all the help he could. George finished the letter to Esther by confirming his high regard for her and his commitment to being her "servant."

A warm goodbye — George's brother found the letter a little formal but approved it has having nothing objectionable for the eyes of a model young lady. That meant that George's business there was over, and it was time for him to go. In a warm parting gesture, his brother insisted on accompanying him part of the way home. They would take a coach, have dinner, spend the night somewhere, and have breakfast together. And so, after a hearty reunion and an equally warm goodbye, the two brothers went their separate ways again.

Chapter 64 — Esther's Narrative

Quiet wedding preparations — With £200 from her guardian, Esther now quietly set about making the necessary wedding preparations. Neither she nor Jarndyce told anyone about it, except that Esther informed Mrs. Woodcourt, who went out of her way to be helpful and who in general had adopted a much milder, more pleasant attitude. As far as Esther was concerned, a private wedding would be the best thing. In any case, the date would be set for after the Chancery term. That gave Esther some hope that, with the existence of the new will, Richard and Ada might be better off by the time she got married. But Jarndyce, true to his usual stance, refused to believe that anything good could ever come of the Jarndyce case.

An unexpected journey — Close to the beginning of the term, Jarndyce was suddenly called to Yorkshire on some business related to Mr. Woodcourt. Esther had been out visiting Ada when he left, so she only found out about it later through a written dispatch from her guardian asking her to meet him the next day. It was the last thing she was expecting, and she had no idea why she was being summoned to join them.

A happy reception at the station — When she arrived at her destination the next evening, her guardian was waiting for her, beaming as cheerfully as ever. Whenever Esther saw him in this state, she attributed it to some kind action on his part. She had made the same statement earlier in the story, and much of her love for him was founded on the pure goodness and generosity of his character.

The purpose of the journey — Jarndyce decided to not keep Esther in suspense, so he explained over dinner that out of gratitude and appreciation to Allan Woodcourt for being such a great help to so many people, he had decided to find him a little house in Yorkshire, for which he would pay the rent. He had been working on getting it ready, but not being sure of himself in the housekeeping department, he had summoned Esther to inspect it before surprising Woodcourt. Esther was so moved by her guardian's kindness that she couldn't speak for a moment, though her tears and smiles spoke for her.

A miniature replica — They visited the house the next morning, and Esther immediately noticed how the flowerbeds mimicked the pattern she had laid out at Bleak House. The garden, with its fruit trees and fresh, beautiful views was delightful, and the house itself was a charming little "doll's" house that, like the flowerbeds, had been arranged in a way that imitated Esther's unique style. Only one thing worried her. She silently wondered if it wouldn't remind Woodcourt too much of her, and she thought that might be too hard on him. Her guardian, however, unaware of these thoughts, was excited and pleased with her admiring reactions. But he had one more thing to show her: there, over the porch, stood the name he had given the little home: "Bleak House."

An unexpected revelation — The time had now come to explain the real purpose of the visit. Jarndyce took Esther over to a bench, and after they sat down together, he began to unfold his thoughts. Once, when Esther was still a young girl, he had dreamt of marrying her, and in writing her his recent letter, he had almost fulfilled that dream. At the time, he was thinking of their mutual happiness, but when Woodcourt returned from abroad, he quickly perceived that Allan loved Esther, and he was reasonably sure that she loved him, too. Esther trembled as she listened to her guardian, but Jarndyce asked her to hear him out. He knew that she would have sacrificed herself so completely for his happiness that no one would ever have known that she had sacrificed anything at all. But that wasn't acceptable to him. He wanted her to experience true happiness. That meant not only being allowed to marry Woodcourt, who had already confessed his love for Esther to her guardian, but it also meant being thoroughly accepted into Woodcourt's family. For that, Jarndyce would have to convince Mrs. Woodcourt to set aside her prejudices about lineage, and that was why she had come to live them with at Bleak House for a while. Her task, in view of the fact that her son loved Esther, was to observe Esther closely and to evaluate her on her real merits. It worked. Mrs. Woodcourt came to love Esther as much as anyone else. Moreover, Allan's profession of love to Esther was done with Jarndyce's knowledge and encouragement.

A gift of love — During this talk, Esther noticed a strong light about her guardian, an almost angelic radiance. And now, having made his speech, her beloved guardian presented Esther to her future husband, who suddenly stood in their presence. Both Esther and the miniature version of Bleak House were Jarndyce's gifts to the compassionate young man who had already contributed so selflessly to the welfare of others. It was characteristic of John Jarndyce's own unselfishness that he deemed this the happiest day of his life. He would go back to being a bachelor, knowing that things were as they should be. The wind, he said, was now blowing from the west.

A visit from Mr. Guppy — Naturally, this produced great happiness on the part of Esther and Woodcourt, but they would have to wait to move to their little home until the matter with Richard and Ada was settled. In the meantime, Esther and her guardian returned to London, arriving late the next day to find that Mr. Guppy had called three times and planned on coming back that night. That prompted Esther to tell Jarndyce about Mr. Guppy's marriage proposal and how he had changed his mind after her illness. With that amusing anecdote in mind, Jarndyce decided to admit him at that late hour, and no sooner had he made the decision than Mr. Guppy appeared with his mother and Mr. Jobling.

Another proposal — It slowly came out that Mr. Guppy was there to make another marriage proposal. He was now a full-fledged attorney about to set up his own business. He had bought a house (pronounced "ouse"), which he would be sharing with his mother and Jobling. He had thought earlier that his desire to marry Esther had waned, but it was still as strong as ever, so with his improved social status and her reduced looks (though he never said this outright), he figured there was more of a balance between them.

A definite rejection and an irate mother — Throughout the first part of this conversation, Guppy's mother kept grinning and rolling her head. That changed when John Jarndyce made a tactful but definite rejection of the marriage proposal on Esther's behalf. In response, Mrs. Guppy became suddenly furious, repeatedly lunging at Jarndyce and telling him to get out (of his own house, no less) and to go find someone who was suitable, if her son wasn't. The meeting ended with Mrs. Guppy yelling her way down the stairs as Guppy and Jobling escorted her out.

Chapter 65 — Beginning the World

On the way to court — With the onset of the new term, Esther and Allan decided to attend the session, to be held at Westminster. The discovery of the new will might bring good news, and Esther expected it to at least create a stir. Richard would certainly be there and in need of support. And as always, Esther thought of Ada, who was about to give birth and must also be needing support in spite of her admirable strength throughout the whole ordeal.

A chance meeting with Caddy — The walk to court was unexpectedly delayed when Esther and Allan suddenly heard Caddy's voice calling Esther from a coach. Caddy was doing well, with plenty of dance students, and she had received Esther's note about all that had recently unfolded in her life. She was overjoyed to see Esther and went on and on about all the good Esther had done for her. Esther even got in the coach for a few minutes in the hope that Caddy would calm down, but that never happened. Even as the coach pulled away, Caddy's affection and excitement never waned.

The end of a farce — That chance meeting made Esther and Allan late for court, and by the time they reached Westminster, the hall was packed, and it was difficult to tell what was going on. Occasionally, there would be an uproar, and some of the counselors would burst out laughing. When Esther and Allan asked a nearby gentleman, they were told that the case appeared to be permanently over. That was soon confirmed when the crowd broke up and emerged from the hall, still laughing. Legal clerks were bringing out massive amounts of paper, and when Esther and Allan again asked an official, he laughingly confirmed that the case was indeed over. Things finally became clear when Mr. Kenge and Mr. Vholes appeared, and on questioning them, Allan was able to deduce that the entire estate had been eaten up by legal costs. No will, valid or invalid, made any difference now. Mr. Kenge presented this ridiculous situation as though it was a triumph of the legal system, the evidence that England's greatest legal minds had diligently applied themselves to a difficult case and been remunerated accordingly. But it was Allan Woodcourt who put in plain English.

Woodcourt quickly attends to Richard — Woodcourt's first thought on hearing this was for Richard's well-being. Mr. Vholes, who gave Esther the impression of having taken his last vampiric bite of his client, informed them as he was leaving that Richard was still in the court. Woodcourt therefore determined to go see him alone and advised Esther to tell her guardian and come over to Richard and Ada's place later. Agreeing, Esther immediately went home to disclose the news. To John Jarndyce, the end of the case was a blessing, but like Allan and Esther, he was concerned for Richard and Ada.

Esther goes to visit Richard, who is weak and ill — Esther went to visit Richard and Ada later that day, and she found Richard lying on the couch in a dark room, with medicine by his bedside. Earlier in court, Allan had stopped him from confronting the judge in anger when he noticed blood coming out of Richard's mouth. Ada informed Esther that Richard had asked for her, and though pale and weak, he smiled in his old way when he opened his eyes and saw her sitting there. By evening, John Jarndyce had also arrived, and there was a reconciliation between them.

Beginning the world: Richard's last hour — The bright spot in Richard's state was that he had finally learned his lesson. He had been forced to let go of the Jarndyce case and was sorry that he had put his dear Ada through all the useless torment and trouble. For all his weakness, he now spoke of the future — his desire to be at Esther and Allan's wedding and especially to see their house, where he was sure he would quickly grow strong again. The old Richard seemed to be coming alive again, though weakly, and he spoke of "beginning the world." He was ready to learn from his former guardian and looked forward to visiting him at the new Bleak House and — John Jarndyce hoped — the old as well. He even looked forward to teaching his own child in that happy setting. But as he buried his head in Ada's breast, embracing her as he asked for forgiveness, he smiled his last smile through his last tears in this world and moved on to the next.

The symbolic end of the Jarndyce suit — Late that evening, Esther learned from Miss Flite that she had set all her birds free.

Chapter 66 — Down in Lincolnshire

Silence reigns at Chesney Wold — Chesney Wold's days of visiting cousins are gone, and a general silence has fallen over the estate. Whatever talk there is of Lady Dedlock's death is likewise hushed, and only those most closely involved know what happened. Lady Dedlock's remains lie buried in the family mausoleum, beneath the trees in the estate park, and Sir Leicester, accompanied by Mr. George, regularly rides out there to pay his respects.

Boythorn's old right-of-way war continues, with a twist — Sir Leicester has aged a great deal since the unfortunate tragedy, but he still has his dignity. Out of compassion, Mr. Boythorn considered ending the right-of-way war between them, but Sir Leicester was so insulted that Boythorn, again out of compassion, went back to his old combative ways, though only as a pretense to humor Sir Leicester. Sir Leicester, for his part, remained completely unaware of that aspect of their argument, just as he had no knowledge of the tragic connection existing between them in their relationship to two sisters, both since gone.

Mr. George, his mother, and his friends — Mr. George now lives in one of the estate's lodges, and he is not alone. With him is Phil, whose job is to polish George's trooper mementos, along with the stirrups, chains, and whatever other metal he can find in the stable. On Sundays, George brings his mother to church, and there is a comforting, kindly relationship between the two of them and Sir Leicester. The Bagnets also visit George in the summers, when the two girls — now older — wander in the park, and the two men sit and smoke their pipes. Sometimes, Lignum plays his fife, and of course, the "old girl" is there, too, with the same old trusty gray cloak and umbrella.

The contracting state of Chesney Wold — Chesney Wold is now no longer open to the public, and most of the house has been closed down. Sir Leicester still sits by the fire in the drawing room in the evenings, while Volumnia reads to him from some boring treatise on the relative merits and demerits of Buffy and Boodle in relation to England's welfare. Sir Leicester, who is gradually fading, sleeps through most of it, and Volumnia has learned how to disguise her yawns. But she plods onward, having discovered some note indicating that she will someday be financially rewarded for her efforts.

Volumnia, a remnant from another time — The general dullness of Volumnia's life is occasionally interrupted by bored cousins participating in shooting sessions on the estate grounds. Otherwise, the most excitement Volumnia sees is some annual politically related event in a large, stately, otherwise vacant assembly hall some fourteen miles from Chesney Wold. On those rare occasions, Volumnia is in her element — a shabbily elegant remnant acting out the graces (though clumsily) of a disappearing era. Her state is mirrored by the room, whose former elegance is falling apart bit by bit with each disappearing chandelier drop.

A dull, depressing emptiness — But rarely does Volumnia get to bask in the glitter of another time. Most of her days are relegated to the dull, depressing vacancy that is now Chesney Wold, a house so dreadful and cavernous that even a maidservant yields to depression and ultimately leaves. And so the story of Chesney Wold, except for a few signs of life, ends in silence and emptiness.

Chapter 67 — The Close of Esther's Narrative

The fates of those directly related to Bleak House — By this time, Esther and Allan Woodcourt have been happily married for seven years and have two young daughters. Ada has a baby boy, who is the joy of her life and a source of healing following Richard's death. Not surprisingly, the little boy's name is Richard. John Jarndyce has appointed himself as their guardian and is ready to welcome them to the old Bleak House, their permanent home, at any time. At the same time, Ada and her son are always welcome at the new Bleak House. Charley has grown up and is married to the attractive miller, whose mill can be seen from the new Bleak House. Charley's little sister Emma is an exact replica of her at the same age, and their brother Tom has become the miller's apprentice.

Caddy Jellyby and her family — Caddy Jellyby is happy, prosperous, and busy with her dancing school. Her husband Prince, though a good husband, is lame, and Caddy's daughter is deaf and dumb. But Caddy makes the best of it and does as much as she can for them, including learning the "deaf and dumb arts." She has since moved to a more fashionable area, where she is often visited by her father, who still sits in his old habitual pose with his head against the wall. Her mother finally gave up on her African quest and is writing even more letters for the cause of the female vote. Peepy is prospering in his job at the Custom House and has developed an excellent relationship with the elder Mr. Turveydrop, who still maintains a lifestyle of Deportment.

A special place for John Jarndyce — As soon as they could, Esther and Allan added a Growlery to their home. Esther mentions here that she cannot write about her guardian without tears welling up in her eyes — so moved is she by his goodness and generosity. He is a father figure to all his wards and their children, and he is Allan's best friend. And for all the changes over the years, Esther's relationship with him is as mutually affectionate and devoted as ever. The only difference is that the east wind is permanently gone — since the day her guardian gave the new Bleak House to Esther and Allan.

A final tribute to beauty and love — Ada is now more beautiful than ever, refined by tragedy; and her little boy has adopted Esther as his other mother. Allan has continued doing much good and is loved in the community and by his wife for his compassion and dedication. Allan and Esther are not rich, but to Esther, the knowledge of doing some good is true wealth.

In fact, Esther's whole life revolved around Allan and those she loved. Whatever praises she received, she attributed to her husband, and whatever beauty she once had outwardly, she saw in others. But those who loved her didn't see it that way. In the final scene, Esther is sitting on the porch looking up at the moonlight and remembering her former looks, when her husband comes home and asks her what she is thinking. She tells him openly that she is amazed at how much he loves her even with her changed appearance. He laughs and questions whether she ever looks in the mirror and then tells her that she is prettier than ever.

Of course, she doesn't believe him. Yet she concludes that all the beauty and goodness around her more than compensate for any outward lack, assuming there is one … but she never finishes her sentence.

About BookCaps

We all need refreshers every now and then. Whether you are a student trying to cram for that big final, or someone just trying to understand a book more, BookCaps can help. We are a small, but growing company, and are adding titles every month.

Visit www.bookcaps.com to see more of our books, or contact us with any questions.

[i] Dickens, Charles and Tatiana M. Holway (Introduction). *Bleak House.* New York: Barnes & Noble, 2005.

Printed in Great Britain
by Amazon

ISBN 9781500515843